The Bending Moment

Also by David E. Hawkins and published by Palgrave Macmillan

Sun Tzu and the Project Battleground
(*with Shan Rajagopal*)

The Art of War by Sun Tzu has influenced many generations of business leaders as well as strategy gurus. Yet for many people in businesses and students of management the translation of strategy into business execution remains a mystery. This book provides a fully comprehensive account of this work and the influence of Sun Tzu in creating project strategy effectively to translate good strategic thinking into accountable and achievable plans yielding desired results. The book gives the reader the opportunity to benefit from the knowledge that successful implementation of business strategies is supported by excellence in project strategy execution.

THE BENDING MOMENT

ENERGIZING CORPORATE BUSINESS STRATEGY

David E. Hawkins

palgrave
macmillan

First published 2005 by
PALGRAVE MACMILLAN
Houndmills, Basingstoke, Hampshire RG21 6XS and
175 Fifth Avenue, New York, N.Y. 10010
Companies and representatives throughout the world

PALGRAVE MACMILLAN is the global academic imprint of the Palgrave Macmillan division of St. Martin's Press, LLC and of Palgrave Macmillan Ltd. Macmillan® is a registered trademark in the United States, United Kingdom and other countries. Palgrave is a registered trademark in the European Union and other countries.

ISBN-13: 978–1–4039–9838–5
ISBN-10: 1–4039–9838–8

This book is printed on paper suitable for recycling and made from fully managed and sustained forest sources.

A catalogue record for this book is available from the British Library.

A catalog record for this book is available from the Library of Congress.

10   9   8   7   6   5   4   3   2   1
14   13   12   11   10   09   08   07   06   05

Printed and bound in Great Britain by
Creative Print & Design (Wales), Ebbw Vale

Dedicated to my wife Christine for her love and support
throughout my career, and to my mother for encouraging
me to grow in many ways

Contents

HARNESSING THE POWER

BREAKING THE PAIN BARRIERS

MOBILIZING FOR ACTION

GAINING ILLUMINATION

FEEDING THE FORCE

Preface

On a cold February evening, returning with my co-author from a business meeting having just concluded the contract to publish *Sun Tzu and the Project Battleground*, a study in strategy, my mind was focused on the subject of developing business strategy. In the best tradition we stopped to enjoy a beer and began to explore the subject of why, when everyone talks of strategy in business, it so often fails to mature into positive results.

With a wide background of experience of working for, and with, a range of organizations, it was interesting, when delving into some of our personal anecdotes, to find the many common trends that emerged. Then, as conversations frequently do, the subject became more philosophical and drifted into the wider subject of life and the balance that exists in nature, except where man has chosen to change the balance by design or default.

As the scope and range of the discussion expanded it became clear that in the organizational environment of business there was also a balance, which was often disrupted or distorted by the forces at work within any group of people. This energy, from whatever origin (and we all have a perspective on the origin of the power) is the underlying essence of an organization.

There has long been a realization that the strength of an organization comes largely from its people. In recent times it has been the goal of many investment strategists to define and capture this factor, as an indication of long-term sustainability for measuring returns on investment. This has been even more pronounced since the acceleration in globalization that has seen many traditional manufacturers moving from production to knowledge management and outsourcing to capitalize on lower costs in developing regions. The shift is towards virtual enterprises that share their core skills and manipulate the value chain in order to maintain their competitive edge.

The importance of a holistic business strategy has become a crucial part of building for success, and the complexity of the marketplace has widened the range of factors that must be considered. What has, however, often been ignored, as was apparent from our late-night discussions, was that while the focus has been outward in terms of recognizing the terrain, and prevailing external influences, the stresses created by not recognizing the internal forces that, being out of alignment, could dilute or even thwart the most robust of strategies.

Attention moved from the concept of mobilizing an organization to develop an effective process of strategic thinking that matched the business landscape to that of identifying and addressing the internal constraints. The 'bending moment' became the focus of my thinking and analysis. With a background in engineering it provided a model that typified what we had been debating: the bending moment is reached when the external or internal pressures exert a stress that changes the molecular strength of a material to the extent that its natural force cannot maintain its shape.

From this initial visualization I started to model the idea of strategic stress analysis (SSA). There has been a great deal of valuable work done on the concept of stress upon individuals, and the impact of this on business performance. There have similarly been many initiatives in the business world focused on liberating the knowledge and experience of individuals to enhance productivity and performance. I felt that there was a gap in these programmes, namely, the stress and friction that exist when a valid strategic approach fails to recognize the internal boundaries and pinch points within organizations.

It was from this idea that I set out to consider my experience and test the thinking on the business worlds I had been exposed to. I would not presume to suggest that organizations are not already aware of the value they have in their personnel, or that the recognition of the challenges in a global marketplace are underestimated by those trying to ensure sustainable growth. It would also be presumptuous to promote the idea that I had found a magic formula that could eradicate these internal constraints.

With a background in project management and organizational process development, what I have set out to achieve is a platform that encourages the innovative business leaders to test the constitution and cohesiveness of their organizations, in the belief that by recognizing the potential limitations that may be lying below the surface of their operations they can improve the capability of reinforcing their strategic aims.

The Bending Moment brings together personal exposure to business operations from high tech to production manufacturing across a wide range of sectors, and through practical involvement from the shop floor to the boardroom. I have enjoyed an active career in the world of supply chain and outsourcing, allowing me to work with many organizations both large and small, and from every corner of the global marketplace.

The common ground I established is that the only constant is change, and if that change is not recognized and organizations adapted to meet the challenge, then the bending moment will come sooner rather than later. I hope this book will provide the stimulus to look at the potential issues that may well exist within your organization.

DAVID E. HAWKINS

Acknowledgements

The author would like to acknowledge and extend appreciation to Peter Makin, who has always encouraged my writing.

Thanks go to Martin Christopher, Gunther Kruse, Briain Flintoff, David Wright, Anoop Singh, Leon Benjamin, Thomas Power, Satvinder Flore and Andy Scott for their valuable input. Thanks to Shan for his contribution in developing the initial framework for the book.

Finally I would like to thank Stephen Rutt, Palgrave Macmillan's publishing director, for his continued confidence in me as an author, and Elaine Towns and Keith Povey for their skilful editing.

DAVID E. HAWKINS

CHAPTER 1

The force of balance

There can be few that would argue against the basic concept that, for every action (or inaction) there is a reaction or consequence. This interaction has been the root of much scientific and philosophical research over the centuries. In many cases the impacts have been developed into rules or formulas, but many others remain evident, recognized but unexplained. What we do not understand we often tend to attribute to some force that sits outside our sphere of existence.

From the beginning of time it has been common, when not being able to rationalize the true cause behind an event, that humans have attributed these reactions a deity or spirit. In the main these revolved around the cycle of life and the balance of nature. A disaster may be attributed to some failure to please a particular deity, and any positive event would be seen as the result of being looked upon favourably from above. Everyone has their own beliefs, and each person tends to favour some greater influence that binds together the fabric of life. The common element often comes from the natural foundation of life and the balance that must be maintained.

Nature, to many people, often seems to be cruel, but the oldest of stories and skills passed down from the tribal wise men or women recognize that natural balance is the critical factor in all things. The interdependence of every aspect of life was both accepted and exploited by these wise men and women to feed, cure and teach the safe way to coexist with nature. In the simple use of herbs as medicine, the combining of ingredients has been shown in modern times to reflect a balance of elements. It is often suggested that modern man has created an imbalance through science and the exploitation of natural resources. There are clearly some areas where most, if not all, would agree. In the longer term we must wait to see if our exploitation will be rebalanced.

Within all of this there is one fact that remains unexplained, and that is 'the force', both positive and negative, that links events or, some may say, stimulates them. We find this in every culture reaching far back into history, and if the folk tales are true it goes back to prehistoric times. Every culture gives it an individual name, but all commonly recognize the same attributes and influences. In humans we call it the soul, but in the natural world this life energy permeates every facet or entity. While we may not be able to explain it we are certainly aware of its influences and impacts.

It is this force that drives us to explore, invent and create. It is often the collective force that drives us to achieve great things, and sadly sometimes to destroy. We challenge the natural balance of the force and create an imbalance. The bending moment is the analogy that captures the concept of this imbalance, where internal or external forces create a pressure point that changes the existing structure.

This concept of balance, the forces and interactions of these elements on individuals, groups of people and organizations is reflected and explored in this book. It introduces the phases in balancing the force and how these underpin the 'bending moments' that occur within organizations, and it is hoped that by recognizing these forces and the potential impacts, the collective focus of organizations can be adapted and strengthened.

As far back as one is able to go in history, the impact of harnessing and focusing the collective power of man has been apparent: from the enormous task of building the Egyptian pyramids to the development of space travel through the combining of human knowledge and skill. In all the great endeavours, the exploitation of nature's power has been a crucial factor.

The great Pyramids often defy our understanding, for while the physics can be explained and quantified, the organizational skills of building these structures without modern equipment was inspirational. Many such achievements rest not on technology but on the desire and management of the collective force. In the same way, the first human to walk on the moon was not simply demonstrating a technological feat but also one of organizational mastery of vast numbers to consolidate knowledge and skills towards a common aim. Each in its way was a strategic masterpiece that identified and addressed the many challenges that needed to be overcome by exploiting either strength or knowledge.

An important milestone in modern development was the Industrial Revolution, where the harnessing of steam suddenly gave rise to new sources of energy that could be used to streamline traditional skills. It changed the nature of basic human dependence on hunting and farming, but in many ways it still rested on two key factors: the first was nature's ability to provide the fuel and the ore from which to produce iron; and second the need of human beings to organize themselves into an alternative culture (see Figure 1.1). It is perhaps an amusing aside to consider that while industrialists were promoting and exploiting the power of new technology they

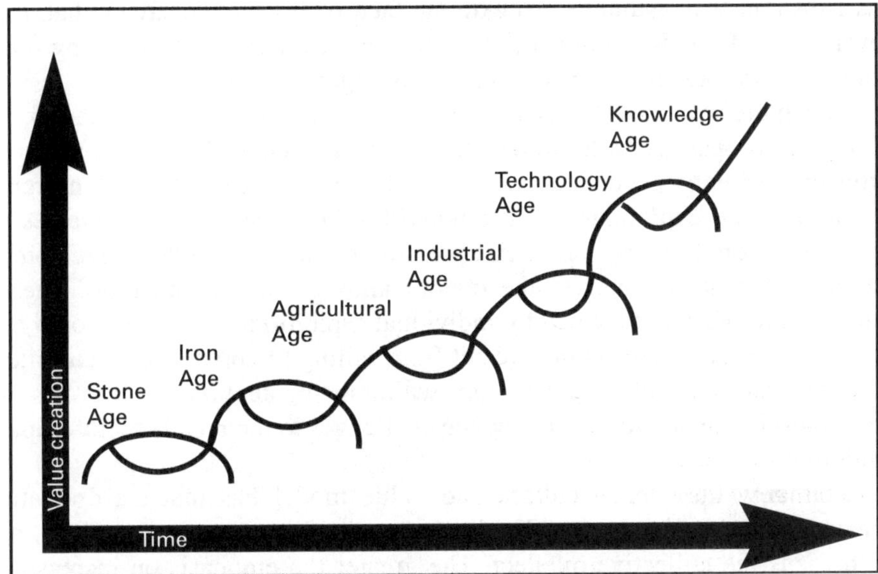

Figure 1.1   Eras of change

were dependent on people digging deep under the ground with crude tools to extract coal that nature had taken millions of years to develop.

The developments in harnessing the workforce had as their foundation the traditional hierarchical structures that had grown from early tribal society, which had then evolved through the disciplined infrastructures of military-led civilizations: command and control, either by direct force or via the control of resources. Wealth was generated through the exploitation of slavery, either as a result of military action or, as in the Middle Ages, through serfdom. As technology advanced and the focus shifted to skills, the power of the skilled partisan became a new measure of value combined with machine power. In today's knowledge age the value of an organization may be measured as much by its human assets as by its physical ones.

What is generally recognized in all these developments is that technology is only a small part of the equation, the true value being in the skill and knowledge of the people, and the ability of organizations to harness and deploy these capabilities, whether it is the skill of the stonemason building a Pyramid or a scientist designing the next space vehicle.

Many times we have heard chief executives stating that organizations are only as good their employees, and it is the people that make it successful. What I have also encountered in my career is that the reality of this often fails to be reflected in the manner in which organizations recognize, consult or involve people. Sometimes this may be by design but, being charitable, perhaps it is as a result of other external factors. It is an old saying that, for every pair of hands employed, you got a brain for free, but releasing that capability or engaging it challenges many organizations.

The more we move towards knowledge-led structures, the harder it becomes to operate the traditional command and control structure and the greater the interdependence, both vertically and horizontally, within organizations. The exploitation of the individual or collective force creates a reaction where failing to recognize pressure points can result in developing stresses that are counter to the overall aims of the organization. These stresses are often not created by individual aspirations, though it would be wrong to ignore these, as they result from failing to appreciate or consider the implications of broader strategies within the context of how individuals or groups in the organization view the challenges to their, and others', capabilities.

This new knowledge culture and value model has made a dramatic change in the leadership profile that is required to energize organizations and focus the collective intellect. The greater the emphasis on increasing the skill level, the higher the probability that individuals will themselves have a wider expectation and focus – not simply in terms of reward but more importantly in terms of recognition and satisfaction derived from contribution through consultation. The dilemma, then, is that as one strives to build an organization based on knowledge, the higher is the probability that one might also be creating internal pressures which, if not addressed, may undermine the overall objectives.

The wisest generals of old knew that they needed the best-trained troops who were also well-equipped and disciplined. They had to be hungry for rewards but sufficiently afraid so that they would fight well, then they needed to have faith in their general to lead them to victory. Today's leadership struggles with warriors who are intelligent and free thinkers wishing to be considered as contributors to strategy rather than as simple executers of policy. The paradox for management is to seek collective input to focus the force of the organization without creating collective inertia through paralysing death by analysis and debate.

Part of the challenge stems from the traditional view of assessing one's internal positioning and power. In the old ideas, knowledge is power, and status is derived from a perspective that the more people reporting to a manager, the more important s/he is. Many will scoff at this idea, but those working with organizations and companies in the twenty-first century still see this culture prevailing.

If managers want to maintain their position then maintaining control over staff is based on restricting information and effectively filtering the

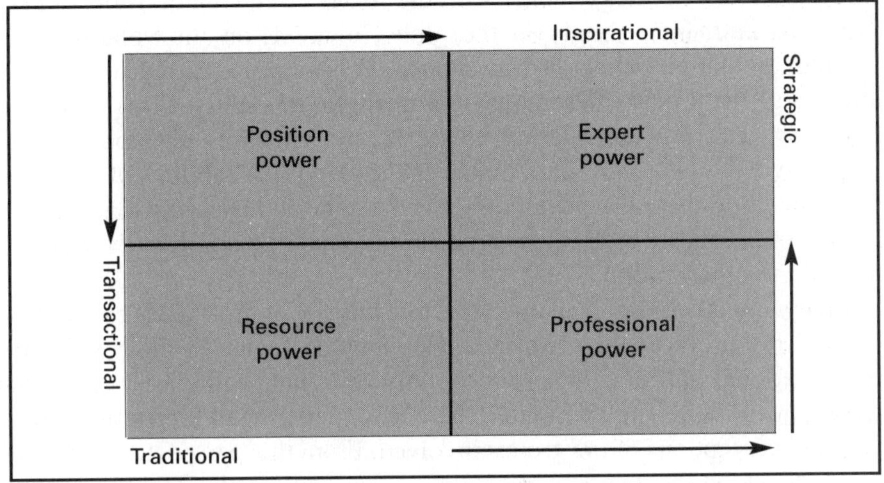

Figure 1.2 Positioning management power

communications flow to the resource pool. At the same time, influencing strategy is based on the control of these resources, the traditional view as shown in Figure 1.2. It must be said that the emerging dependence on e-mail is to some extent restricting this style of management.

Management by hierarchy can be equally disruptive, since the senior position may command authority but it is no guarantee of respect. The military, once again, recognize that leadership is about inspiring people to push beyond their own perceived limitations. Too often those who have limited knowledge or experience of the realities of their aspirations of the limitations of the organizations that will be required to achieve the result are responsible to define the business strategy.

The impact of professional power rests largely with traditionalists, who will base their strategy on historical experience. This may be a valuable contribution but is often relatively rigid in its perspective. The professional engineer, for example, is trained for excellence and strives to deliver the highest possible quality product. This may, however, not reflect the flexibility and demands of the market.

In contrast, the experts derive power from knowledge and tend to focus on inspiration to lead and direct, developing strategies that will inevitably stretch those around them but often failing to recognize the limitations of others, whether real or perceived.

Clearly, the optimum strategy is created by organizations that are able to draw on all these characteristics while maintaining a balance that reflects both external influences and internal capabilities. Frequently, organizations concentrate on strategy based on the external evaluation of market demands, and, increasingly in the global context, on the volatility and complexity that globalization has created. Focusing on the 'customer pull' effect and the capabilities of the competition is clearly a major factor. However, ignoring the internal pressures and conflicts that the strategy might evoke may well undermine the overall probability of success. Understanding the influence of effective balance and ensuring that the critical stress points are addressed is crucial in terms of exploiting the capabilities of the organization.

Many organizations lean towards the project approach to consolidate internal resources and develop a single strategic focus. In today's diverse organizational culture, where not only internal boundaries but also geographic diversity are common, there is a greater need to assess the realities and perceptions of the groups involved. From this perspective I evolved the concept of the bending moment to encapsulate the idea of internal stresses and the practical application of strategic stress analysis as a means of improving the identification of these key pinch points. With a long career operating in the project environment, and being an advocate of process and strategic thinking, I sought to develop an approach that could concentrate the internal focus of organizations and help to prioritize actions effectively.

To provide a structure for my thinking, and assist in the understanding of my research and conclusions, I have focused on four key phases. This approach provides a framework to draw together experiences across a range of industries which, despite being diverse in terms of business sectors, geography and culture (both national and corporate) prove to be very consistent. The exposure to many organizations has shown that what we each as individuals experience are common traits across industry. From this experience base I defined the four phases and the key elements that formed the basis of analysis (see Figure 1.3).

The first phase, 'Decoding the force' is focused on identifying the factors that create pressures on an organization. These look at the impacts of collision between internal groups or individuals, then consider the implications of internal resistance that often stifle innovation and change, which can impinge seriously on imaginative strategic thinking. Perhaps the biggest disruptive influence, however, is the impact of misinterpretation of directives or information that leads to a false baseline for assessment. The key to all successful strategy is that those required to take action understand the basic elements of what, when, where, who, how and, in a knowledge-based environment, why.

Next we move our attention towards what I refer to as 'Energizing the force', recognizing that organizations seek to exploit the force's resources

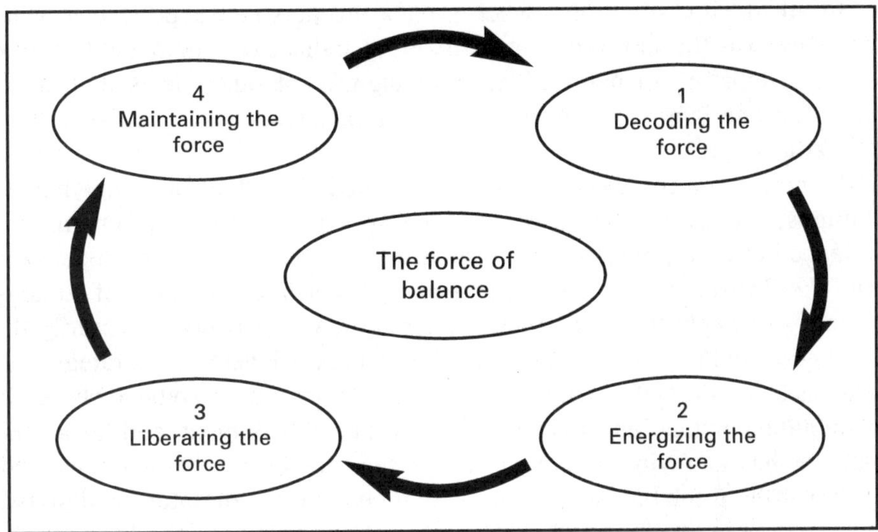

Figure 1.3 The force of balance

– in particular, in the form of people. The challenge has always been to release the know-how that exists without creating anarchy, moving this process forward to cultivate synergies across the organization where internal frictions may well act as sea anchors to progress. Finally, organizations need to harness the power of their operations to focus on common objectives by developing joint approaches that consider individual pressures and constraints, developing implementation programmes that encourage success rather than simply demanding outputs, which do not reflect in any way the capabilities of the group.

Having established a sound understanding of the pressures and drivers, an even greater challenge comes from 'Liberating the force' and releasing the organization to press forward. This includes the need for leaders to work on breaking down the barriers that constrain progress, and preparing the organization to take on the challenges ahead, increasing understanding and deploying approaches that address the concerns and limitations of the organization.

The final phase is structured around 'Maintaining the force'. Since the business landscape is not constant, any development or strategy will only survive if it is capable of adapting to change. In the global environment perhaps the only constant is change, which is a process, and not an event. By recognizing that change is inevitable, organizations need to feed the force and enhance its capabilities to face the next paradigm shift in the market, to maintain a competitive edge.

In all my investigations, when comparing personal experiences, what was clear was the similarity between the force that exists in an organization and that existing in nature. The most significant outcome is that, as in nature, if one ignores the need to maintain balance, events are likely to be unpredictable.

In many ancient works that have formed the basis of many human cultures, the essence of their thinking was founded on optimizing the balance between physical and spiritual forces. When working on *Sun Tzu and the Project Battleground*, I gained a greater understanding of strategy in terms of exploiting the balance; learning that it was not necessarily the strongest person that prevailed. In this context, developing strategy was seen as being crucial to winning, but that strategy must also be anchored in a sound understanding of capabilities and the environment, and those who believe they can win are likely to be successful.

In nature, if the balance is disrupted, then the force of nature will invoke events to counter the trend. The more we interfere with the balance, the greater the risk that we shall eventually distort the future, perhaps irrevocably. In our business environment there are many factors that we cannot control, and we have to have strategies that allow us to adopt a flexible approach. These challenges are increasing, and to compound these by not optimizing our organizations or ignoring the implications of internal stress will lead to an erosion of the chances of success.

Effective business strategy is a complex process of evaluating a combination of external influences and drivers alongside internal capabilities and constraints. Failure to recognize these attributes and pressures will inevitably drive an organization towards creating pressures where the bending moment will occur. This may be a dramatic event or it may simply result in progressive failure to achieve optimum results. Either way, organizations should be looking to identify and address those influences that they can control, and free resources, skills and focus to meet the influences that are less predictable.

Decoding the force

The force that exists or builds within an organization has a major impact on how that organization, or group of individuals within the organization, perform. The stress levels that can be created not only affect people at a personal level; they also introduce tensions between fractions or functional elements of the organization. The resulting diversion of focus then impinges on the overall performance of the venture.

The first stage in the process of harnessing the force and redirecting it towards the strategic aims of the organization is to decode or interpret where the stress points are and what may be the catalyst that is inducing them. In my experience and analysis of many business operations, I have collected these under three main categories.

The first of these is captured under the heading of **collision**. This represents those elements of the operation and activities that induce a narrowly targeted approach or individual agendas and generate friction. This pressure, whether intentional or by osmosis, creates pinch points that deflect from the overall objectives of the business. It has to be recognized that people are very different, and whenever a group are brought together there will be clashes of thinking and approach. This conflict environment can be harnessed to create innovative new ideas, but more often than not it exists by default through wider influences on the operating structure.

The second analysis is **resistance**, which often emerges as a result of change encroaching on the comfort zones of individuals or groups within an organization. This aspect has become more common since the 1980s, as globalization and technology development have introduced significant volatility into an increasingly competitive marketplace. Change is now seen inevitably within the business landscape at every level, from corporate global strategy down to the pressure on the working environment, technology, and more recently the optimization of resources through outsourcing to enhance competitive edge.

The third stage of assessment is focused on the impacts of **misinter-**

pretation in the context that, as the marketplace platform expands so the influences from outside an organization increase. National cultural differences introduce social friction within organizations, as do alternative business cultures and methods. The adoption of one may cascade through the organization and develop gaps between various sectors, functions or divisions. Globalization is part of the business environment and is becoming a common factor in all business strategy; the exploitation of opportunities also introduces new risks and the influence of stakeholders' considerations, including features ranging from profitability to corporate social responsibility.

To manage the force, its influences must first be identified within the organization by decoding the impacts, many of which may be obvious, but others are perhaps driven by operational approaches.

COLLISION

CHAPTER 2

Corporate silos

How often does one hear the marketing pitch, 'one organization focused on an integrated response to customer needs'? With globalization, this concept has been extended to encompass the idea of 'global but local'. It may be very convincing marketing where major corporations promote a wide product range tailored to the end-to-end support of customer operations. This has been further developing into alternative services propositions that aim to integrate themselves into the customers' business. This has been a more recent phenomenon particularly where the customers themselves have been looking to contract back into their core activities.

This concept of building holistic capability is one I would support wholeheartedly but the implications for many corporations and companies is that the current ethos and structure is incapable of supporting such a transition. The holistic approach requires a complete paradigm shift in mind-set for most traditionally-based operations that have been evolving sometimes over a hundred years or so. The silo effect, where vertical management constrains cross function working, is one that is visible in most organizations with which I have been associated, and it draws its strength from the traditional command and control management style that emerged from the first days of the Industrial Revolution.

Management structures are generally built around functional performance, capability, location and skill sets. The command structure then devolves from this core segregation throughout the organization. The measures of success and responsibility that have traditionally been employed reinforce this structure, and with them the first level of stresses, as in Figure 2.1, that create conflict, division and resistance to change.

These stress factors do not operate in isolation and a companies' performance is delivered through a combination of its capabilities and resources. Working in project environments, these external stresses are often faced by the project team, while inside the team the focus is on complementary activity towards common goals. The essence of any organization is in its leadership and one can easily recognize that when there is no integration at

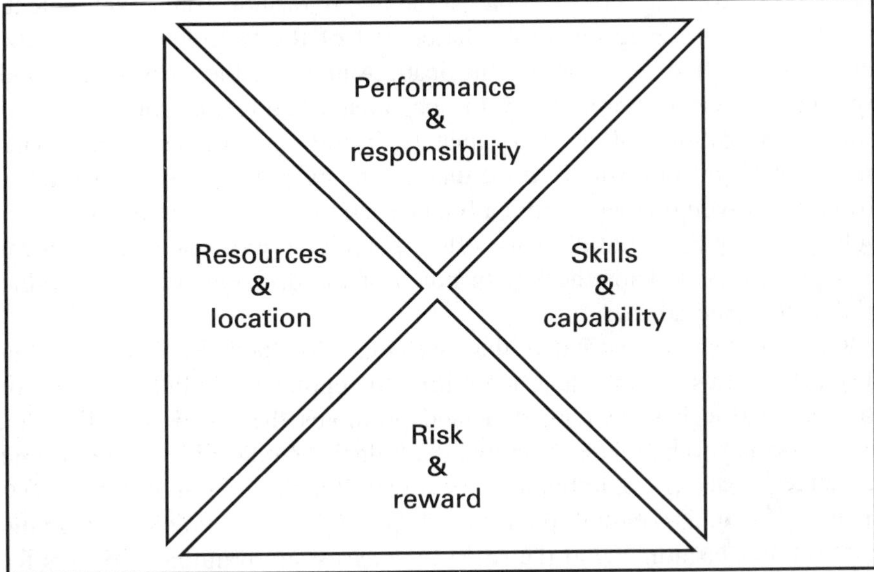

Figure 2.1 Key strategic stress factors

the top, there is never likely to be successful interaction down the chain of command.

The stress between functional groups can be epitomized for most of us by the perennial conflict between sales and operations. The driver for sales is to conclude contracts, and the responsibility for delivery rests with the operational groups. I am sure we have all experienced situations where contracts have been concluded, but where the operational group either is not fully aware of the contents of the deal or is being asked to deliver beyond current capability.

It would, however, be unrealistic to assume that this was the only area where these conflicts arise. The status of any functional group within an organization depends on a number of factors, which often evolve from the necessary core capability and skills in that business, or from the particular traits of the management or marketplace.

In the industrial age the specialist was considered to be superior to the rest of the organization, whatever the industry. This creation of an elite is natural, and rewards would reflect the dependence on that skill. In a similar way, society in general places great store on the professions (such as doctors), based on their importance to human well-being.

This focus on skill is perhaps understandable and justified, but what is perhaps less easy to understand, and perhaps more divisive, is the trend-based importance profiling. For example, at the height of industrial development, the engineer was king but in the latter part of the twentieth century, the financially skilled were taking the lead. And later, the information and communications technology (ICT) specialist became the cornerstone of many organizations, often, unfortunately, in my view, linked to the financial power. It is not difficult to see that, in an engineering environment, the stresses that would emerge from a finance-led management structure might well prove quite painful. This often perceived fad-based hierarchical management is perhaps the key to much of the division and stresses that arise within operations.

The problem is, perhaps, that we tend to specialize our training programmes to such an extent that failing to appreciate the holistic needs of an organization becomes inherent and promotes the creation of barriers. There also has to be recognition that the longer the educational process and investment made by an individual, the greater the desire to have that investment appreciated. A case in point is perhaps engineering which is becoming less and less fashionable at the same time as we are training engineers for excellence, so this training often conflicts with the commercial needs on the day. Having worked for many years in the project and procurement field, the constant challenge has been to balance cost and performance needs.

Engineers want to provide the best possible solution to a requirement, irrespective of the customer contract or needs. Similar challenges arise when considering the competitive exploitation of outsourcing manufacturing, where often generations of manufacturing skills are in conflict with the potentially more cost-effective overseas manufacturer. Part of the conflict is that purchasing policy has generally been focused on low price, rather than on total cost, and the technologists are defending their training and status.

Those who have experienced this conflict will appreciate that the best deal is one that considers the whole range of factors when making a selection of product or supplier. One element in this is that often the purchasing group has been built up without focusing on the truly necessary skills, and frequently under the guidance of financial management that looks only at the bottom line.

Divisional barriers are one aspect of the corporate silo that would be recognized by anyone working for or with a large organization. Again, one sees the pressure building up around status, which can often come from senior managements' own career path. If the chief executive officer (CEO) emerges from one particular sector of the business this will often lead to a special positioning of that division. The second, and perhaps more divisive, factor is internal competition in terms of both performance and investment.

What is most frustrating is where the complementary effects of the different groups are ignored in favour of individual targets.

These artificial boundaries can become predominant features of an operations culture, and a major cause of stress in every aspect of people and product development. Competition is a good stimulus for innovation, but it must be balanced against the overall objectives of the business and energy redirected, where it is being deployed in a counter-productive way. The automotive industry is one example of how internal investment programmes are driven towards specific operating units, where failure inevitability leads to job losses, and future collaboration between operating centres can be seriously impeded.

Territorial boundaries are also a significant factor in the perpetuating of the silo effect. For while it makes sense to define clear operating territories to optimize resources and overcome duplication of effort, the way in which these are recognized and managed can be instrumental in the building of silos, particularly when, in many industrial sectors, the global nature of investment and development operates at a higher level. A case in point is the mining industry, where customers, plant locations, engineering houses, contracting parties and financial institutions may range across all five continents. The question often faced is who owned the deal, and in several cases, while the internal debate raged, the real work was being overlooked.

This challenge of interlinking multiple companies, particularly in a global context, is one that certainly fosters the silo mentality, for while CEOs may proffer a one-company concept, their generals perhaps have other agendas. This often shows when there is an opportunity to deploy complementary products to provide a composite solution. Each entity, focused on its individual technology, production and margins, fails to integrate and as a result often misses the entire opportunity, or worse – astute customers play on the division to improve their own positioning. Personal experience with major global corporations, such as ABB and Siemens among others, has highlighted time and again the constraints of internal territorial boundaries.

Clearly, one should not look only at the management structure as being the only influence on these internal barriers. The impact of globalization has led to many organizations being multinational, and with this come the historical relationships and the implications of cultural diversity. These traits, which we all recognize in some way, are the feedstock of the silo society; the social undertones that often inadvertently support the more focused drivers for division.

Anecdotal reports from many pan-European organizations have highlighted the stresses that fostered silos based on national positioning. The differences generally attributed to the English and the French is no secret, but even closer to home regional differences pervade management structures. In Asia, similar frictions exist and even within the USA the regional or state cultures provide challenges to a truly homogenous platform. Whether organizations can become truly global is perhaps a far more philosophical debate, but these factors are part of the challenge in balancing the force of an organization.

Working in the industrial sectors emphasizes particularly another key factor briefly touched upon earlier, and that is the comfort zone. At a management level, the culture in which individuals trained will greatly influence the way they react to change or the influence of management from outside. When working around the world, one does develop some degree of adaptability, but often one is faced with such a level of in-built traditional culture that conflict is inevitable. The interesting facet of this is that the lower one's expectation of understanding the culture, the easier it is to build communication bridges. The less apparent the cultural differences, and the harder it is to recognize the amount of stress that pressurizing comfort zones will generate.

Traditionalism is perhaps one of the major factors in the spectrum of stress influences and corporate silos as in Figure 2.2 that can impede the deployment of new ideas and strategies, and thus disperse the force that

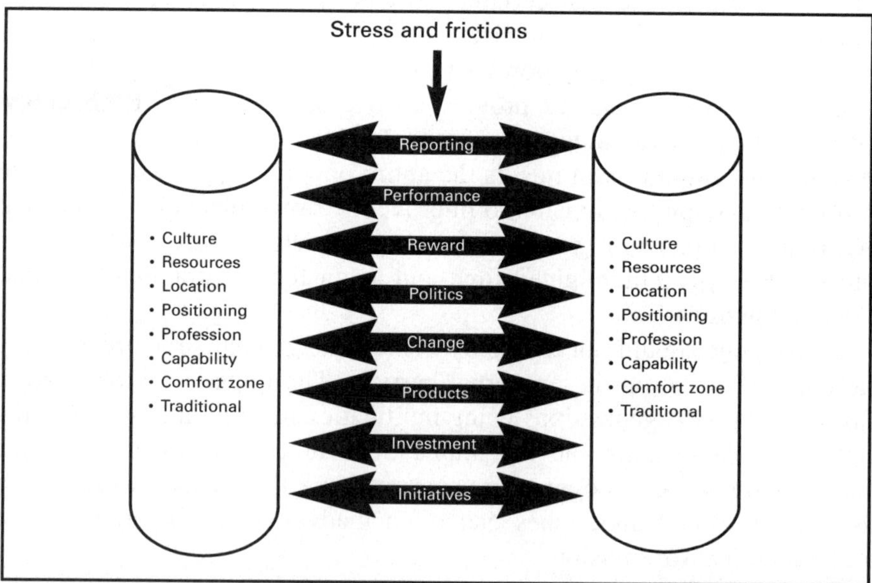

Figure 2.2   Corporate silos

should be focused on moving forward. When introducing change and innovation, which is a crucial facet of survival in the modern business arena, so often the comment is heard 'but we have always done it this way'. There may be tacit agreement to change, but the real motivation and drive is held back by this underlying concern that change will dissipate if it is allowed to run its course.

Often this concern is based not on a failure to recognize that change is necessary, but more on the capacity to grasp the nettle and rise to the challenge. It is interesting to consider this against a range of different national and regional environments. The more integrated the operation within the local community, the harder it is to grasp change, particularly where this might impinge on the local infrastructure. There is also the impact of the historical relationship of the venture: the older it is, the more change it has seen, but it has also seen change come and go, so with an opportunity to do nothing it might just pass away. Sadly, this frequently results in the balance being totally skewed and an opportunity to move forward being lost. The silo maintains its influence only ultimately to disappear against increased competition.

Perhaps the most significant factor in the creation of the corporate silo syndrome, however, is one that is a clear necessity for management but engenders more conflict than any other. Financial reporting and management has to be the most volatile aspect of any business venture. There can be no one in the business world who does not accept that the goal of a business is to generate value for its stakeholders, however that value may be distributed. It would also be generally accepted that one of the key measurements of success and performance is monitored through financial reporting. Unfortunately, this same reporting structure and the success or failure attributed to it is probably the biggest single factor in creating the silo culture within organizations.

The divisions of reporting and methodology define how every business sector, functional group and individual performance is measured. From this is generally derived how rewards are distributed and efforts acknowledged. Little wonder, then, that the way in which this is done affects the whole ethos and interaction between various parts of the organization, and even more the recognition that maximizing returns and optimizing resources within these financial regimes underpins the silo culture. More importantly, when the organization's strategic approach is based on integration, and the finance approach is focused more locally, the balance of the organization is seriously affected.

The natural focus for any manager is to concentrate the efforts of the group on the home territory, whether this is geographic or product-based. This in turn will affect the amount of cross-company activity and support that could or would be provided. Where organizations are self-supporting operating units this has less effect than when the divisional structure is based around expertise, products and skill sets. Thus any conflict between local needs and cross-company support will certainly affect the overall balance and probably create baggage that will surface when the flow needs to be reversed.

The sharing of profits across boundaries is also a factor within this financially structured, divisive approach. Inter-company pricing has always been a major obstacle against greater integration. Since local profits support local budgets and incentive programmes, maximizing margins is a key to performance measurement. All attention is focused on home needs and the silo walls thicken. In one organization in the power generation field there were four divisions and the strength of feeling became critical when three announced high returns but failed to recognize that their primary internal customer was the fourth division. Getting the forces of all four focused externally required a major change in mind-set which was driven by a shared financial reporting and incentive programme. This example is not uncommon across multi-divisional organizations.

In addition to the financial programmes, key performance indicators often engender a focus on continuous improvement but fail to recognize the interdependence that exists across the organization. Divisional, group or functional structures interact at some point, and the way each performs can have a significant impact on their internal partners. The conflict between supporting external customers directly or meeting the needs of internal customers for fewer direct external relationships proves the point that most silo cultures are too focused, to the detriment of the organization's ability to concentrate its force towards the market.

In all of this one should not ignore the implications of individual career programmes and the promotion of personal recognition that helps to support the traditional silo ethos. If one is measured principally on the performance of the group one manages it is likely the best efforts will be concentrated on those results. In many institutions, corporate gaming is the fundamental energy.

In analysing those major corporations that have gone into decline it is easy to see the amount of effort being focused on positioning. This in turn leads to a group trait that is encouraged to protect the silo and optimize how it looks to the internal world as opposed to focusing on external performances for customers and shareholders. Around the world we have seen so many examples of self-focus being the main driving force that it has overtaken the benefits of measured performance, and these organizations are crumbling because of imbalance.

Other factors that help to support the corporate silo paradox is the skills gap and national salary structures. Working with companies across Europe, the USA and Japan there are many myths that should be exploded regarding capability, dedication and application. National traits are often discussed, but in practice it comes down to the organization and the individual, though some cultural foundations may never change.

There is, for example, a perspective found on both sides of the Atlantic regarding business approaches and skills, and from personal experience these stereotypical views are far from being consistent in terms of both good and bad traits. However, this often causes stresses between organizations needing to share working environments and information. Thus the effort is not put in, the gulf widens and the silos harden. On one side there may be the view 'Why should I train someone to take my job?', while on the other, the view that without global-level wage structures the work put in is not being properly recognized.

These personal considerations provide, and perhaps define, the character of each working group, which is then directed by a management that is self-focused and driven by financial forces. And occasionally the complication of political differences between nation-states provides even more material for the silo builders. For example, when the USA has an embargo in operation, sister companies may be used to function outside national boundaries but still be required to report and function through USA organizations, and once again the local silo finds a focus for protectionism.

Finally, the shareholders' expectations and customer needs are being used either to support the silo or, more often than not, they are suffering from the implications of the corporate silo effect.

Many attempts have been made to address the paradox of the silo, which is created partially as result of trying to build in responsibility and accountability, and to incentivize individuals and groups. The 1990s saw the evolution of matrix management approaches, but these failed to meet the challenge effectively. The holistic concept works on paper but still does not compensate for those who seek to manipulate it to their own advantage. Perhaps there is no answer, and all organizations can do is to promote an effective ethos at the individual level. And then monitor where these silos are creating a negative force on the balance of the operation and take local action.

CHAPTER 3

Customers and competitors

There are two major external stresses on any organization: the first is the relationship with the customer base, and the second comes from the performance and approach of the competition. This is not new thinking by any means, but what are often ignored are the internal stresses that are created by failing to understand these drivers and having a common strategy and approach in dealing with them.

For many businesses the concept of 'build it and they will come' has permeated many internal strategies. Working, for example, with engineering companies, where product design is the lifeblood of the operation, it has frequently created a challenge of thinking when external supply is shown not only to be superior but often more competitive. Engineers put so much of themselves into the products they design that they find it hard to accept that others may be providing a better package. Many times external relationships with customers have been strained or broken because of the technical debate between conflicting engineering viewpoints.

There can be few in the business world who have not witnessed the conflict between sales and operations when a sale has fallen through. On the one side the product champions maintain that they have the high ground technically and the customer does not know what he wants, while on the other hand, the sales organization rests on the standard responses of the price being too high, the company is technically out of step, or the competition has the inside track. All of this may in part be true, but more effort is often expended on justification than on addressing the problem. Whatever the reality may be, the customer, as the old adage goes, is never wrong. However, this internal conflict burns up resources and prevents organizations from capitalizing on skills and knowledge.

The push/pull complexities of the marketplace have long since become part of the business strategic profiling agenda. On the one hand one presses into a market with an existing product and battles against all comers to promote its virtues or value. On the other, the smart money is on those few who are able to create a market desire for a product or service that every-

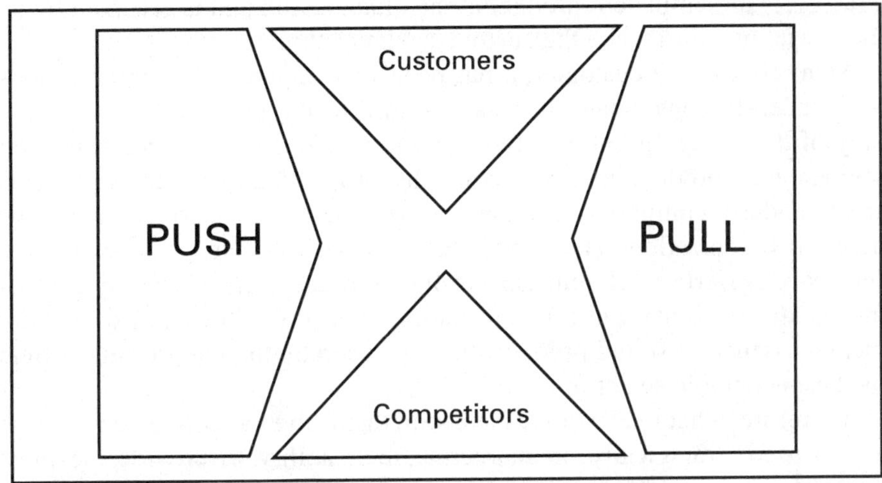

Figure 3.1 Market pressure

one wants. One current example has been the success enjoyed by the front-running mobile phone producers. In earlier times the personal computer (PC) companies created a demand that sucked in sales. This is the territory where the PR and marketing industry has often made its name, by building demand rather than satisfying a need.

Again, none of this is new, but I did not set out to write a new 'sales and marketing' manual. The objective is to understand how the interfaces with the outside world can build stresses within an organization that may dilute or derail internal strategies. Having experienced both sides of the trading table, as customer and supplier, it is easy to identify how organizations compartmentalize the functions of sales and operations, thus creating the first significant stress point in the overall operation.

One would accept that these roles might require very different skills, but if they are examined closely they are not that dissimilar, and the most effective approach is to work more holistically in both directions. It must always be remembered that while the customer may develop individual relationships, generally they see the organization as a whole, and the more astute customers will spot the cracks and exploit them.

It is crucial to have a firm understanding of customers' requirements and to be able to adapt the proposition on offer to meet these needs, whether real or perceived. It is this second factor that often creates the biggest hurdle, in that what guides a decision may not be based on real need. What is even more important is to ensure that this knowledge, and the appropriate strategy, is disseminated throughout the organization and is accepted by all those who may influence the customer relationship.

Many times, as a customer, it has been very apparent that organizations have failed to consolidate their sales effort, to the endless frustration not only of those buying but also those trying to sell. Major corporations that segment their product range by geography, production locations or products create endless complexity for the customer. It is not uncommon for one umbrella organization to have three salesmen visit the same customer in the same week offering different aspects of their range. This is not only confusing for the customer and time-consuming, but it also breaches the fundamental essence of sound product strategy, whereby the widest range offers the best economic selection.

Therefore, what readers may have seen themselves are organizations that are focused strategically on marketing their ability to provide the most comprehensive service to the customer going on to undermine that strategy at the interface through a lack of co-ordination. The internal impact of this is also to drive wedges between sectors of the business that either want to promote their individual product at all costs, or blame others for damaging the customer relationship. Once again, the smart customer will capitalize on the fragmentation to exploit gaps in the sales profile.

This lack of focus is not only diverting efforts from successful sales; it is also likely to be demanding ever-increasing internal efforts and resources to fight contests that have no positive contribution to the business strategy. The larger and more diverse the organization, the wider the potential to engender stress within the fabric of the operation. Several major multinational organizations have grown and then collapsed under the stress of internal boundaries, divisions and customer ownership issues. These are matrix organizations that spend the vast majority of effort reflected inwards towards self-justification and positioning.

The second common facet of customers influencing internal operations derives from the conflict between the future strategic developments of the customer and the internal assessment of where future strategic investment should be going. There is certainly a trend in many sectors of business for organizations to focus on the core activities and find partners or outsource non-core operations. It would therefore make sense for those marketing to that business sector to re-align their business to be more service-orientated.

An example of this is mining, where the real expertise of the major operators and the principal value is in the end product sales, whether the product is copper, gold, platinum or diamonds. Acquisition takes over from exploration, and a reducing global skill base constricts available resources, and there emerges the strategic concept for the life of plant operations being handed to third-party organizations, many of which market externally their ability to provide a complete service to the customer. Internally, however, their structure, capability and historical operating approach is focused on the manufacture of equipment and supply. Many traditional corporate divisions are most actively confronting the global strategic movement in favour of their individual product line or localized skill set. Those selling the concept inevitably clash with the traditionalists and again we see the strategic stress deflecting what was a sound customer-driven market position.

What is interesting in these circumstances is that smaller organizations, recognizing the market opportunity, look to build partnerships with complementary organizations to provide a complete service. Since they are not in conflict with their partners and have a firm focus on the strategy they can prosper, while their bigger competitors implode. So the concept strategy was valid; it is just the dependence on effective relationships and internal structures that defines the winners and losers.

It is similarly important to integrate customers' future strategies into the internal developments under consideration. Very often the perception of where the product, service or organization should be developed is driven by internal assumptions. Many organizations have lost significant ground in the marketplace by following internal convictions for investment without testing these on the existing customer base. Alternatively, organizations take a stance on developing new markets without understanding properly the suitability of the offering.

As has already been said, the focus for any market initiative must come either from understanding the customer needs and plans, or by developing a desire that future offers are geared to satisfy. The forces within an organization frequently become negatively charged because of this. Where the development programmes are focused on internal desires and the customer-facing operations are trying to influence the investment based on interpreting the customers' focus.

One interesting example was in respect to a major provider in the power industry. A product left for a number of years because of a lack of investment came up for discussion and, as in many industries, the 'buy or build' debate raged. The technologist won the day, but the target competitive levels for the new product were based on external testing. This ignored the demands of the market, and after eighteen months the programme was stopped because not only was there a reality check made on the customer investment profile but also advances by external suppliers demonstrated that the previous assumptions would not be competitive.

The result in this case was not only a considerable waste of effort but also a lack of concerted focus to optimize alternatives. The power bases we discussed around corporate silos have a major impact in this area, around the effective directing of corporate force and energy. In a highly competitive market the biggest impact on the bottom line is waste and so often this comes from a lack of integrated strategies.

There does, of course, have to be a consideration of strategic positioning, where often having one's own technology base provides an advantage. The question is whether the skills and knowledge are maintained but no commitment is made to the production that is a strategic issue. In similar circumstances the outsourcing of production may provide a competitive advantage, but this has to be balanced against the lost of a skills base for the future.

There has been much written since the mid-1990s about the benefits of greater integration throughout the value chain, and I shall discuss the implications of partnerships and alliances later. However, with respect to internal developments, the targeting of internal resources towards customer-focused activities is yet another cause for internal conflict. In most organizations, one sees the complexity of personal drivers ranging from 'Why? We have always done it this way' to the visionary who looks forward and says, 'Why not'. Understanding the customer's position is as important as identifying internal conflicts.

When these forces build up within an organization the strategic imperatives become very vulnerable to the impact of negative forces, which are often not visible. The one thing for certain in these types of arrangements

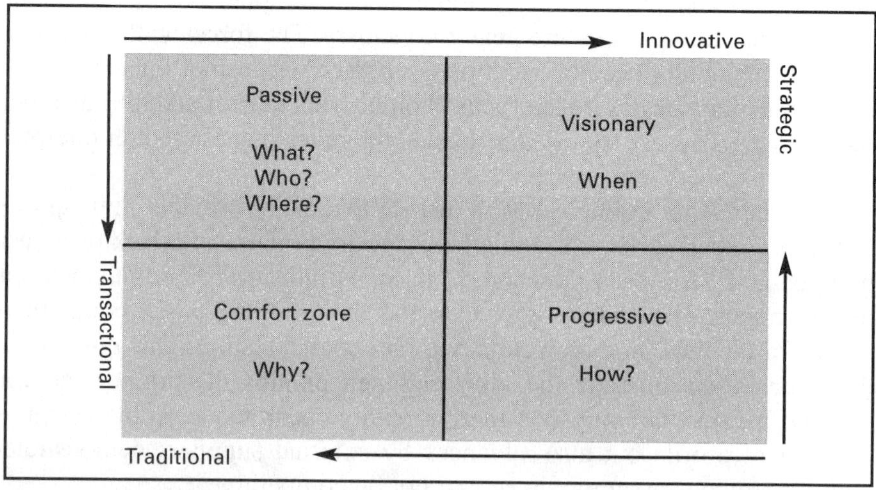

Figure 3.2 People positioning

is that there has to be complete consistency of approach across the organization. The closer one gets to the customer, the more visible are the internal divisions and the more vulnerable the organization.

The development of a new delivery programme to meet the desires of a new customer may demand internal changes that, rather than being seen as evolution, are resisted in favour of protectionism. It is also unwise to assume that customers will not have their own traditionalists, whether for choice of products or methodologies. I worked on a refinery project in the Middle East at a time when microchip technology was exploding into the marketplace and the passion was for the latest and best. The customer rejected this in favour of more mechanical controls because, in their view, their company had the skills to support this approach. The result was a major internal battle on what the customer should be offered, the new technology supporters won the day and the customer went elsewhere.

These pressures from the customer are not only restricted to technology and scope of service. The nature and culture of the customer can be a major factor that needs to be absorbed and utilized by the organizations internal force. Those who have had experience of working in both the public and private sectors will appreciate the distinct differences in corporate culture that thread through the operations and approaches. Take these differences a stage further into the global market and add the next level of national culture to the complex mix of relationships and one starts to see the external forces that can drive into organizations at every level.

Looking at a range of countries, it is easy to see how the local customer may come into conflict with those who are comfortable with established methods. More importantly, one begins to appreciate how the deployment of a strategy can be compromised because of a lack of consideration for the frontline challenges being faced. When the home office fails to deliver they may see this as a small impact, but to the teams in the firing line the results can be serious.

Working with construction organizations around the world, one gets used to the divide between site and home office, and the more remote the location the stronger the likelihood of conflict – not because people want to fight, but because each is failing to appreciate the customer-driven pressures that are being applied. It soon evolves into a 'them and us' situation, where customers are frequently exposed to internal divisions through frustration. The force is then diluted, and the possibility of executing a strategic approach crumbles through the division of energy and focus.

The balance of internal forces is therefore critical to an organization, and when any imbalance affects the external relationships with customers there is a serious challenge to business success. Unfortunately, while these situations seem clearly counter to what most companies would promote as their common focus, I have seen many times the stresses that can be created by failing to maintain a balance, not only diverting internal focus but also often damaging external perceptions.

Having looked at the customer influence, it is just as important to address the impacts that competitor pressures can apply to internal stability. The most interesting aspects of this are the internal strategies that are developed around what the competition is doing, and the perception of how good they are. This was highlighted recently when, being involved with a major merger, I had the opportunity to sit across the table from previous competitors. It became apparent very quickly that the assessment of the skills, capabilities, technology and operational performance each had of the other had been greatly inflated. They say the grass is always greener on the other side, but when you reach the grass the reality is often quite different. It was certainly so in this case, and my research suggests that it is a not uncommon trait within organizations to underrate themselves and inflate the capabilities of competition.

Customers often fuel this perception as a means of strengthening their own negotiating positions. However, the message that goes back into the company is often couched in terms of 'well, if they can do it, so can we'. The truth is often that what is being suggested is not entirely correct and a rabbit is set running without any real research. A large amount of effort is expended and pressures created between interested parties – for example, sales and production – when energy should have been focused on understanding the reality of the situation or developing an alternative solution.

Following the competition is never a good long-term strategy, and failing to understand properly the challenge that the competition is inducing, will create the imbalance that allows them to move forward while your group chases its tail. I would not suggest for one moment that it is not important to match or surpass the expectations of the competition, but the benchmark of where the competition stands must be rationalized, since what the customer or market is seeing may be reflective of many issues that are perhaps not similar in the case of your organization.

From a wide experience in the field of procurement, the hardest things to grasp are the peripheral issues that have an impact on price and the performance of a supplier. The strategic focus of the competition may be directed towards any number of targets, from filling excess production capacity to market or customer penetration, where the focus is on a long-term initiative. Their performance may be based on a more aggressive risk management profile or contracting strategy, which seeks to capitalize later on a low-cost starting point.

Certainly, the competition helps to set the trend and provides a series of measures to set the market rate, but these are dangerous if viewed in isolation. Even more destructive is the pressure that can be transmitted internally by treating these indicators as absolutes. It does, however, happen quite frequently across organizations, which then find themselves embroiled in internal debates and defensive barriers that deflect from the main task of winning. There must be a balance that accepts information from external sources and validates the possibilities in a concerted way.

The most common failing is that one has to be sure that like is being compared with like. In a more consumer-focused environment, where the market price and value proposition is initially declared more widely than perhaps the bespoke arena, the analysis of the competition has to be measured and properly considered. Effective network and market testing is an essential ingredient of any marketing strategy. Performance feedback is another crucial element in the equation, since the customer relationship is not only based on the immediate price differentiation. The competition will not set out to make life easy, but if by chance their strategy is to destabilize a company's operations then balancing internal forces is crucial if these forces are not to be misdirected.

One major company I experienced at first hand was so far behind the competitive market that they eventually gave up trying to squeeze their traditional approach and manoeuvring into a competitive position. Many months of development work, picking up various elements of performance and cost, with the various functional groups and much internal conflict had failed to improve matters. The approach was then changed to work on anticipating market levels and risk winning without a defined programme for actual delivery. Certainly this was a risky strategy, but it resulted in winning a major contract and the company then mobilized the entire force of the organization to find ways to meet the challenge. Thankfully, they succeeded.

Established players are part of the spectrum, but more difficult to evaluate are the newcomers. With increasing globalization these more and more frequently challenge traditional organizations. There is always a tendency to assume that the market will have some degree of loyalty, or at least view new competition with a degree of reluctance until they have been seen to perform. The reality is that many times the customer will not seek to employ new players immediately, but they will certainly use the offerings to set new benchmarks in terms of price, scope and performance.

The most influential aspect of competitor positioning is that which stems from close relationships with customers, and in particular where these may have established partnerships. The closer a competitor is to the customer,

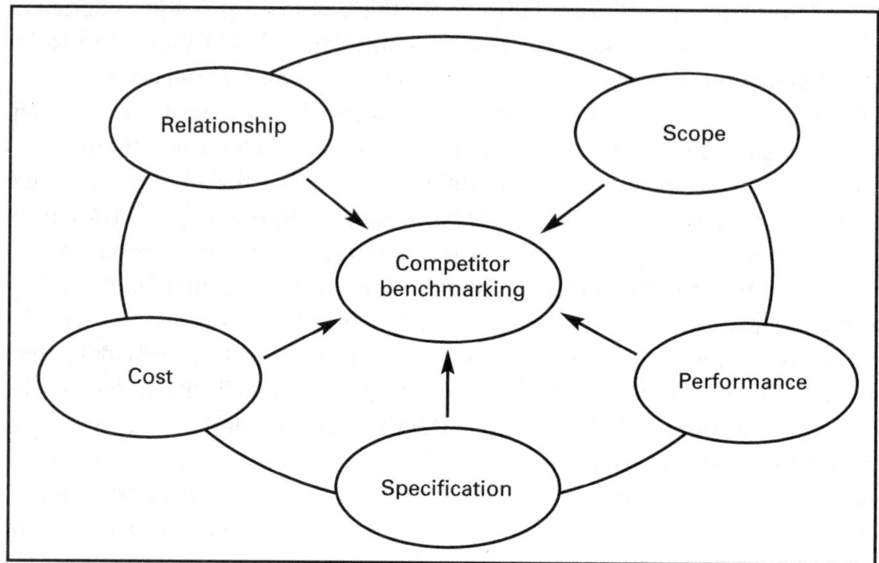

Figure 3.3 Competitor capability

the harder it is to prevent the distorting of information. It has often been a policy to 'power map' customers and try to develop an interconnection with key competitors. This helps the process of understanding the drivers for aspects of performance, and thus the evaluation of trends and demands.

Competition is the essence of a free economy market but it has to be measured against the organization and not used as a club to beat through options that might in the long-term be detrimental to overall performance. It should also be recognized that, in many markets, the underlying networks or national traits can be a factor that have little to do with competitiveness.

Those who have worked in the global market will appreciate the support and tight relationships that can influence customers' choice. Whether this is on a personal basis or through some national preference, we all perhaps appreciate the benefits of a global free market, but over several decades there have been many occasions when the reality has been far from what was seen in prospect.

The public face of the competition and its real capabilities may, as with one's own company, be totally different. The pressure to meet these expectations can drive wedges into even the most carefully orchestrated business strategies. The impacts across an organization may be significant, and the dilution of effort and focus that comes from chasing false goals debilitating.

This challenge of maintaining the balance of forces between competitive leapfrog and simply tearing the organization in pieces to follow a localized competitor trend is a major issue for many in the global market, even more so when amplified by the pressures of the internal silo, impacts that utilize these trends to further other agendas. It is interesting that most organizations analyse why orders were lost but few analyse why they won them. Yet it is the benchmark of winning that sets the future programmes. Frequently, winning was a combination of factors that might shield the true competitive position.

I would be the first to agree that lively competition is the lifeblood of product and service improvements, but at the same time it must be recognized that it produces considerable internal stresses if not evaluated in context. The assessment of when and how to react to the competition in a holistic manner is a key part of maintaining the right balance and focus on the forces of an organization.

CHAPTER 4

Business environment

In today's marketplace there can be few, if any, businesses that are not only dealing with the intricacies of their own industry sector but also the effects of globalization. There are those who suggest that we are seeing a major business revolution in the wake of increased globalization. Tom Peters, in his book *Liberation Management* said 'Globalisation and information technology are bringing about the most dramatic transformation in the history of business'. In reality, we believe that we are simply experiencing the next evolution of business.

Global trading is certainly not new, but recent advances in travel and communications have created a much faster pace of change. These factors have accelerated the impacts of global variations and as a result appear more dramatic. What is certain is that, within the boundaries of most organizations, the implications and pressures brought about by globalization and strategies reflecting this environment are severe.

When simply reviewing the world news media that brings issues into the office or home as they happen, it is sure that some influences now encroach on the business community at a much lower level in the hierarchy than was previously noticeable. These new impacts did, in the main, eventually bite into localized operations but now the transition is immediate. Some issues in the past would, through time delays, often have been marginalized and had limited impact. Today we have to recognize the global implications on our operations, which is very complex and volatile.

I spent most of my career involved with both customers and suppliers in foreign countries. Those who have shared similar backgrounds will appreciate the frustrations and intriguing nature of these interactions. Technology may have opened the door to many opportunities in terms of optimizing global business operations, but it has also created many challenges for those in the organizations associated with that trading community. The Internet has provided access to new customers and suppliers, but at the same time it has failed to overcome the challenge of the 'wired' relationship, both internally and externally.

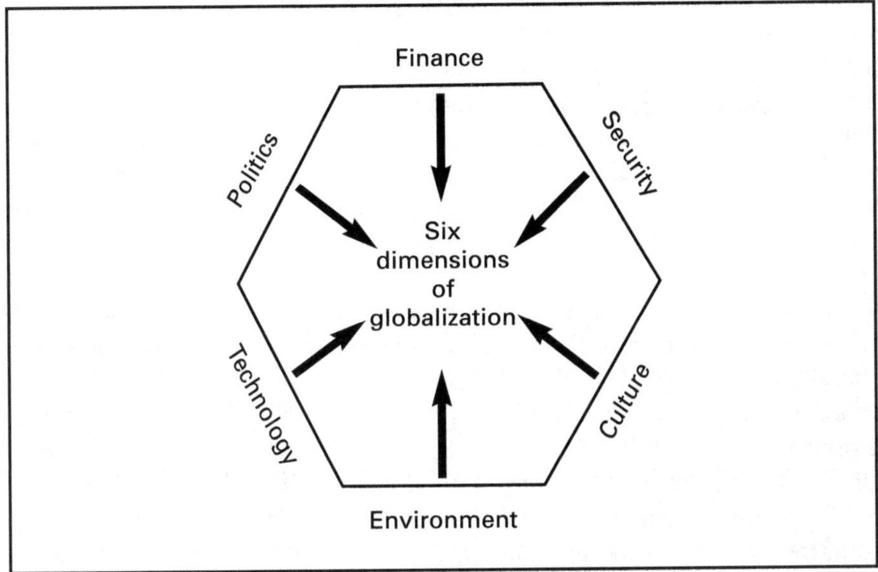

Figure 4.1 Global pressures

The drive to capitalize on low-cost manufacturing has left many struggling to meet customer expectations, and internal groups trying to rationalize the strategy. Since, despite product and national loyalty, customers will always maintain a close link between price, quality and service, whether at a business or consumer level. Those that have mastered these linkages have been forced to abandon traditional sourcing patterns in order to harness the competitive edge as well as having to address the internal stress implications.

While technology may take one part of an organization forward, it creates a negative effect in others. Competition grows as standards and reliability improve, so the pressure on price overtakes differentiation. The customer will always look for the most commercially suitable deal, and so the supply profile is a constantly changing platform. The automotive industry presents a clear and graphic example of this. The growth of imports from the Far East has progressively overcome initial resistance and customer perceptions. The importation of more streamlined manufacturing techniques and business models into Europe, for example, brought further erosion of the market share, and customer acceptance increased pressure on established local manufacturers. Today, even these advance operations are suffering from competition from newcomers emerging from their own regions, therefore even high-tech and advanced manufacturing investment can be seen to have enjoyed only a limited period of success.

The nationality of a motor vehicle can now only be attributed to the manufacturer's name, and the heritage is only assumed by the average customer. Brand has taken prominence over the historical relationship with origin. Traditional manufacturing and supply networks have been abandoned and local producer networks at every level have been forced to merge, globalize or close. As quality demands increase and price levels decline the pace of global exploitation increases. Effectiveness in delivering on this exploitation is dependent on focusing the internal forces of an organization to adapt.

The Internet allows both large and small companies to appear equally proficient and attractive to a potential customer, and the ability to search and compare provides choice and information as never before. The challenge for organizations is to master the trust barrier and deliver as promised. In the short-term, the impact is creating benchmarking that pressurizes the traditional supplier and the organizations behind them.

The historical colonial model of exploiting natural resources in foreign countries was of an ever-changing battlefield. Wars have been fought across the globe for centuries in an effort to secure profitable resources. Today the new global war is one of economics, which challenges rich and poor alike. The generals now are the leaders of industry and finance, the front line is the organizations that must absorb the strategies and develop a focused approach.

The value of companies, investments and tangible assets can rise or fall without the past benefit of time to evaluate or temper the realistic impact. Major shareholders may be on the other side of the globe and have no national loyalty. Their decisions (and sometimes their gambles) can have immediate and dire consequences. Once again, we can identify the volatility of the market and the effect it can have in undermining strategies. Exchange rate changes can turn success into failure without any consideration of the effort that has been expended. Customer loyalty at every level of the market can wane quickly against a backdrop of personal risk or impact appraisal.

As the industrial economic climate has become harsher, so major industries have reacted with rationalization, merger and acquisition. The bigger the player, the greater the spend profile and thus the greater the opportunity to capitalize on economies of scale. Traditional loyalty has no place in this economic juggling act, and the focus for organizations must be on optimizing their operations within this minefield.

Politics has seldom been a friend of the market. The saying goes that a day is a long time in politics. Compound that understanding with the fact that instant communication can engender dramatic changes in moments throughout the world trading markets. Political changes can be debated over long periods of time, such as the World Trade Organization (WTO), or erupt overnight and completely change the market complexion for both large and small operators.

In addition, random acts of terrorism can destabilize trading positions in hours, and along with those impacts comes the whole issue of global supply and political acceptance or boycotts. The regulatory differences across the globe can be a source of both opportunity and high risk. Those who have had the experience of working in many different countries will appreciate the complexities that need to be overcome. Changes in legislation around the world may be motivated by protectionism, political differences or a desire to localize investment, and the raising or lowering of trade barriers has to be managed in both the short and the long term.

The front-line impact of globalization is in the aspect of competition. As the industrialized market achieves a greater acceptance of overseas products and cost benefits, so the opportunity for newcomers to join the race for market share increases. The traditional models of the multinationals manufacturing in the Third World under their direct control and the trader importing on a speculative basis have now more than ever been opened up to direct competition.

In the latter part of the twentieth century the growth in direct competition has changed the face of market share. On the other side of the coin the perception of the wealth in the industrialized countries by those in the Third World has eroded the opportunity for export profitability to these poorer centres. Education, information and communication have homogenized the market place, increasing the desire for Western technology but only at local price levels. Again, we see the traditional manufacturing-based industries being squeezed in both directions. Therefore, the liberalization of the market that is certain to continue will be constantly 'moving the goalposts' for the business community and unsettling business strategy.

It is not to infer that globalization is entirely negative; like most situations in life there is something positive to be considered. Globalization and communications have opened up a vast new potential customer base. Industrialization and consumer awareness means that opportunities can be developed. As these developing markets grow, so the opportunity and the desire for higher living standards creates expectations and a purchasing drive. The exportation of technology and brand replaces hardware, which in itself would be beyond the growing economic capabilities. The need to develop localized capabilities is an opportunity but also a potential threat, for once knowledge is transferred a partner may become a competitor overnight.

In reality, we have already passed this stage of evolution with the major competitive markets. Today more advanced versions of original technology are flowing backwards up the trading rivers. Perhaps the next major evolution will be joint ventures focused on exports to the next emerging areas of the world. Some examples of this can already be seen and more will surely follow. In this environment the common focus of the organization is a threat that must be recognized, and the challenge is to maintain the flow of the energy within an organization. The challenge for the global organization is not so much in identifying the capabilities but in merging them into an effective organization.

Globalization may be a blessing or a curse, but one thing is certain, it is here to stay. The role of leadership is being stretched to meet these obstacles and opportunities. The rules of engagement have been widened and the exploitation of the market rests not only on traditional conventional relationships at home but must now encompass dimensions that many not have previously been confronted. The skills and awareness needed to capitalize on meeting the global challenge must generally be raised to new levels. Many may suggest that we already buy in the world market and have done so for years, but other organizations have maintained their historical approach and will find themselves increasingly disadvantaged.

As outlined already, the commercial world is getting smaller, and the challenge of the market and the impacts of globalization are beginning to squeeze business ventures both large and small. This arena is more complicated than many will have faced before. Even those who have moved around the world realize that they have to modify their approach to be successful. For those starting out on the road, or having to change direction in order to meet the growing international dimensions of business, cultural awareness is a crucial factor. It may seem obvious to suggest that different nationalities require different approaches but sadly very often organizations fail not because of marketing issues but because of a failure to recognize the alternative cultural aspects of a business environment. The appreciation of local knowledge and guidance should never be underestimated, since what might be very effective in one location can have the absolute opposite effect in another.

It is sometimes easy to recognize someone from another region by their appearance and language, but it is not so easy to appreciate their attitude and approach to business. For example, working in China is less culturally difficult than in, say, northern Europe. This may seem strange, but when the statement is analysed, in China it is obvious that people are different so people immediately compensate for the possibilities of language and cultural difference. Yet being part of the EU and having a relatively common business environment together with, say, a good use of English by both parties, the expectation of reaching an understanding is much higher. As a result, the effort put in to communication is reduced and often the results are correspondingly less successful. Taking these differences back into the flow of an organization is crucial if support is to be maintained.

It is dangerous to assume that there is a common culture depending on which part of the world one is in, as cultural diversity is the result of a homogenized blend of many factors and traits. We tend to classify these into three main groups: national; business; and corporate (see Figure 4.2). This ignores the personal dimension, which is a common element the world over and would be far too difficult to categorize, since we can all appreciate, even on our home territory, that there is a wide range of personal traits which result in individuals melding with some and being rejected by others.

Starting from the broadest perspective, people are generally a reflection of the environment they frequent, therefore it is useful to have a knowledge of the local terrain before venturing into any discussions. In the Far East, access to information about the West is usually gleaned through the media, so there is always an impression that Western companies have deep pockets.

On the other side of the coin, many countries viewed from the West and entitled 'Third-World' are seen as being unsophisticated and limited in experience, but nothing could be further from the truth in the real world. Many of these countries have trading histories that dwarf those in the industrialized

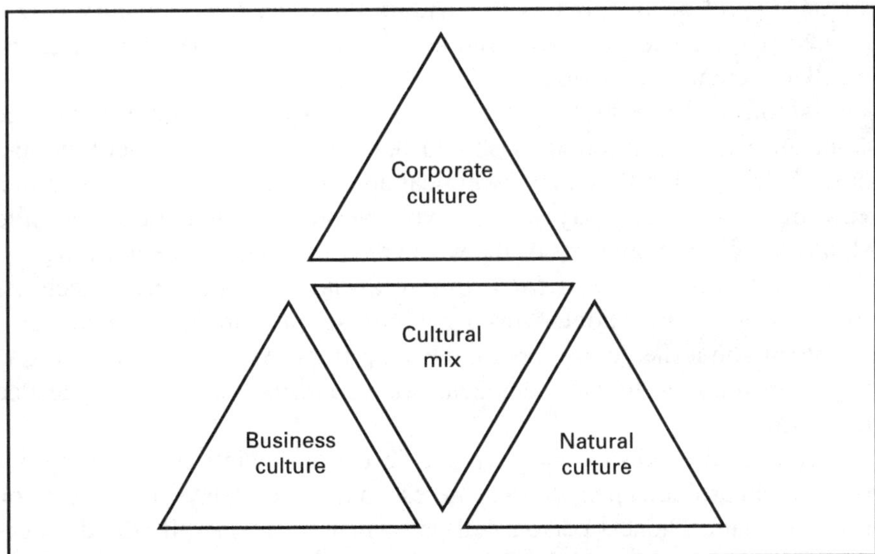

Figure 4.2 Cultural stress

West, often dating back thousands of years. In a trading environment they have almost genetic capabilities in terms of handling very complex negotiations. They also have cultural approaches that in the West may be considered antiquated or even questionable, but these are their ways and are something that must be accepted.

To use the local market as an example, one can consider, say, a small cost increase that most Western businessmen would handle by credit card being equal to the local inhabitants' annual salary. The perception therefore is that the number is a big one and the exchanges may be very difficult. From another aspect, local governments may place much greater penalties on an individual for failure, therefore resistance to acknowledging or accepting changes will be fought simply at a personal level.

In more general terms, the subjects of religion and politics are always to be avoided, or if raised, handled with great care. In some parts of the world the two are inextricably linked and this can cause great tension. Finally, be alert for emotional outbursts. These may not be understood and can cause great discomfort and confusion. It may be a good thing to show how one feels, but make sure that this is not focused or received in a personal way. In some cultures it is seen as a weakness or impolite, but in others it is considered as a normal discussion mode.

Moving on to the business cultures, which can be even more bemusing, people tend to view the world from their own organization's position and culture, the assumption often being that what is right for them must be the correct way to behave, but this is seldom the case. Every country is at a different stage of development, and may be following a path that might be widely different from another.

It is constantly frustrating and often annoying when people pronounce about the way other countries should handle their business activity, and these views, though they may be ethical and correct at home, have no real place in other cultures. By way of explanation, there is the case of child labour, where in many parts of the world the difference between eating and starving may be the need for a nine-year-old to work heavy machines instead of going to school. Working with a supplier in India, there was a complaint about the youngsters on the shop floor. As a result, the next day they were missing, having been sent home, and they lost a badly needed day's wages.

Second is the question of payment: in certain countries their religious background prohibits penalties or interest charges for delays in payment, on the basis that an honest person will pay when he/she can. If s/he does not have the money s/he won't be able to pay, which is not very comforting for the chief finance officer (CFO).

The tricky area is that of facilitation payments, or bribes in Western terms. This is frowned upon quite rightly in the industrialized world, where the intent is corruption. Yet it is common practice in many parts of the world and while in most it is legislated against, it is condoned. The logic is often difficult to follow, but if you start by assuming bribery will happen, then keeping people low paid compensates for the impact and the net result is a wash.

Often simply to get your papers to the top of an approval pile, say in a bank or government office, requires some special incentive. The clerks are underpaid and have little opportunity to improve their lot, so your papers are no better than any other. Clearly there are much bigger and more questionable arrangements being made, and individuals and organizations must set their own parameters.

Understanding these and the many other anomalies that will be encountered around the world are crucial to being ready to undertake effective developments outside your comfort zone. What is more important is that this understanding is shared across the organization, to ensure that actions are not taken that will constrain progress in terms of strategy deployment and implementation.

The last of the three constituents of the cultural mix is the corporate culture, and here one has to be alert to the implications of globalization. As multinational organizations spread their influence, they also take with them the parent company culture to some extent, which may be partially or fully absorbed. It may be wrong to assume that an international name creates a similar culture wherever it goes.

It is also dangerous to assume that individuals in a foreign company fully support or are integrated with the local organization. Travelling around the world, I have found that in many cases the local people have been educated in one of the major established universities and their skills should not be underestimated. One should also recognize that the standards of education in many (so-called) Third-World countries are based on equal, and often higher, standards than those one may consider to be prestigious. In sum, the answer is not to make assumptions wherever one travels, and to take the progress of discussions forward carefully as one builds a profile of those with whom one is dealing.

One may make sweeping nationalistic projections of a particular style or trait, only to find the individuals being dealt with, in the Middle East, say, have spent most of their lives in the USA and absorbed much of that business culture. There are many publications that will enable one to identify the key traits and styles to look for and lay down some basic rules of etiquette, which will influence the relationships and the general style of the region.

What will very quickly be appreciated from any personal experiences is that national differences produce significant subsets of criteria, and even at a national level countries will produce their own variations based on their history, education and development progress. Therefore it is most important that this data and any similar information is used only to highlight the relationship structures and not as a definitive analysis. Unless this is understood and managed, success in building relationships is likely to be limited: consider the implications of three companies trying to conclude a deal – one from each region – and then add local influences and politics.

It is also important to recognize the degree of development that has taken place in the supply chain in the industrialized world with respect to procurement practice from the traditional horse trader through to the most sophisticated e-business ventures. Though each of these remains valid, they require very different styles of relationship.

At the same time, one also needs to look at the long-term objectives for each of the trading partners. Developing a strategy that can meet these expectations is a challenge. In the West we still tend to focus on the deal today, whereas in the Far East trading is expected to be hard but is always directed to the long-term relationship.

The business environment is complex and should be properly understood and integrated into an organization's strategic thinking at every level. Failing to understand the implications and pressures this environment can induce will have major impacts on the effective implementation of any strategy. For those organizations that have a significant involvement with overseas customers or suppliers it is important that those not in the front line understand these pressures. Many times I have experienced internal conflicts and pressures that stem from a failure to fully appreciate the wider business environment.

RESISTANCE

CHAPTER 5

Mergers and takeovers

In the context of the many business operational challenges, the issues of maintaining the balance of an organization throughout a merger or takeover is probably the most volatile. These two situations are often linked together, though in the strictest of terms they are two separate conditions. A merger is usually associated with the mutual joining of two organizations, where one may be more prominent but it is the common focus that is aimed for. On the other hand, a takeover is generally associated with the aggressive purchase of a company. From experience, both tend to generate the same complexity in terms of impacts on the internal energy of the organizations and create a significant challenge in terms of maintaining balance and focus.

I shall discuss acquisitions in the next chapter – while these involve many of the same issues, they do tend to have different drivers. The business environment drives these marriages, basically from two perspectives – on the one hand in today's market the strength of competing organizations is reducing, while on the other, the combining of complementary companies or business operations opens new opportunities to exploit the joint customer base.

What is observed as a common feature of both mergers and takeovers is that the newly-combined organizations generally have largely the same management in place afterwards, stemming usually from the senior partner. They do, however, face the same market challenges under their new combined name. There is also the factor that, while there are two corporate operations combining, there are within these corporate entities many sub-organizations operating, which means that refocusing two operations into one is very complex. In fact, more often than not, the two organizations have to face even more challenges once the merger has been implemented, particularly where shareholder value and expectations have been used to fund the transfer. Delivering the promised rationalization, optimization and complementary developments and increasing profit potential proves hard to realize. Statistically, less than 30 per cent of mergers in fact deliver the promise that was promoted during the merger negotiations.

These pre-merger expectations cascade throughout the organizations involved, either creating resistance to change or promoting power struggles as people try to capitalize on the opportunity and manoeuvre to maintain or re-establish their previous position. Pleasing the internal stakeholders is seen as less of a priority than placating the shareholders. The defusing of focus and destabilization of balance impedes the drive towards promised growth.

The challenge with any merging of operations is that, first, there will almost certainly be one party that is the stronger. Clearly, most often this is the party that led the merger proposition, though it may not necessarily be the larger organization. This is a natural outcome in terms of traditional risk management thinking, of master and slave, which are further underpinned by the desire to appoint trusted officers to management roles. As a result, the predominant management ethos is carried forward and to some extent imposed despite most promising a common and mutual focus to meld the organizations. This also ignores the potential impact of national cultures, business cultures and in many cases the balance of resources between one company and the other. Who holds the power decides the way in which the merger is perceived, and thus supported, across the organization. The asserting of previous positioning and the conviction that 'our way is right' builds an image of superiority that can undermine the executive strategy of merging the two organizations. Preventing the illusion or reality of one absorbing the other is a key challenge if the focus and energy of future development is not to be diverted towards internal wrangling and the creation of new corporate silos.

Investigations and experiences show that in the majority of cases merged organizations falter during the first 100 days, then take between twelve and eighteen months to develop a new stability. Some fail to make the transition and never recover, eventually being further absorbed or broken down. This was not a result of the strategic decision to merge being at fault, but it was because the implementation had failed to recognize the importance of harnessing and capitalizing on the joint forces that drove them as separate organizations. The more traditional the background of the organizations, the harder it is to blend the two into one without damaging the balance, energy and focus.

In many cases, a merger takes place between previous competitors, and this in itself creates a range of potentially conflicting dynamics that must be addressed. These organizations may have been fighting each other aggressively for a market share or driven by awe at the other's performance. Both of these situations create almost instant stresses across newly-merged operations.

The earlier issues of management style and ethos of superiority compound the complexity and thus the potential to create closed ranks at every level. When the reality of past-assumed positioning or capability is found to be flawed, then the dilution of enthusiasm may be an even greater hurdle when energizing the value of the merger. This was the truth around what had previously been a driving influence.

One interesting facet of many mergers and takeovers is that the driving organization is often the smaller partner. Commercial strength often rests with the smaller organization, since it is not hindered by a large infrastructure and thus is more dynamic and viewed as potentially more profitable. This market valuation and strength, however, often masks the inexperience that exists at management level to move on from the family culture or corner-shop mentality to managing a much larger operation. Thus the incoming management is found to be lacking by other organizations and the impetus is quickly lost.

The resulting stress that builds up comes from the inability to recognize that the bigger and more diverse the organization grows, the harder it is to manage the business, particularly when the traditional operating model has been structured around small and close-knit management teams. The reverse is also true when faced with a takeover by a large multinational, which assumes that its newly-acquired smaller partner is not geared to meet the demands of operating within a huge infrastructure. Either way, the impact on the people within those new operations can be severe and dilutes the energy that the organization should be directing towards the market challenges.

This 'big brother' syndrome can be even more dramatic when the new management structure crosses national cultural boundaries. Those who have worked with other nationalities will easily understand how often cultural differences and work patterns can create conflict, even at the basic levels of dress style or how to address each other – from the very formal Japanese style to relaxed North American familiarity. The business environment is now very much a cultural mix, but on their home territory established organizations find it hard to bend their traditional approaches. They then bring their culture to bear on merged organizations, building friction and frustration.

These differences pervade every aspect of trying to homogenize two organizations into one. The name above the door may change quickly, but the national and business culture might take decades to adapt. When this is combined with the tensions of a merger or takeover, the differences can become major obstacles to driving the business forward. The lead has to come from the top and be applied consistently throughout the new organization, with every effort being made to neutralize the 'us and them' distinctions.

All this may be stating the obvious, but as an example of how easily the strategic intent can be defused, during a presentation following one major merger, the CEO made a great play of the desire to unite the groups. However, he failed to notice that one of his presentation slides carried the incoming organization's old name and all his work was immediately undermined. Mistrust of the incoming management is the leading reason for people not to focus on the future, but rather to seek to defend past practices and status.

The financial markets have moved noticeably since the mid-1990s from evaluating tangible assets to a wider focus on the knowledge and skill base potential of organizations. Rationalizing organizations leads to conflicts among the teams, particularly where the merger is bringing together complementary organizations where neither in fact has direct experience of the other's markets. Recognizing these intellectual assets and refocusing them are two very different issues. The classic challenge in this respect comes when, say, one organization is primarily producer of a standard product and the other leans more to bespoke. The outwardly common industrial sector hides a diversity of skills and history in meeting the market demands.

Many organizations have in recent years leaned progressively towards more of a solutions-based approach, looking to develop their market profile to extend the range of support available to a customer. The bespoke operation is clearly more attuned to customer-driven demand, whereas the production-based operation is more focused on standard product configurations and supply support. The two approaches may appear to offer a complementary integration but in fact in operational terms they are diametrically opposed to one another. The overall strategy may therefore be flawed, because unless the skills gaps can be bridged and focused, the potential to integrate may be limited.

In a number of major merger programmes, the perspective of integrating the customer base may also carry some constraints in terms of the traditional approach for the market. An example of this can be seen in a number of mergers within the minerals processing environment, where the needs of customers range from aggregate quarries to multinational mining operations, including the specialist needs of refined white minerals. The degree of commonality would appear on the surface to be relatively close, but the reality of the customer profiles and industrial approaches creates very different operational needs.

The history of servicing specific customer segments engenders a style and pace that is peculiar to that industry sector. The friction that can then build when, through a merger, organizations look for economies of scale and the rationalization of resources, can be significant. The transfer of business methods and cultures then starts to project the focus in one direction or the other, and subsequently one or both markets suffer from a lack of focus. It is also important to remember that individual trading relationships are a valuable part of the business backbone and are frequently protected avidly by those who have built up the relationships. The result is that individuals lose the focus that drove them previously, and the energy is diluted. Combined market knowledge may then be a divisive factor rather than the foundation on which to build a composite future.

There is in any merger a need to maintain a focus on the customer, which after all is the main focus of the business environment, but frequently the strategic imperative of the merger is based on an assumption of the benefits for customers. Major mergers are very public affairs, where customers often have a more open view of the organizations they have been dealing with over many years. This starts with the realization of the market value of a company. In one example case, in the power industry dealing with Chinese customers, when the merger went through, the valuation of their supplier was significantly lower than they had perceived. The result was that ongoing negotiations became very difficult and the pressure on the team increased significantly.

The merger, or takeover, is often viewed by customers with a great deal of concern, since confidence is a major factor in supporting trading relationships, and the advent of new owners may bring alternative strategies. Customers also recognize that, when change affects the people they are dealing with, so performance is potentially compromised. This then builds into their being more cautious and as a result greater stresses occur in existing activities. The implications of the new structure on their needs can often generate a risk profile that moves them towards alternative sources that, while perhaps not the most favoured, do not have an image of instability. It is these factors that often add to the pressure on merging organizations and are reasons why they lose ground in the early stages of the merger.

Customer perceptions are a major factor in any business operation, and in the aftermath of a merger they take on a more influential perspective. Rationalization is a common commercial driver within a merger, and as such customers see potential risks building. Where the interfaces with their existing relationships are involved any lack of confidence will readily be visible. The other factor is the comfort zone within which customers operate, which over time results in certain product names being favoured over others. When two competing organizations merge, customers are faced with the complexity of which will emerge as the stronger front-line deliverer.

Organizations invest considerable amounts during the merger process to build up a profile of benefit for both the financial investment market and for customers. They often, however, fail to recognize that most customer relationships are built around individual people on both sides of the trading table. When these come under pressure, or worse are totally ignored, the stability and projected value of the merger can be seriously affected.

The greater the financial dependence of success for the merger on rationalization of the organizations, the stronger the deflection of energy and customer focus. When these pressures are further complicated by internal positioning, the prognosis for success is even more suspect. The market may have become more focused on valuing the wider aspects of organizations, but as yet the recognition of corporate style is largely directed to towards the credibility of the leadership. Leadership is certainly a major factor in driving success and creating confidence, but most business leaders will acknowledge that they are dependent on others throughout their organization. How mergers are orchestrated and conveyed to the workforce and skill base greatly influences the probability of success.

The complexity of mergers on relationships and performance are further complicated by interfaces with the supplier base and partners. In the evolution of business models there is an increasing recognition of the benefits of outsourcing rather than acquisition. The announcement of a merger that may result in these relationships being changed means that the pressure on the operating teams will increase significantly. We shall look at these relationships more deeply in Chapter 7.

The future focus of the merged organization has to be well-developed and conveyed both internally and externally to ensure that the fundamental energy of the merging organizations is not diluted and deflected from the core drivers of the business. The renaming of an organization may not at first mean changes to the product range, but it must to be clearly defined at an early stage to ensure that there is a clear focus.

There will always be winners and losers, and the question of who stays and who goes will slice through the operational teams. The greater the lack of definition, the greater the probability that many key players will look outside the company for their future, with the net result being that the strategic prospect becomes damaged by inaction or lack of definition.

One further aspect of mergers and takeovers relates to those that take place across organizations rather than merging with external organizations. As business operations evolve, the rationalization of internal groupings becomes more frequent. These internal mergers carry with them many of the influences that emerge from external mergers. However, they are frequently given less consideration because they are viewed merely as organizational development. In the light of these being internal affairs they do not attract the attention of external stakeholders, but they can have equally significant impacts on operational performance.

Divisional mergers and takeovers often promote greater internal tension, since clearly existing positioning and power structures will certainly be affected. The changes in management approach and tensions of relationships can cause major upheavals to the stability and direction of internal energy. Again, it is often the strategic decision that is sound but the problem lies with the timing and definition of the implications that emerge slowly and filter out into the working operations.

There is little doubt that the strength of an organization is dependent as much on its employees as it is on the systems it operates and the products it produces. As the market investment profiling involves a greater recognition of these less tangible assets, so do the implications and manner in which mergers are executed.

The deployment of strategic mergers and the value creation prospects of takeovers can be major victims of the relationships and energy that underpin and drive organizations. Capitalizing on the knowledge and skills of an organization is not simply a process of acquiring the shares and resources; it is more reflective of how separate organizations can grow together and increase their internal forces, while maintaining the balance of existing operations. Mobilizing the joint capacity of both operations means recognizing how those internal power centres can be linked and motivated rather than demotivated by failing to address the strategic pressure points that may be created.

CHAPTER 6

Acquisitions

When setting out to shape the profile of the first phase of this book, I decided that while acquisitions carry many of the same characteristics as mergers and takeovers, they did as a subject warrant separate attention. Certainly in Europe, the development of growth through acquisition is a major strategic approach, compared to the general business culture in the USA and Far East, where growth strategy is based more on organic development.

As with mergers and takeovers, the level of success derived from acquisitions is generally less than 30 per cent. However, in the main, acquisitions are in themselves not generally focused on integrated optimization but more directly towards the exploitation of assets, technology or adoption of customer service base.

Acquisitions engender all the complications and difficulties of mergers, but these are amplified because the general intent is not to consolidate the organization but more to capitalize on its immediate realizable value. To this extent, the valuation of an acquisition carries a greater dependence, and cost, for what is generally regarded as goodwill, the difference between the asset value and the market valuation of the company. Compared to organic growth, the acquisition process is focused much more on the short term, and its success is very much dependent on how quickly those assets can be absorbed or divested.

Reviewing the annual evaluations of corporate value based on corporate returns, the implications of acquisitions can be identified relatively easily. The growth of an organization, while maintaining its staff costs, has high levels of depreciation generally reflecting the acquisition strategy at work. Continued growth then depends on maintaining a continuous flow of acquisition targets, with assets that can be exploited.

In a wider sense, there are a number of drivers for acquisitions, ranging from specialist complementary products through more basic concepts of the undervalued operations, where the tangible assets in fact outvalue the market valuation. This is particularly significant in cases where companies have large property portfolios with more value as development prospects than being maintained for current use. On the product side of the equation, the value is largely dependent on technical advantage, and perhaps on whether these can be integrated into existing production facilities.

Clearly, there are cases where smaller, highly focused companies are unable to exploit their own technology or patents without expansion, because they are too small to raise investment capital. One industrial sector that is very prone to this profile is pharmaceuticals, where the larger conglomerates often eventually absorb small developers. The multinationals have the resources and market reach to facilitate exploitation.

What is difficult to assess in terms of acquisition strategy is the relative values of a company between assets and knowledge, and where in all of this is the true value of the energy that underlies the performance of an organization. This is where the acquisition focus is generally concentrated solely on what can be realized from the acquisition compared to building from the combination of resources and assets. A company's intellectual property is only one aspect of its value, and often it is the individuals who make up the organization that are the real assets. This was highlighted during the emergence of the dot.com boom, which saw companies composed of one or two talented individuals being valued in multiple millions, but where the only asset was the perception of their talent. In fact, many had only a concept in place, but were still able to attract substantial venture capital. As we know, the majority of these companies failed because the business proposition was impractical, having failed to address many of the basic fundamental processes that traditional businesses have built up.

Developing the profile for a strategic acquisition, then, must establish clearly what the prospect is for the amortization of the assets and capitalization on the investment. As outlined already, the product acquisition may be to fill a gap or extend the range. The customer base may be to integrate the wider opportunities of exploiting the established range of customers, which of course depends very much on maintaining customer confidence, particularly if absorbing the company is part of an overall strategy.

Rationalization of resources is a common driver in acquisition situations, and it is this challenge that starts to deflect those with the knowledge and skills that drive the organization. Once future plans become vague the tendency is for the best to look elsewhere. The operation of approaches such as 'golden handcuffs' contracts tend to send out the message that while one or two people may be considered valuable, the rest are expendable. What soon becomes apparent, from experience, is that management decisions, far from being constructive, tend to reflect their desire to protect the specifics of the deal. As a result, the organization quickly falls into decline and the acquisition value starts to dissipate.

In acquisition mode, the major challenge is for management of the new owners to engender the right kind of culture and an approach that promotes future potential. Often, however, when the strategy is one of capitalizing on assets, the general style of management will be negative. The impact on staff being that even before any sell off or closure the organization has already started terminal decline. One inept manager reflected exactly this approach: he tried to enthuse people by suggesting that their future was in doubt, but if they failed to work constructively they would accelerate the situation. The energy within the operation was dispelled immediately, and those he wanted to transfer left before he had a chance to make them an offer.

The value of an organization, as already outlined, is much dependent on the strength of the energy that is created by the working culture. When another organization acquires that operation, harnessing the balance of focus is an essential aspect of maximizing the acquisition value. Goodwill is a large and expensive part of acquisition strategy, which is generally written off in a short-term growth programme. If the acquiring organization has an optional strategy to liquidate or develop it is important not to displace the balance of energy in the early days, since this intangible asset that drives an organization will be difficult, if not impossible, to rebuild.

Any business today is a combination of fixed assets, internal knowledge, skills, resources and external relationships among both customers and suppliers. The acquisition strategy has to recognize these various contributors to a company's value, and the contribution made by the focus or ethos that drives the organization. The strategy is then vulnerable to the implications of upsetting the balance of an organization, which can dilute its operational value greatly long before asset capitalization can be implemented. Even worse is that, if a long-term strategy has not been defined, the decision may well be induced by failing to maintain the internal drivers. The best resources look outside and the less dynamic relax their efforts.

Closures, cost savings and focus on economies of scale that can help to improve the situation within an acquired organization may also be the catalyst for creating the imbalance. The way in which these approaches are delivered and presented has a significant impact on the way they will be received. Changing an organization has to be centred on a clear vision of the future, and even then, as we shall discuss later, it may still meet resistance. When such even justified rationalization approaches are presented as 'do or die' the probable perception of staff will be negative.

The choice of language is crucial, as is the recognition of the value of the force within an organization. If the objective is short-term, then some value will clearly be accepted as being lost. If the strategy is future growth and development, then the acquisition profile needs careful consideration and deployment to avoid diluting the asset's worth. Worst of all, when the backbone of an organization is its knowledge base and relationship profile, these are assets that may be costly to lose or rebuild. Understanding the potential to waste an asset must be a key factor in developing strategy and avoiding the stresses that can often inadvertently be created.

CHAPTER 7

Partners and outsourcing

The growing trend since the mid-1990s has been towards the greater use of outsourcing to optimize business operations. This adoption of outsourcing has increased as organizations have looked first to reduce their cost base, divesting non-core activities (which may range from internal facilities management aspects to the complete transfer of manufacturing or product processes). The second driver has been the recognition that global competition and low-cost labour have provided an environment where, through enhanced communications, even customer-facing activities may be relocated economically, with considerable cost advantage.

There have been many high-profile outsourcing programmes, such as the transfer of call centres to India. For many years the IT industry has looked to optimize software development to centres in India or Mexico and other countries. In the manufacturing world, the opportunities that can be exploited by focusing production in areas of low-cost operation have been developed extensively. In certain cases, the drivers for outsourcing have come more from the need to develop facilities local to the developing customer locations, benefiting from the reduction in logistics and distribution costs.

At whatever level organizations seek to consider or implement outsourcing programmes, there is no doubt that it can provide a significant strategic opportunity. It also brings with it considerable challenges for organizations to address, and developing this channel of diversity may be affected by the implications of strategic stress. It may well be a high-level strategic driver to enlarge outsourcing programmes, but the day-to-day operational implications of these strategies generate a wide range of internal pressures. These pressures, if not recognized within the overall strategy implementation, may create an imbalance within the operation that undermines the strategic objectives and dilutes the advantages that originated the concept.

The risks of transferring aspects of an organization's performance to external providers are themselves significant. In many cases these have been addressed by the introduction of partnering and collaborative networks, to which we shall return later. It must, however, always be remembered that customers do not recognize the external providers: they only see the organization they deal with. In the same vein, when internal support activities are outsourced, the recipients of the service tend to be much less tolerant when service levels fall.

There are many areas of the business environment that have been the focus of outsourcing programmes, and this trend is likely to continue to grow. The increase in globalization and the diversity of the marketplace makes investment programmes hard to manage in terms of acquiring assets around the world. The more organizations try to spread their marketing and development, together with the increases in competition, mean that the business environment is constantly changing, thus flexibility is crucial to survival.

The drive to meet competitive challenges means that traditional business models are being broken down in favour of more complex but competitive networks of complementary organizations. Whether this is the provision of internal support operations such as accounting and IT, through more basic building maintenance to the fundamental aspects of production, service delivery and even research and development (R&D), we see so many aspects of the business world drifting towards the outsourcing approach that it would be impractical to try to address them all. From our experiences however, many of the issues that this strategy invokes have common foundations and impacts on the optimization of the strategy.

The first principle of outsourcing rests on the premise that others, being more focused on a single aspect, can provide a more comprehensive and competitive solution. Organizations start by looking for cost savings, either directly from competitive supply or in the case of many internal service programmes, indirectly by reducing their overhead cost base. There have been many examples in the media, particularly associated with the public sector, of private operations taking over activities and in many cases the existing staff.

This strategy has many benefits to the organization but the success of these approaches is often tainted by staff reaction. Frequently there is also a backlash from external customers or general public opinion. Where these programmes start to show the impacts of diverting energy is the personal and social relationships that existed and the inevitable perception that while external providers should give better levels of service than would be accepted from previous colleagues, even where in some cases the same colleagues are now externally employed. These stresses then build towards contractual disputes that may eventually derail the initial strategy and its projected benefits.

The implications of a strategy that looks to reduce the workforce in one country in order to exploit the potential of lower-cost markets provides potentially a much more stressful situation. For example, the number of cases associated with the transfer of call centres that have created both internal and external pressures on an organization will highlight the failings of organizations to recognize that the strategic implications have perhaps not been fully considered. Today, customers are more active and more critical, not only in their buying habits but also in using their power as purchaser and shareholders to challenge the strategies of organizations.

The internal and external pressures that can be invoked from outsourcing programmes today for most organizations stretches also into the arena of social acceptability. The exploitation of low-cost marketplaces by many global names, such as Nike, Marks & Spencer and McDonald's among others, has faced the strength of feeling that comes from failing to address issues such as child labour or animal farming. The implications of pushing strategically towards these low-cost markets may well have a sound economic base, but the dilution of energy and business focus that can result may well negate the benefits.

Outsourcing decisions may have more simplistic but equally damaging impacts. For example, an organization that puts a third-party company before the customer takes the risk that their performance is a direct reflection on their image. Take the common issue of distribution through external companies, where the customer will see the performance being driven by the supplier. Internally poor performance may be dismissed, based on no longer having a direct relationship with the logistics operation. Energy and balance within an organization is a crucial element of overall effectiveness and performance, therefore integrating external organizations is not simply a case of passing the activity to others. We may not always share the views of colleagues but since they are part of the same organization the overall business process is dependent on collaborative working, a feature that may be missing from the external relationships. The supply-chain risk factor is one that every organization has to consider, in terms of those related to the specification relative to customer expectations, hazard and complexity, criticality and probability. This has to be balanced against the supplier in terms of experience, reputation, confidence and past performance.

From my experience in the engineering and manufacturing world, the major obstacle to effective outsourcing is in the definition of scope and specification. There are a number of aspects to this situation, the first being that traditional manufacturing organizations frequently developed an unofficial methodology derived from years of experience. So many times we have seen in reviews of companies that, while there may be established processes in place, the practical adjustment of these on the shop floor results in an improved approach that is not recorded through technical feedback.

When the strategic decisions are made to outsource activities there is a natural reticence among the workforce to support transfers of work, which is then compounded by the failure to communicate custom and practice knowledge. The result is that a new provider works to what is specified but the output falls below requirements. The transfer of knowledge is a key factor in successful outsourcing, but often this knowledge relies on the skills of those who are likely to lose out through the strategy.

Expectations in following an outsourcing strategy are also a crucial part of the assessment and implications. I have often been involved in discussions where the conceptual benefits of outsourcing become the benchmark for success. The idea that transfer to Eastern Europe or the Far East can reduce costs by 30–40 per cent based on comparisons of labour rates frequently fails to recognize the cost involved in knowledge transfer and training, particularly where the activity must be integrated into some wider product or service application. The investment strategy needs to reflect the progressive transfer of activities and the cost of providing parallel support.

The outsourcing contractor may well be highly skilled and equipped to meet the technical needs of the work, but whether the approaches of the two organizations can be integrated effectively is less obvious. Certainly I have experienced the confusion and conflict that can result from differing cultures, language, terminology and work methods. Re-creating an effective business process that spans organizational boundaries can dilute the focus and energy that should be directed towards success. In one particular case, when visiting an engineering contractor in India and being shown, and impressed by, a comprehensive computer-design capability that had been installed to meet the demands of international customers, the owner protested that the investment versus the traditional contract drafting on drawing boards had in fact made them less competitive, because the investment could not be sent home when there was no work. Thus the potential benefits of outsourcing where lost through trying to integrate.

Outsourcing is very much a part of the business-strategic toolbox and a most valuable aspect of developing programmes to meet the demands of the marketplace. However, while it may be obvious at a strategic level to recognize the potential of driving the outsourcing route, the wider implications of transferring activities to external organizations must be balanced against overall performance and sustainability. In particular, the ability of organizations to maintain key skills associated with the outsourcing activity in order to be able to evaluate and manage future relationships.

As already noted, the key resource within organizations is people. The implications of outsourcing may be poorly presented and thus generate negativity among those who have the skills to exploit the potential strategy and thus can often prevent the success or realization of a strategy. It is hard to accept that you are being required to train people who ultimately will take over your job. This strategy may be right for the organization overall, but for the individual the implications may be far less attractive and often it is their special knowledge that will be necessary to effect the transfer. Failing to recognize and address this underlying risk to the energy of the organization may result in failing to realize the expectations of outsourcing.

The utilization of partnering and collaborative relationships was mentioned earlier as one approach that can be adopted to meet some of the difficult challenges that outsourcing creates. The concept of partnering is not new, but the term has been well used in the past decade or so to the point that perhaps those who adopted the term simply as a marketing ploy have devalued it. For those who have invested time and effort in the development of partnering relationships, the benefits are clear. When two companies agree to work in a closer manner, and outsourcing sets the mode, the commercial benefits are dependent on creating a new delivery process that crosses organizational boundaries. In fact, this becomes a virtual organization where the energy and balance of each has to blend to ensure that the joint objectives can be realized, reflecting a transition from a traditional product-based industry towards relationship-based networks.

Partnering approaches focus on the releasing of costs and resources by providing an open platform of relationships. The organizations share risks

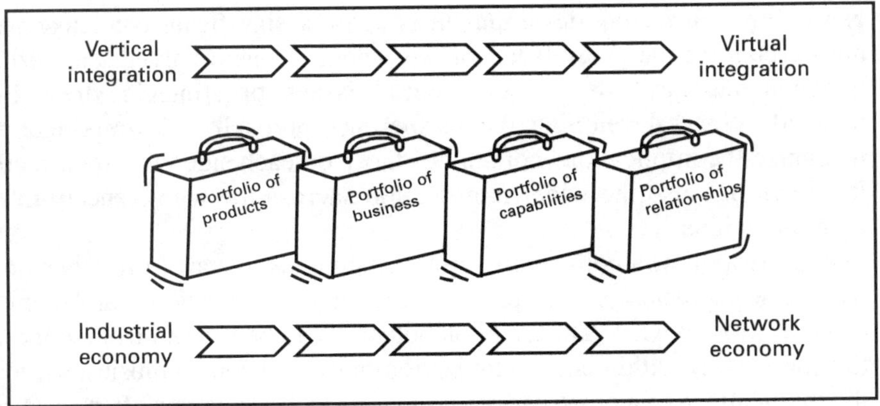

Figure 7.1 Evolution towards a network economy

and rewards, for their mutual benefit. The development of common objectives and processes allows organizations to share skills and knowledge, and to accept joint responsibility for performance. Thus as a business approach it fills some of the less obvious gaps that can be created in outsourcing programmes. It can, of course, go much further, in that when organizations jointly approach innovative reviews of the products, services and processes it is possible to create new propositions for the market.

What supports effective collaborative relationships is the development of a culture that allows the participants to harness the energy from both organizations. This does mean, however, that there is also the potential to create imbalance through this merging of structures, culture and ethos. The sharing of knowledge and skills can provide the most effective way to ensure that outsourcing programmes are successful. It requires organizations to recognize, however, that unlike the situation in traditional contracting relationships, there is a greater need to support both individual and joint objectives.

On the strategic side, the adoption of partnering also provides a long-term environment where knowledge transfer and training can be seen as an investment for the future. So long as the partnership continues to add value for both parties, the progressive integration at the working level will inevitably create a focus on innovation. It does mean that organizations need to have a more holistic view of the market and a more detailed perspective of each other's operations. This openness takes time to build up the trust that will enhance the energy of both operations and focus it towards mutually agreed objectives.

The strategic deployment of partnering is clearly an option for those organizations where knowledge transfer and integrated processes are key factors in the business environment. Moving from the strategic concept of partnering to effective development is again a significant challenge that must recognize the many facets of the organizations involved. Partnering arrangements have the same potential issues of strategic stress but doubled. When developing the partnering approach it is important to recognize the implications not only of those on each side who are directly involved, but also the wider ramifications across the whole spectrum of both operations.

The creation of a collaborative relationship has to start from a perspective of what makes sense for the individual organizations, and then a consideration of what value creation potential can be derived from working together. Many within each organization may not be so enthusiastic about the implications of a close partnering relationship, since this often means a significant change in the traditional confrontational trading approach and may require some degree of preferential trading. There are many aspects of effective partnering that those not closely involved see as negatives.

Careful assessment of the organization is a crucial part of deciding whether it is culturally ready to bridge the gap between distance trading and integrated business processes. If this analysis is not done, what often results is that, as the partnership progresses, the negative energy seeps into the programme, which then fails to meets the partners' expectations and so the strategy falls.

We shall look further at the development of allies later, but what should be appreciated at this point is that, if partnering is a strategic initiative, it should not be assumed that simply by declaring an intent to work more closely together will make it happen. First-hand experience in a large number of partnering programmes has shown that substantial added value can be created, but it has also shown that failing to address the implications across the organizations can bring considerable stress that both diffuses energy and creates imbalance in the operations.

MISINTERPRETATION

CHAPTER 8

Market knowledge

It would be illogical to consider the formulation of any business approach without taking into account the marketplace within which it is to operate. Since the current state of the market may not only have an impact on a company's drivers and strategy, it also applies pressures and influences on its customers or potential partners. I have separated the marketplace from the business environment, because although they are clearly closely linked, each industrial sector has its own dynamics where the effect of global development may have a greater or a lesser impact.

Each industrial sector has its own rhythms, which reflect the economic investment and development cycle. The shift between customer power and supplier power will vary depending on the traditional rules of supply and demand. Clearly these variables will have a significant influence on the nature of any strategy. For example, in the 1970s the oil industry was being held to ransom by valve suppliers as a result of the rapid exploitation of the North Sea: the demand for supply was controlled by the suppliers not customers. Today the market looks very different and competition is highly aggressive. Meeting internal drivers in this environment means deploying adaptable approaches that harness the organization's forces.

The business cycle is a key factor in the development of strategies. Industries as well as individual suppliers follow trends, which reflect external pressures and influences on development. The cycle time is not standard and in recent years the span has reduced as a result of the emergence of low-cost competition and general economic shifts. A cycle generally tends to run over five to seven years. At the bottom of the wave organizations are in panic, but as the market changes the emotions drift upwards through enthusiasm and excitement until at the crest of the wave there is euphoria. The downward cycle starts with complacency, leads to despair and then again to the bottom of the wave and panic.

It is important to understand where an organization is currently placed, as clearly when the cycle is down, opportunities for more open-minded ideas increase. However, the reverse is also true – when a company is down the potential for buying into an alternative is also increased.

It is interesting but not surprising that during the low points of the cycle two things generally happen. First, there is an upsurge in the profitability of consultants, who focus on organizational re-engineering as a solution to the depression, and the second common event is an increase in mergers to optimize reduced market demand. Thus it must be recognized that the relationships and strategy for agreements may have to encompass more than simple one-to-one interactions. The market environment and business terrain can undermine even the most carefully planned strategies, while at the same time building stresses into internal operations.

Some influences are common to many industrial sectors being driven by national and political changes, but again they are factors that should not be ignored in the quest for balance. These may have an impact on both immediate results as well as on the long-term aspects of development. The dynamics of change in the marketplace provide a complex backdrop to strategy development. Technology has certainly had an impact on communications networks, but perhaps more influential is industry convergence, both in terms of consolidation and in merger and sector migration – for example, supermarkets into banks. Clearly the changing political environment and the resulting regulatory changes have an impact locally, nationally and globally. Economic volatility and growing customer needs have opened the way to greater competition within a liberalized global market.

Many organizations are part of multinational groups and as such are affected not only by local pressures but also by the domino effect of wider changes in the market. The drivers can come from outside the immediate range of discussion, and cause relationships to follow alternative routes. For example, when governments change their stance on a political issue, the implications can cascade down very rapidly.

There can be few companies in the industrialized world today that are not at the back the call of the financial markets and shareholders. In recent years there has been a significant change in the valuation process to reflect greater consideration for corporate structures as opposed to assets. At the same time the growing trend in recognizing corporate social responsibility has opened new dimensions in the interdependence of trading relationships.

To set out a business strategy one needs to understand not simply what are the local objectives but also to be cognizant of the wider perspective. The business strategy battleground (Figure 8.1) reflects some of the key issues. Whether at company, group or international level, each has an influence on how the players may react or what options and safeguards may have to be considered. Understanding what drives your organization and

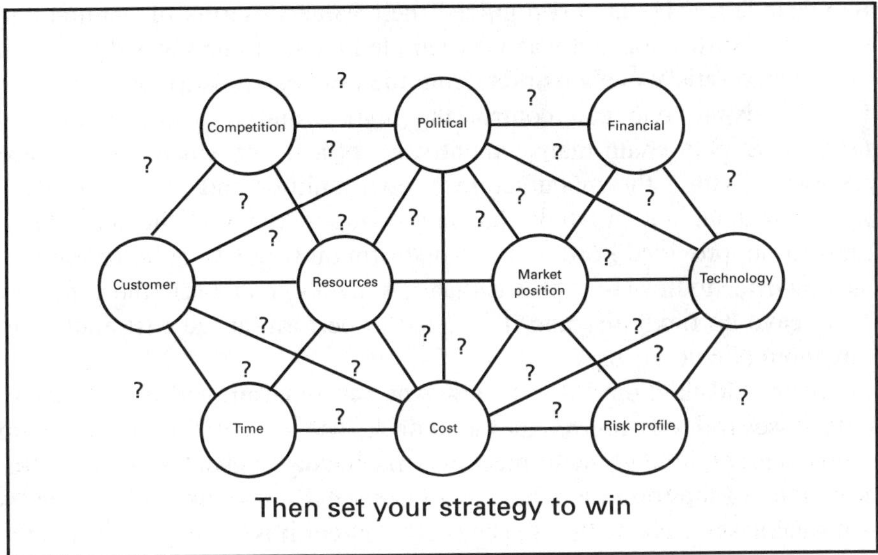

Figure 8.1   Business strategy battleground

that of the customer or supplier are important features of the development process. The whole spectrum of the marketplace will influence events and if these are not understood then opportunities may be missed and the risk profile increased. It is perhaps therefore also worth looking at the horizon to see where the individual industry sector or business trends are heading, since these long-term developments may well spark the opportunity to exploit current interactions.

The history of the Industrial Revolution is well documented and this provides a backdrop to considering how business models have changed over time as an introduction to what the next stage in evolution may be. We can certainly go back much further to demonstrate that tomorrow's ideas are simply a revitalized view of yesterday's. The transition from farming communities to industrial complexes was by the scale of history relatively fast, perhaps 150 years, but the changes over the next decade will probably be instantaneous by comparison, but the future business model may be more recognizable to those looking back to the start of the industrial changes we have seen in more recent times.

The business concept created by Henry Ford and mirrored around the world was in many respects an industrial version of the feudal systems that existed over millennia. Though many will argue that, unlike the barons of old, Ford did not own his workers. That is perhaps just semantics, since those who gathered around his ventures in some ways had the same dependence and interdependence. He also recognized their value in terms of maintaining focus. The Fordist concept was very simple in that, if one owns directly all one needs to satisfy one's market, from the raw materials to the marketing and advertising, one can control the market and to some extent the customer. Supply chain management was not a factor, since performance was totally within the manufacturer's own abilities and resources. This, together with an innovative product, a growing market appetite and limited competition, provided Ford with the platform on which to build an empire. The downside to this concept was that, if market demand fell, the company would have no flexibility and if it failed to perform at the customer level there would be no excuse.

Having said this, the Fordist view was valid and proved its robustness through several downturns in the world. The model was copied and deployed around the globe to meet ever-increasing consumer demand. But the rigidity of the formula, while creating strength, was also building in its own weaknesses. The bigger the beast, the harder it is to keep it fed and the more difficult to manage the changes in the market drivers. It is interesting to consider whether such an approach could be successful again.

In the meantime, perhaps this is a good area in which to consider the changing face of the market by comparing changes in this one sector of industry, because as it developed it was clear that the key factor in productivity was worker participation. Later examples of the same approach showed its vulnerability to union and mass labour negotiations.

The post-Second World War development of Japan saw the first significant introduction of just-in-time (JIT) production methodology and a whole new set of challenges for maintaining balance. This concept enabled a more competitive cost base and started a new chain of business thinking. The extended model is structured around exploiting the JIT principles but now, instead of subcontractors simply delivering to the plant on demand, they were integrated into the process. The most significant factor was, however, the change from adversarial supplier management to collaborative mutually beneficial long-term relationships.

This effective single model of manufacturing collaboration certainly makes all participants totally dependent on each other. The development of supply chain integration was focused on knowledge sharing and a mutual need to advance the companies' joint position in the market. Even so, this model still cannot fully meet the pressures of the market;, many markets are looking for alternative models. The trend towards optimization of the supply chain is, again, not new – every trader since time began has realized that the less paid for parts or products, the greater the potential profit. And the less paid for the parts and materials needed, the greater the flexibility in maintaining competitive pricing and margin. The rise of purchasing as a net contributor was not based on trying to reduce costs but was more about maintaining market position. The new challenge for many organizations is to face the 'buy or build' dilemma.

The development of outsourcing introduced the benefit of reducing investment and establishing a more flexible response to the ebb and flow of the market. Many companies achieved short-term profit gains simply by reducing their asset portfolio and labour profile. The downside in this progression was that in many cases expertise had not been developed to handle the complexities of this new dependency.

Product quality and delivery delays cause serious damage to market reputation as well as causing directors to have sleepless nights when predicted improvements are eroded. Today, the professionalism that has been brought to the management of supply chains has in the main overcome many of these problems, and it is also likely that customer acceptance is much higher.

The latest market evolution is to look at the outsourcing of non-core activities. In many cases, the infrastructure demands are a cost constant. There is a move to pass non-essential activities to subcontractors whose costs could then be handled more flexibly though demand-driven contracts. The market jigsaw has become more complex. Many service and facilities companies have grown up and moved into the space in the market. It may be fair to say that in many cases the results, while commercially attractive, did not always deliver the best return. Expectations always rise when service functions are brought in, and many times the contractor failed to meet demands.

The focus has shifted to the core manufacturing and assembly of products. The progressive drift to low-cost markets worked well for those organizations that have the foresight and investment capital. For others, the challenge is to maintain competitiveness without major investment through outsourcing at a more fundamental level of the business.

Meeting the volatile demands of the market and maintaining competitiveness is the Rubicon that many in the Western industrial regions had to face and cross. Labour costs climb and legislation forces increasing demands on the employer. The option was to find ways of taking the skills and knowledge accumulated sometimes over a hundred years or more and transplant this to other side of the world. This trend started the knowledge-based society, but this knowledge has to be extracted effectively.

This is not an easy transition, and companies has to find contractors who can maintain the reputation of the business, then create adequate training and specifications to support production. One of the major hurdles is that most established manufacturing plants have evolved and much of what was done in the past was passed around through internal networks. Once you have trained a subcontractor, how do you control the intellectual property? Today's low-cost provider becomes tomorrow's competitor.

The successes have prompted others to look progressively beyond their traditional trading relationships and explore the business process. This has enabled companies to venture into short-term relationships with one objective while maintaining their individual overall business strategies. The market has then travelled full circle, though of course, as is always the case, people make it more complex. In essence we have reached the point where the traditional local network of specialists is now re-established, but at a corporate and global level. This evolution is the background against which to understand the influences on internal developments, and subsequently the balance of forces within the organization. At the same time the competition is taking similar actions, and what they are promoting could be to your disadvantage. The marketplace is a complex killing-ground.

CHAPTER 9

Strategic stakeholders

There has been much discussion in recent years focused on raising awareness towards the multiplicity of stakeholders that are part of the business environment, which as a result has become even more complex. This complexity added new dimensions to both strategic thinking and development. It has also introduced multiples layers of concerns and stresses that must be addressed, while delivering customer satisfaction and shareholder value.

The stakeholder concept encourages organizations to recognize that they operate within a holistic environment where action and interaction can influence the balance of the wider community. As business leaders become more socially aware, so they must also appreciate the pressures that strategic commitments might bring to their operations. Much of what has been outlined so far has been reflective of the internal frictions that can be created by ignoring the implications of strategic programmes.

These have focused on the staff but it should also be recognized that these employees are also members of the local community, which may engender conflicts between corporate loyalty and their perspectives for their wider community. We shall talk more later about the implications of sustainability and corporate responsibility, but when looking to consider the strategic implications of stakeholders one must move away from those with purely commercial interests.

The traditional perspective for the business community was perhaps a little narrower than is generally accepted as being the case today. Owners, shareholders, customers and in many cases, staff (though the latter was often less considered) provided the background framework to putting stakeholders into strategic thinking. This linear and somewhat limited profile was much easier to address, but as the net widens so the implications for conflicts, friction and the dilution of strategic focus become more apparent.

The mapping of stakeholders that can have a direct strategic impact on the business is an important element of the leadership's background assess-

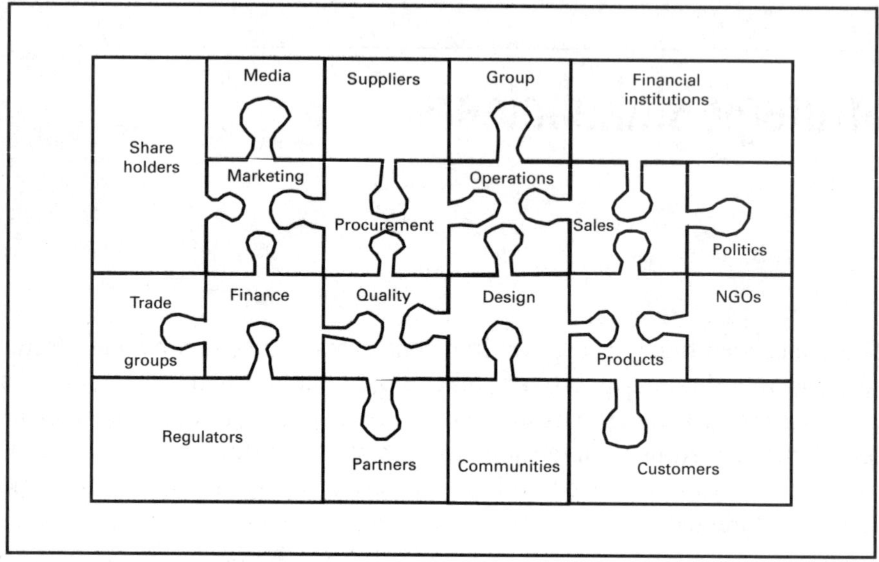

Figure 9.1   Stakeholder influences

ment. Clearly, there are internal and external stakeholders. Internally, we have raised the prospect of the corporate silos, but the concept of recognizing employees as major stakeholders has perhaps only emerged since the 1990s. There is no doubt that recognition of knowledge and skills has helped to raise the profile of employees as a key ingredient in business success. In many cases they may be shareholders, customers and members of the communities in which the business is based. This means that, in many industrialized countries, there is legislation that empowers individuals to participate in the management and governance of the organization. They will all probably also have strong views on the environment.

Shareholders are one of the traditionally accepted stakeholders in a business, and their investment approach has a major impact on the strategic approach that business will take. The major institutional investors often hold a level of stake that means they can influence every aspect of development. These are the more visible strategic influences and considerations.

Individual shareholders provide a far less tangible influence, since they frequently demonstrate no interest in the business other than to sell when they consider the investment is not returning a suitable dividend, or out of protest over some course of action taken by the leadership. Anticipating these trends and drivers induces business leaders to develop expensive programmes, which they believe will create the profile that will maintain share value and support. The cynic may suggest that there is very fine line between corporate responsibility and continued shareholder support, which some business leaders may exploit. In truth, one would hope that there is a mutually driven programme, since business leaders are also part of the global community.

The strategic stress that the shareholder can induce is, however, a significant factor for most business operations. When investment return and social responsibility come into conflict it has an effect on business operations. Trying to satisfy corporate programmes that maintain the right public profile while continually improving costs, margins, profitability and share dividends can stretch most organizations. These pressures also increase the friction between groups within the organization that have different performance goals. Time after time the boardroom strategy sets conflicting objectives, and as a result the energy of the business operation is diluted by pulling against itself.

It would be good to think that, in time, the business community could establish a global code of conduct that levelled the playing field, but having spent many years in various industries around the world, I think this is a pipe dream. There will always be some organization somewhere that is ready to bend the rules, and shareholders need to be very clear as to how they expect their investments to be managed and used. Taking the moral high ground while demanding the highest returns is likely to add to the stresses of the business and compound the loss of focus.

It may seem strange to consider the media as a business stakeholder, since most people think their role is to report or entertain, but as we all know they frequently adopt approaches that create news or trends. We should recognize that these are also businesses in their own right that have the same conflicts and trials as any other. The media is also one of the principal routes for advertising, and one often wonders how revenues and bad news are balanced by media operations. We are not suggesting a lack of integrity, but the media is a clear example of strategic stress whereby delivering their primary objectives of news could be seriously undermining their commercial stability.

For most in the business community the media can be both saint and sinner, and managing the balance while keeping the positioning business positive can be a significant challenge. After all, the more positive profiling that goes on, the more opportunities may emerge. However, the downside is that once in the media sightline, any negative aspect will certainly gain even more space. This affects not only the shareholders; it also influences customers and can in the worst case reflect back on the staff. Nobody wants to be recognized as part of an organization that is receiving negative reactions from the public. So, for example, when a company appears to be exploiting the environment or some Third-World community, it makes news and the internal energy of the business is likely to be diluted.

Trade groups set standards, codes of practice and lobby for regulatory change. Regulators on the other hand take government policy and turn it into rules for business to follow. Both are stakeholders who can have a significant influence on business strategy, and thus affect the balance and energy of a business operation. Trade organizations, whether national or international, tend to seek consensus among their members when developing standards or voluntary codes as a result a business work within these structures, but with a wide range of application from compliance to excellence. The latter clearly has an impact on cost and performance levels.

Working within the guidelines of these trade organizations may be desirable to the business leadership, whereas strategy in their operation is more likely to be focused on minimal regulatory compliance. This conflict is one which has frequently arisen between the business community and legislators. Both sides may well agree on the specific objective in principle, but will take opposing positions regarding how to encourage or enforce delivery. More often than not this results in lengthy debate and compromise while the business world moves on.

Thus the strategic approach of the business will be directed towards meeting shareholder aspirations, which frequently means considerable energy being deployed to mask compliance or shift operations outside the regulatory influence. The implications across the organization are that stresses are created between the drivers for the business and the wider environment. This stress will certainly have an impact on the focus and energy of the operation, and major shifts in operational location will certainly create some imbalance.

The next level of stakeholder is those whose own business activities are interconnected. Most organizations, either directly or indirectly, support multiple tiers of suppliers. Every strategic move will have an impact on this community, where some may gain and others will certainly lose. For example, consider the transfer of purchasing overseas or the consolidation of buying power for economies of scale that create barriers to traditional smaller suppliers.

These supply relationships clearly have to remain competitively driven, and people would certainly not support programmes that do not underpin basic good practice. But these changes in spending profiles often ignore the wider interactions of local reliable suppliers, the loss of innovative smaller organizations that are the mainstay of development and of the relationships that have clearly grown in a regional community. This also fails to recognize that for those in business there are pressures caused by the loss of comfort zones, reliability and perhaps personal standing in the community.

Supply networks are a crucial part of every business operation. For many, the external spend far outweighs the internal cost profile. It therefore would not makes sense to ignore what can in many cases be the difference between success and failure of a business by exploiting the value chain to its fullest extent. The strategic decisions must, however, also recognize the wider implications that may flow from a simple 'let's go overseas' philosophy. In many cases the interdependence of the supply network makes suppliers not only a significant asset in the delivery process, but they also become stakeholders in the longer-term development of products, skills and knowledge. Their influence may emanate from their individual positioning and the relationships that hold the market together.

The long-term supply relationship will probably have evolved into a partnering relationship even if the concept of the name partnering is not currently part of the operational profile. In such cases where the operational boundaries have been bridged there is clearly a stakeholder position held by these partners. We discussed these relationships earlier but it would be wrong to exclude them when looking at the network of stakeholders.

Group companies should be included within the context of stakeholders. This is on the basis that in a multinational business environment there are significant operations operating under one prime holding company effectively as independent companies. These complex business structures often combining totally uncomplementary businesses still have an impact on each other and to some extent remain interdependent. A major failure or strategic change in direction can have a significant impact.

Local communities that provide infrastructure and resources for a business site are clearly stakeholders in that business, whether it is a traditional industrial site or some new development in one of the lower-cost markets. Businesses and the community have a mutual responsibility to consider the implications of any strategic decision. Certainly those employed from the community would probably contribute more enthusiastically if they feel that this interdependence is both recognized and supported where this is practical.

It should also be recognized by community leaders that in running public business operations they have a mutual responsibility to support and help local businesses to grow. Traditionally businesses grew and alongside that growth the local community expanded. In today's industrial marketplace, where flexibility and global supply are common features of most business operations, the traditional long-term integrated community is less obvious. On the other hand, the development of Third-World sources has meant that multinationals are now back in the role of community benefactors. The more they invest in the location, the more entrenched they become and the greater their social responsibility towards the community.

This interaction between business and the community has given rise to a wide range of non-governmental organizations (NGOs): environmental, animal rights, human rights and many more. Some may consider these to be a blight on the business playing field and certainly people would not support any that fail to recognize the legal right of a business, its leaders and employees.

Many of these organizations, while holding firm views on the way things should be done, accept the rights of business to function and make profit. They seek to influence business and governments rather than force them through violence. These groups may often be considered unwelcome guests at the feast, but there is no doubt that they have positioned themselves as stakeholders in the wider sense, as such strategic developments can hardly make any progress without taking their considerations into the equation. In many cases employees may hold similar sympathies and again they expect their employers to act responsibly or risk creating an imbalance.

Financial institutions clearly exert a significant influence on the business world through investment, insurance and banking transactions, and at the higher end of the investment scale in supporting major developments such as government projects around the world. As such they represent one of the front-line stakeholders in any business venture and the financial interaction at every level of the operational activity has a direct bearing on strategy development and deployment.

In many ways the financial sector has been able to influence changes on behalf of the smaller stakeholders. Ethical practice and environmental conditioning of investment loans are structured carefully to protect their own public positions and reputation relative to exploitation. All these aspects of tempering business operations will add to the challenges for those within the operation in executing the strategies of their leadership.

Government and business strategy are often closely intertwined, though while clearly on occasion they may be in direct conflict, their activities have a major impact on each other. As such, any significant business strategy will have an influence on government standing and the reverse is also true – that policy may induce business to adopt alternative strategies. Thus each is a stakeholder in the other, and as such has an impact on the amount of internal focus a business directs either towards complying with government policy or developing strategies to circumvent or avoid the implications of government drivers.

Customers, whether industrial, commercial or at the consumer level, are clearly part of the stakeholder community, and we have already explored the impacts customers can have on strategic imperatives, together with how the influence of the customer can promote internal imbalance. In terms of considering the wider stakeholder environment one must also consider that the actions or reactions of the customer base can influence or mobilize others in the stakeholder community. This is particularly true at the consumer level where chain reactions focused on some individual business can have a major impact on that business.

What should be clear by now is that the stakeholder network environment is a significant supporter of the business community, but it can also be its nemesis. The energy of an organization can be diluted or diverted simply as a result of the various stakeholder influences.

Energizing the force

The balance of an organization is an important factor in ensuring the focus of the corporate force and energy the organization produces is concentrated in maintaining its strategic direction. In Phase Two we look at the aspects of creating the integration of strategic thinking, and innovative ideas. At the same time this must include an analysis of capabilities, skills and resources to support the overall strategic goals.

It is, however, not uncommon for traditional strategic and business planning programmes to absorb internal priorities and drivers to the extent that these can in fact become counter-productive. To maintain the balance and counter the impacts of conflicting energies within organizations it is crucial not only to concentrate on wide-ranging stimulation unless it is within a structured approach.

Established organizations generally encapsulate the ingredients and knowledge necessary to achieve all but the most stretching of future demands that evolving strategies might require. Often, however, the internal structures and approaches introduce barriers to **awakening the knowledge** effectively. It is in these cases that very often organizations look to the external stimulus of consultants and business gurus to provide them with a framework that will allow that knowledge to emerge and be activated. Too often this approach, rather than helping, in fact brings about further confusion and stress as a result of its introduction.

In the majority of situations, experience has shown that the most successful organizations find ways inside their own skill and knowledge base to **cultivate synergies** and focus across the spectrum of resources. It is fair to say that occasionally external facilitation can initiate the framework necessary to effect this development. The longer this external support stays in place, however, the less effective it becomes.

One can look to the similarities of supporting poorer nations in famine through charitable funding. To quote the well-known aphorism, if people are fed fish for a day, then the next day they must be fed again, but if they are taught to fish they will feed themselves for ever. Organizations must introduce the philosophy and structured approaches necessary to re-examine themselves continuously and implement improvements.

What has clearly come from investigations is that, in terms of building a robust and dynamic organization that is effective in **harnessing the energy** and then focusing this towards implementing strategic direction, is that the driver must come from corporate commitment at every level. Developing an approach that will draw out the energy that exists and channelling this to meet the challenges of the day must come from internal stakeholders. Avoiding the impacts of not maintaining the balance of these energies must also be part of the managements ethos. Well-intentioned innovation programmes can just as easily create the bending moment if they ignore the need to ensure harmonizing the many constituents of the development programme.

AWAKENING THE KNOWLEDGE

CHAPTER 10

Strategic stress

Strategy development is perhaps the most important factor in any business venture. As with any activity, understanding where you want to go and working out how to get there ensures that you focus resources most efficiently towards progress. My earlier work, *Sun Tzu and the Project Battleground* developed thinking around the work of the famous Chinese military strategist. Despite what some may think, Sun Tzu's perspective some 2,500 years ago has a lot to offer the strategist of today. His premise was that if one created the right strategy then success would be assured, and that winning was a reflection of strategy not strength.

> The one who figures on victory at headquarters before even doing battle is the one who has the most strategic factors on his side. The one who figures on inability to prevail at headquarters before doing battle is the one with the least strategic factors on his side. The one with many strategic factors in his favour wins, the one with few strategic factors loses – how much more so for one with no strategic factors in his favour. Observing the matter in this way, I can see who will win and who will lose.
>
> Sun Tzu, *The Art of War*, circa 500 BC

The importance and value of strategy, and equally important the development of strategic thinking, is based on the assumption that organizations understand the true nature of strategy as opposed to tactics and planning. It is even more import to ensure that strategy is developed in an effective manner. Readers may argue that this is obvious, but in interviews with several CEOs on the subject of strategy it has become clear that they used the term 'strategy' but in most cases their strategy was totally focused around tactics and planning.

Frequently, the strategic thinking that senior executives are able to undertake is in the main constrained within the executive and senior management of their own organizations. This situation leads them to fall into a morass of organizational positioning and resource, and functional and personal agendas. The result is that, as the objectives and ideas are evaluated, they are moulded by preconceived cultural pressures as opposed to being allowed to grow from the organic assessment of the external influences that will ultimately shape success.

It is also common for the CEOs, like any other leader or ship's captain, to be seen as the fount of knowledge and to instil confidence. The result is often that more innovative ideas are not put forward by the CEO in order to avoid appearing fallible. It is even more common that goals are set at a very superficial level such as a percentage of profit or market growth. This then is cascaded through the organization, which in turn adapts the prime goals to match localized aspirations. The net result of failing to drive an effective strategy development programme is that organizations spend a considerable amount of effort on the programme but with little hope of any major strategic benefit ultimately being forthcoming.

Strategy is the most critical factor in the creation of a balanced organization that is capable of exploiting its energy and forces. Fundamentally, if one cannot get the overall focus of the organization centred around a common and integrated set of objectives, then inevitably there will be stresses created that will dilute or misdirect the energy and effort. From personal experience, the number of organizations is quite high that, while promoting a comprehensive approach to business planning, in fact waste resources. On the other hand, many of the more successful organizations have dynamic leadership that is prepared to think the unthinkable and then inspire the organization to deliver.

Getting the business strategy and subsequent planning programme to operate effectively is the single most important factor in mobilizing the assets of an organization. It is also the point at which a foundation can be created that ensures a cohesive approach is implemented and that avoids the dilution of energy through internal stresses and conflicts. The framework of traditional business planing hierarchy (Figure 10.1) development in moving an organization from an established mission through to effective implementation remains valid. Unfortunately, as in most situations, it is in the detail and deployment that the idea becomes deflected or diluted, and the crucial linkage is in the strategy.

A clear mission statement, though today perhaps seen as a hackneyed concept, allows an organization to measure and focus its business at every level against the common focus set from the executive level. It also provides a hook for every individual to understand the ultimate aims that their activity and effort is directed towards. Some years ago the competition between

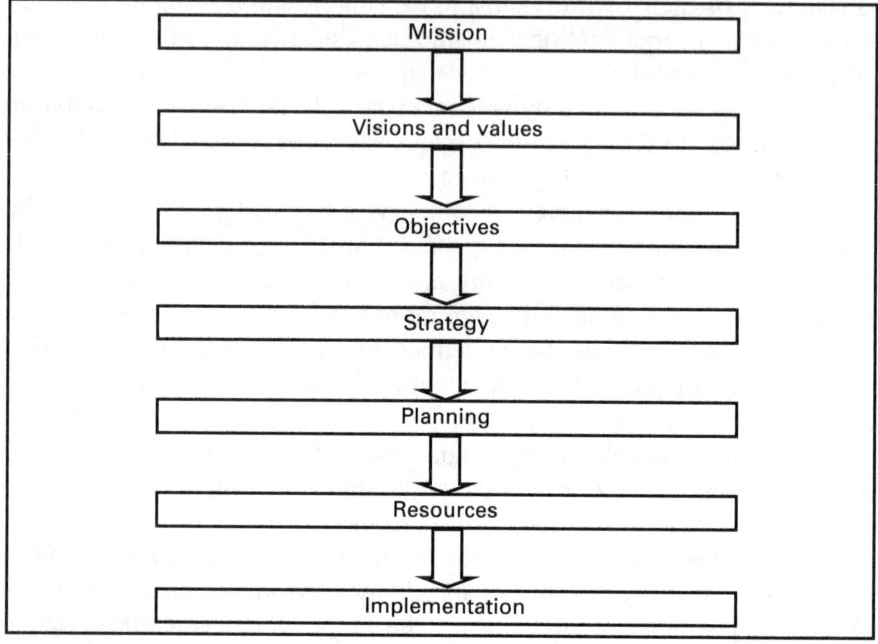

Figure 10.1   Business planning hierarchy

Fuji and Kodak had reached its peak and Fuji declared its mission as 'kill Kodak', and this left every member of staff in no doubt about their focus. In today's climate it is perhaps not very politically correct, but it illustrates the impact and focus that can be generated.

The definition of visions and values has again often been seen as very lightweight and no longer pertinent in the aggressive global marketplace. In fact, as an approach it is probably more pertinent today where the culture and nature of business is a key factor in meeting the demands of the many stakeholders. The greater the focus on the wider ranging implications of corporate social responsibility (CSR) and sustainability, the more important it is for organizations to declare their primary values in order to set the environment within which every trading activity should be considered internally and evaluated externally. We shall look more deeply at the whole issue of strategic sustainability later, but at this stage it is an important consideration in the overall strategic programme.

Clearly, the driver for every organization will be meeting the expectations or aspirations of its stakeholders, in the commercial world translating into share value and dividend returns. It will be these objectives that create the benchmarks of success, and where contributors at every level should be able to recognize their efforts and, it is hoped, appropriate rewards.

Up to this point the linear process makes sound sense, but it is the way in which organizations approach the next steps that sets winners and losers apart. Many organizations adopt this framework and implement elaborate business planning programmes that are designed to capture the knowledge of the organization and allow integration of the strategic intent. Unfortunately, it is at this pivotal point where strategy becomes confused with tactics, planning and financial reporting matrices, that will govern responsibility and performance measurement going forward. It should therefore come as no surprise that in the majority of cases organizations do not fully meet their business objectives.

Strategy may well be shaped by available resources, market conditions and investment profile demands, but it should not be driven by these factors. Effective strategic thinking starts with an objective then assesses the factors that will influence the successful outcome. Analysis of these influences and resource constraints may well provide the stimulus to seek alternative strategies from those traditionally pursued.

The constrained approach is likely to result in a conservative strategy, which will not meet objectives and as a result will create internal stress. The blinkered approach to strategy is equally flawed – when organizations set objectives without considering the realities. Clearly, the ideal is to foster a free-thinking process that allows innovative and out-of-the-box brain-storming, which create an opportunity to think beyond the traditional limits.

This separation between strategy and planning is crucial if organizations are not to bind themselves within historical constraints or allow the process to become steered by the fears or aspirations of corporate silos, functional groups or individuals. Even more tempering for the strategic process are the implications for resources, particularly any strategy that might reduce elements of the organization, which will probably work hard to defend their position even when the strategic imperative is clearly pointing the other way. Similarly novel approaches may be ignored as a result of resource limitations in terms of either capacity or skills. If the strategy is right, then resources may need to be reconfigured or complemented but it does not mean that the strategy should not be progressed.

No doubt there are many who have faced the dual business planning paradigm of increasing sales and profits while reducing internal operating costs – which in the main means people. Given these two potentially conflicting approaches, is it any wonder that strategic planning gets bogged down in protectionism and confusion. The key is to set the strategic platform without limitations then balance the possibilities against practical demands and constraints. Only when these have been bedded down should organizations look to develop the future key performance indicators (KPIs) and financial reporting benchmarks.

In most cases the process is very time-consuming, and thus organizations try to integrate the whole programme without appreciating that perhaps they are losing the edge they hope to gain. Here are two examples of how the benefits of integrated strategic planning failed. In one, the whole strategic profile of a major European organization was ultimately driven towards units of output and machines sold. This was completely contrary to the declared objectives that focused on moving the company towards a service and solutions-based market profile. The result was therefore driven backwards from the production matrix with the effect that 'service and solutions' became an internal joke.

In the second case, with a Japanese company, the focus on strategic business planning was so well-structured and demanding that every year 30–40 per cent of management time was spent on deciding where the next strategic planning programme was to be focused. The effort and focus on driving the real business forward was constrained between the release of the current plan and the creation of the next one. It should also be noted that the five-year plan changed every year.

The cascade approach is, of course, crucial to ensure that the strategic development is integrated effectively into the whole organization at every level, from the key aims of the executive to the recruiting and development programme in its most remote outpost. The problem, as already highlighted, is that when the programme fails to separate strategy from planning, the feedback process will certainly attract local influences that will be difficult to disentangle. It therefore further underpins the need to develop strategic frameworks before trying to move to the planning and tactics of implementation.

In the majority of organizations, strategy is a few key objectives passed down from above. In many cases it does not even reach that level of strategic guidance, but simply reflects anecdotal ideas such as reducing costs by a combination of downsizing and outsourcing. This is perhaps in part a result of the influence of financial management as opposed to operational interfaces of technology, sales, production or service. In many companies in the 1990s, the whole strategic focus was hooked into the hysteria of web-based business models.

We are only now seeing the true integration of technology after the dot.com boom. Much earlier, we saw the drive for automation and huge investments in integrated computer systems that would sharpen the focus on reporting and give better financial visibility. These examples of missed strategic focus do not mean that we do not appreciate the value in many of these ideas and initiatives. The stresses that these strategies invoked were very significant and detracted from the real focus of the businesses they were supposed to help. They consumed large investments and vast amounts of resources. It is reported that, in the world of technology, fewer than 20 per cent of improvement projects deliver satisfactory results.

All this leads to one basic consideration in the development of effective business strategy, which is that it must be created within a holistic environment and not driven by the traditional conflicts of matrix approaches that create stress between operational and support organizations, and even between the aspirations of those groupings. The strength of any one particular group or function can distort the overall balance of the multiple functions that will be required to deliver the whole proposition. Evaluating interaction at the strategic level without the definition and detailed jigsaw of performance measurement, reporting and predefined goals will be likely to open up the opportunity to consider a wider range of options and solutions. Objectives clearly have to be established at the most senior level, but the way in which these are achieved can vary and are dependent on many factors.

The most effective and balanced development of strategy comes from accumulating and assessing the maximum amount of knowledge across the organization. Too often these holistic assessments are pre-empted by objectives that define the route forward. For example, achieving a desired increase in profitability can be derived from many different approaches, such as market growth, cost reduction, operational improvements, product redevelopment, and additional products and services. Cultivating the synergies and assessing the correct combination of actions must be based on holistically matching strategic options then ensuring that all fractions and stakeholders share the final vision and objectives. Only from this position can organizations fully exploit their potential and avoid an internal dilution of energy and focus.

The traditional starting point for any strategy development is to build from a SWOT analysis, though many fail to capture in this approach the wider implications of the political and economic landscape within which this analysis is undertaken. The STEP analysis complements the more focused business review. Collecting the inputs across the organization provides a benchmark for creating the organization's overall thinking and the platform on which to develop a gap analysis in respect of the objectives being pursued. (See Figure 10.2.)

This approach is not rocket science, and many will say it is old hat, or

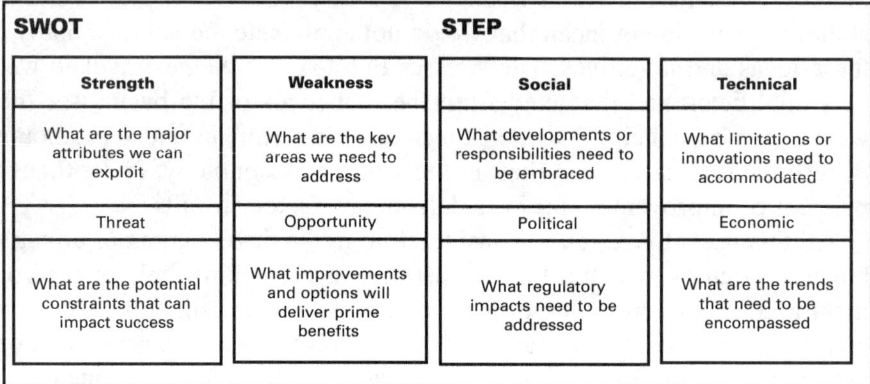

Figure 10.2 SWOT and STEP

that it is part of their strategic development process. The challenge comes when, in larger organizations, these analysis approaches become very specific and are seldom consolidated centrally to identify potential internal conflicts. The result is that while there is a comfortable feeling that everyone is working to the same end, the reality is that they may well be focusing on different routes, which in themselves could dilute the efforts of others. It is clearly important that every part of an organization develops a level of strategy that ultimately feeds back and forth, vertically and horizontally within the operation.

Frequently, even at a very early stage, we see organizations taking overall strategic objectives and goals, and disseminating these to the contributors, while at the same time building incentive schemes that will benefit from meeting these targets. This again creates a situation where the central strategy may be acknowledged but the implementation can be fragmented, based on the group's, function's or individual's ability to respond to these targets. This is often based on a negative defensive position, or worse, by directing the focus towards others and damaging the integrated commitment to the overall objectives.

Objectives must be real and measurable, but until the overall approach is defined they should remain as a common goal. The following is offered as one example of the negative impacts that can result from the early defining of strategic measures from personal experience.

One company recently took a rigid approach to decreasing costs by defining the staff reductions that would be necessary to meet the board's objectives. The first reaction was to focus on a reduction in headcount numbers without looking at the operational impacts or cost–benefit analysis. As one might expect, clerical staff were lost first, forcing more mundane activities onto senior personnel; this in turn reduced efficiency but at the same time these staff members became dissatisfied, so performance dropped. The reduction benefit failed to match the strategic objective and in fact brought the operation into an even less profitable position.

In a similar vein, the conflicts between growth through changing a product and service focus failed because of the desire to make short-term operating-cost reductions. Those longer-term development projects that could not deliver immediately were the target of divisional reductions instead of the rationalizing of traditional product operations, which gave short-term benefits. The net result was that the strategic directive failed to materialize; it was either the wrong strategy or the process of directing the organization was flawed.

The key strategic imperatives should be tested and then implementation planning undertaken to drive forward change while protecting the core programme. The moment that tactics and planning are merged with the strategic development process, the stress that is created will unbalance the organization and divert its energy to meet long-term aims. It is hard to harness the power of any organization when the conflict is, in effect, built into the strategic programme being followed.

The classic situation is the demand for growth without recognizing an increase in budgets or investment is needed to meet that challenge. Many will argue that improving productivity is not always a case of capital investment, and as a firm believer in the value of process mapping and optimization, agreeing the principle is not difficult. Where the conflict occurs is in the sequence with which actions are evaluated and taken. What most will appreciate is that even investment in training can be an early target for cost reduction programmes as part of overall development, while strategic changes in direction will almost certainly create the need to retrain or raise skill levels.

Simply asking people to deliver more without addressing the infrastructure, resources and skills base makes little or no sense. At the same time, increasing sales without ensuring that products taken to market are competitive and meet demand is futile. In a similar vein, investing in R&D that is not linked to market needs or demands, unless tied to a strategy where creating new demand is an imperative, is simply a waste of resources. Markets and customers must be at the centre of any strategy, and failing to recognize this will mean ultimately that the strategy will fail.

What is also frequently missed in strategic assessment is the development of a risk profile that should be established as a reflection of the strategic imperatives. So often organizations consolidate their business strategy based on euphoria. As noted earlier regarding the dot.com boom hysteria, most of the early web-based business propositions would never have passed even the most rudimentary risk analysis.

Certainly in a large corporation there are real implications of risk being generated by individual strategies. Both for the particular part of the operation but more importantly cross infecting other aspects of the business. What then may seem attractive to one group can ultimately undermine other initiatives.

While accepting that most experienced business managers might find much of this perhaps too simplistic and maintain that it is nothing new, experience and investigations suggest that many do not follow even these basic rules of engagement. It is my contention that many, even at high levels of management, still confuse strategy with planning and tactics, and the success of the venture is potentially being imperilled by moving too quickly to implementation. Without fully understanding the implications holistically within their organizations of strategic imperatives, companies risk creating stresses that will deflect energy and build in imbalance.

Harnessing the power of an organization is a crucial part of developing a successful operation. This energy comes from ensuring that not only are individuals and groups encouraged to be innovative and creative, but these programmes must be meshed with the aspirations and activities of others, whether directly associated or not.

CHAPTER 11

Holistic self-assessment

Many of the issues outlined so far are not new concepts for organizations both large and small. In discussions with executives across a broad range of companies the implications of strategic decisions are often acknowledged. What may be apparent less frequently are the efforts being put in place to identify these key stress points and thus be able to evaluate them and take action. The old adage, 'you can't fix what you can't see' holds true in this strategic stress environment.

Organizations perhaps sense that a sound strategic plan pushed through will eventually carry itself forward, while there may be some casualties in terms of people, performance and objectives overall. Certainly there is some value in this approach, particularly where there is sufficient critical mass. However, the failure of organizations to realize their full potential can often be traced back to the failure of strategic development and deployment, which is undermined by the internal conflicts it creates.

From my own direct experiences in the project environment and having often been called upon to assist organizations with strategy and organizational development, the amount of energy that is diverted towards many of the issues identified is quite alarming. Having enjoyed the benefit of working with a large number of organizations globally, I identified a number of areas where this dissipation of energy can materialize. When I tested this knowledge and analysed my research I consolidated these into a group of sixteen specific target areas.

Clearly, every organization is different. Its evolution and development are peculiar to that entity, but despite multiple variations, common 'hot spots' consistently emerge. To move any venture forward and address the weaknesses in its approach, the first major step is to identify the crucial elements that are out of balance with the overall objectives. Creating this visibility means taking a hard, critical inward look and bring the pressure points to the surface.

This self-assessment must, however, be focused not at the functional level but at the wider holistic relationships across the organization. As any mechanic will appreciate, while one can create the most perfect set of components, it is how these interact that defines the performance of a piece of equipment. The same goes for every organization where even the most efficient of individual operating units can be flawed if they fail to integrate. In the wider context of optimizing the interaction between external elements (such as customers, partners and suppliers), the crucial stage is first to understand your own organization.

Developing and exploiting the wider marketplace must be founded in a well-focused, stable, balanced and energized home base. The concept of outsourcing and the extended enterprise introduces a series of multipliers to the organizational balance. Most, if not all, organizations suffer from similar stresses, which may not only conflict across organization boundaries but may well also accentuate the challenges of optimization and value creation. The holistic self-assessment process, then, is a key part not only in exploiting the energy of one's own organization: the greater the level of balance that exists, the higher the potential success in bridging operations between organizations.

My own profiling resulted in a series of sixteen key areas where organizations should start to focus on drawing out the potential stress influences. These are:

- Goals and objectives;
- Leadership;
- Planning;
- Capabilities;
- Risk management;
- Financial management;
- Business environment;
- Customers;
- Competitors;
- Partners;
- Negotiations;
- Management;
- Change management;
- Communications;
- Marketing; and
- Culture.

You will note that I have already addressed some of these topics, and will over the coming chapters seek to shed more light on these areas of concern. For the present, though, what I aim to do is to look at some of the questions organizations should be asking themselves in order to develop a stress profile which can be recognized and addressed where appropriate.

You will see that I am not suggesting that every aspect has to be addressed. In some cases, the impact when evaluated may specifically be ignored in order to maintain a degree of internal conflict and competition that stimulates more important aspects of the operation. Recognizing these stress points and leaving them alone may work for the internal focus, but once highlighted they can be addressed when appropriate in wider marketplace relationships.

In developing the strategic stress analysis concept and approach I did not seek to create a rigid mathematical model. The concept was driven by two elementary factors: one being that there is not and never will be a perfect organization – the more global businesses become and the more volatile the market, the less likely it will be that one can find a one-size-fits-all solution. The second factor is more a concern that organizations seek to improve scores rather than assess the strategic importance of each factor and work on those that are key to current objectives. In Chapter 13 we shall look at the implications of corporate initiatives and some of the implications of becoming focused on programmes rather than driving forward real needs.

The important factor in evaluating an assessment of an organization is to focus on the balance and conflicts between elements of the operation. The structure, then, of our strategic stress analysis is to concentrate on identifying the pressure points between fractions within the organization that can lead to a diffusion of energy and the introduction of imbalances. Many of these may already be recognized from anecdotal information but by validating these in a structured manner one creates a platform for organizational development that is founded on a profile of each organization rather than on an aggregated model profile, which may or may not encompass the specific needs of individual and diverse organizations. It should also aim to cut, both vertically and horizontally, through the operation division or group, or corporate-wide, to give a true holistic profile. As a model it can clearly also be used across organizational boundaries, partnerships and customers but the first step is to understand the issues in relation to your own sphere of activity, whether this is a company grouping or a specific project arena.

The aim is to compare overall responses, by group, by business sector, functional operation and by every level of the management structure. From the executive board that develops and sets strategy to the organization components that will have to develop localized strategies and implementation. Effective analysis should be concentrated first on the areas where there is clear synergy which can be further exploited, and secondly on the areas where conflicts of perception need to investigated and addressed.

Goals and objectives

These tend to be fundamental causes of stress between parts of an organization, where the visions and objectives have not been disseminated adequately and thus are not fully understood. This leads to the questioning of expectations and an awareness that these may or may not be realistic. This is often accentuated by roles and responsibilities not being well defined, and the tendency is for objectives to be viewed as being unachievable.

Extending this analysis, one can see individuals being deflated by policies and strategies that do not encompass the wider aspects of sustainability, which most people want to see flowing through their business activities. As people are the core resource and asset they also expect organizations to be ready to invest in the future, and strategies which induce a contracting of future investment must be fully understood if they are not to induce a negative balance.

Underpinning these issues is the old chestnut of the management approach to effective communication and a balanced perspective on growth and profitability. The level of effort management deploys towards ensuring the business strategy is understood, and recognition that, where necessary, training forms a part of that strategy, tends to cement the focus on future sustainable development.

Leadership

The key to harmonizing the energy of any organization rests in the ethos created by a leadership that is forward-looking. At the same time they must been seen to be decisive and direct the energy towards outcomes rather than individual tasks. The commitment of leadership to mentor its people is an important measure of true integration towards success. Clearly this attention to the development of people must also be seen to recognize effort and contribution, which will induce a culture where the organization does its best for its staff.

The nurturing of people assets must be balanced by an acceptance that management has both capability and respect as leaders. This can often be measured by assessing the amount of time management direct towards communication that provides diktat direction while empowering its people. The essence of all of this is that leadership that is viewed as proactive will gain the trust of its people and support for strategies that may at times not always appear to be welcome.

Planning

The strength of an organization should be balanced between its investments in people and the effort that it directs towards ensuring there are well-defined business processes. It should not be establishing strategies that it has insufficient resources to support, while in this age of outsourcing a strategy that looks beyond internal constraints a more comprehensive and dynamic perspective can be developed.

The development of planning must be driven to be cross-functional, and where practical consider customers' demands in the overall operation. What often pulls a company down is the amount and frequency of reporting that is required to maintain visibility. This, of course, has a parallel need to ensure that the quality of reporting is achieved as part of the normal process and is not demand driven. Clearly, where a major part of the operation's resources are provided from external sources, then systems and processes must be able to link and incorporate these capabilities.

Capabilities

Based on experience, few organizations or groups would ever accept that they have all the resources they need. This is in part because they should be always pushing to be more effective and create resources to allow development. On a more negative note, there may be some degree of status and resource power being invoked. This focus on resources is also reflective of the operation's perspective on its own and other's performance. There may be other considerations too, such as having the appropriate tools available to meet the objectives and challenges that business strategies present.

It is often interesting to question an organization about is own perceptions of its performance. This performance evaluation splits into the introspective view and the assessment of others. We all in the main have a more critical view of others than of ourselves, and in the cause of balancing the focus of an organization this aspect will be likely to cause high levels of friction.

How one views the organization in terms of skills and training can be a major factor in forming a personal drive towards new challenges. Whether we feel confident that the operation is forward-looking and has an appetite for change is frequently reflective of their investment in people.

Risk management

The way in which we address risk at both individual and corporate level reflects heavily on the confidence of the organization: the more comfortable we feel, the less friction that is generated. An organization that understands its markets and has a structured approach to risk management will probably spend less time looking inwards than one that is by nature risk averse and thus challenges every internal innovative initiative.

This does not mean that organizations pay too little attention to identifying potential problems, but have robust processes to address them effectively. A significant factor in this context is the strength of the linkage between sales and production. This attention to risk must also flow out to key external partners where these are involved in the overall programme. Again, it can be seen that organizations which are proactive in terms of risk management create a culture that is able to adapt and exploit opportunities collectively without the misdirecting of energy.

Financial management

Where the financial operations of an organization are integrated into the operating process they tend to be more appreciative of practical challenges, which in turn engenders a more holistic focus. As a result the financial modelling is likely to encompass a more practical dimension.

Where the financial direction sits outside the realities of the operation and drives from a more simplistic lowest-price, highest-profit analysis, then certainly stress levels will be higher. The overbalanced influence of financial operations on the strategy will certainly drive a wedge into cross-functional integration. This is not to suggest that financial input is not important; in fact, I would promote the contrary but those involved must create a balanced strategy that integrates not divides.

Effective financial management can enhance profitability by helping to optimize elements such as cash flow and maintaining a view on economic trends, even more so when the business profile and strategy focuses on a multi-currency environment. The more integrated the financial operations in the delivery process, the more holistic the solutions that can be created to address multiple strategic drivers.

Business environment

Few, if any, business organizations have the capability of changing the business environment, but those that do not monitor it effectively and analyse the implications for its staff and operations will see conflicts building internally. The more traditional operation will find a high degree of friction when faced with new pressures or less traditional opportunities.

The organization that has an established track record in the marketplaces it is addressing will be able to more readily mobilize its resources to support development strategies. Those that do not have this background will find pressures and resistance in the comfort zones. The same influences arise from stepping outside the traditional customer profile. Thus an organization that has a strategic imperative to open up a new market overseas must first convince its people that it can meet the challenge.

Customers

The implications and influences of the customer were addressed earlier, but as one moves into the self-assessment process it is important to recognize that the perspective of a customer, sector or region may be radically different throughout the organization. The greater the experience base and the more interaction with customers, the lower the stress level. It is important to appreciate that the face of the organization, seen from the customer's viewpoint, must be uniform. If there is strategic move to change the customer profile by opening new markets, then every part of the organization must pull together. The better one knows the customer's drivers and approach the easier it is to address a strategy focused on their needs and satisfy the internal pressures, whether these are change management, risk or management in general.

Competitors

As discussed above, the reality, impression, illusion or perception of the competition can influence significantly the way in which an organization meets the market challenge. What is not often considered is that various parts of an organization might have diverse viewpoints, which can dilute or deflect a business strategy. These internal perceptions can not only affect the way the organization views the competition, but it can also have an effect on internal boundaries and interactions. Assessing these differences is the first step towards isolating perception from reality and consolidating the organization's combined approach and strategy.

Partners

The more an organization depends on the resources and contributions of external contributors to the overall operation, the greater the potential for these relationships to cross over and influence the internal adoption of strategic approaches. In many cases, a key ingredient to supplement an organization's strategic approach is the creation of external alliances. This approach may well cause internal friction where such arrangements dilute the positioning of elements of the company, and these external associations may bring with them additional risks which parts of the organization may not be ready to address.

Organizations that have developed a number of external alliances often find their strategic development and business planning is regularly shared with these partners. Clearly it is important that the organization embraces fully these relationships, to avoid diluting energies through internal wrangling or positioning to exploit the relationships inherent within traditional contracting approaches. The greater the dependency, the more crucial it is to identify areas where internal pressures may deflect the common objectives of these relationships.

Negotiations

The way in which an organization approaches negotiations may often be a good indicator of its general ethos and strategic focus. It should be recognized that most businesses undertake negotiations with clients, suppliers, alliance partners and frequently public organizations, such as those that control permits and licences. The traditional focus on which each of these groups is addressed will likely be different reflecting the various elements of the organization which may be involved in the negotiation.

This can typically be seen where the sale activity is focused on closing the deal with the customer, whereas the approach to external partners and suppliers is to squeeze the most from them to avoid reducing internal margins. Given the greater use of alliance-based strategies, organizations must recognize that the flow from supplier to customer is a crucial part of business success. Organizations that can mobilize a collective approach to vertical and horizontal negotiations tend to experience less internal stress, and pressure is directed to others to achieve results rather than to a collective perspective.

Management

We have already discussed the impact of management structure on the ability of an organization to execute effective strategic approaches. The process of holistic assessment needs to consider these implications seriously. The way in which fractions within the organization view the management structure and capability will influence significantly the focus of its energy. The more authoritative and rigidly enforced the reporting structure, the less of a forum for collective integration and the more potential there will be for silo conflicts. The perceptions of a creative management will encourage innovation and provide a more receptive approach to strategic change or challenges.

Change management

In a volatile world, the inevitability of change is a factor that every organization must recognize and address. Strategic development can often engender wide-ranging change at every level of the operation, which, if it is not receptive and confident of its change management processes, will accentuate the stresses and lack of balance across the organization.

An organization that views change as an opportunity will probably not encounter imbalance when strategies are introduced that move outside the comfort zone. The more widespread this ethos, the more collaborative cross-functional integration there will be to move ideas forward. Where change is considered in a negative light, the probability is that the organization will be more insular in its approach and thus deplete its energy seeking to shift the focus or responsibility. The perspective on organizational change is yet another factor in the harnessing of energy across the organization.

Communications

There is a fundamental necessity in every organization to ensure that communications are both fluid and effective, and the impacts of strategic change or challenges must clearly be supported by an efficient communications strategy. This subject is one that surfaces in every organizational review, but in terms of driving a strategic approach it is crucial that every player understands the focus and feels part of a process that is beneficial.

Marketing

How an organization perceives the way in which it is seen by the outside world is a key part of how it views and values itself. Where there are good relationships with customers, the strategic deployment into wider markets will be taken positively. Operations that see themselves as being dependent on a traditional market sector will find it hard to embrace new challenges, while those that have good internal links between the operations and the customer base and are used to develop customer-focused solutions will find it easier to accept wider challenges.

Culture

The most difficult facet of strategic stress and the imbalances that can be created are driven fundamentally by the overall culture and nature of the organization. The perceptions of management may well differ greatly from the realities of those lower down the hierarchy who will be responsible for delivering that strategy. Innovative organizations are more likely to have a clear focus on their employees and embrace high levels of empowerment. The company's knowledge base will be shared and they will generally be collaborative in their thinking.

These general observations are not intended to provide a benchmark for the perfect company, since in my view this does not exist. The aim of this holistic assessment is to test the understanding and appreciation of the organization to establish where the pressure points may be, and at what level. We frequently find that while there may be a public and management profile that displays the most dynamic of integrated operations, the reality is often less well defined.

This internal conflict and stress can often be seen when asking staff to relate the various functional groups within the organization to key parts on the human body. Each individual has his or her own perception and perspective that, while often conveyed in a humorous way, often reflects a genuine characterization that is derived from some deeper discontent.

To this extent the potential of any organization to perform to its full capability is constrained by pockets of stress, which are not deliberately introduced to stimulate competition or in many cases even recognized by those making the strategic decisions.

As outlined earlier, it is not my view that organizations should seek to resolve every challenge. In the first place, this would probably be impossible, but more importantly the process would only be effective for a short time. As the market and global environment changes, so do key stresses and thus the model organization would only fit the bill for one set of circumstances. What is important is that organizations develop a culture that embraces adaptability and change. Alongside this must be a recognition that the energy and balance of an organization is what makes it successful or not, and that profile will blend and flex over time.

The holistic map of pressure points provides the leadership with a critical analysis that can be evaluated so that specific potential key firebreaks may be addressed to optimize strategic imperatives.

CHAPTER 12

Allies

In today's business world we accept computers and the Internet as offering opportunities to link organizations together to supplement the current need or for the generation of new value propositions. This concept, together with the demands of the global marketplace, means that organizations need to seek out and develop alliances and partnerships to create virtual organizations. These relationships may form the crucial ingredient for a more dynamic business strategy, but they also introduce new pressures that must be addressed.

The current trend in strategic thinking suggests that organizations need not own all the resources they use or incorporate into their operations. The evolution of supply chain developments such as 'just-in-time' (JIT) supply programmes and the adoption of outsourcing has introduced a change from demand and supply to a more integrated delivery process. From a focus on cost reduction in the 1970s and 1980s, outsourcing introduced the need for process modelling across organizational boundaries.

This trend towards the integration of business relationships has been underpinned by the concepts of partnering and the use of alliances. These concepts have shown that independent organizations can operate within the framework of common objectives. The idea of alliances is as old as time itself, where human beings have met challenges by working in collaboration with others. In the future I believe this business model will challenge significantly the more traditional organizational structure, but in doing so it will provide a new source of energy that must be maintained in balance if it is to succeed. With the business community progressing towards more of a network economy, strategic development, organizational structures and skill sets must be re-evaluated.

Having worked within extended supply chain and global project environments, I recognize that I have been working in virtual organizations for most of my career. It is interesting that something companies have been doing for years has been given an up-to-date spin. This experience of procurement and project management has demonstrated that every activity is based on relationships, both within organizations and across corporate boundaries, with success being dependent on effective interfaces.

Readers working with large organizations will know that, paradoxically, rivalry between internal groups, departments and divisions often seems more important than competition in the marketplace. Project structures were intended to combat this tendency by bringing together specialists focused on a single goal, but failures still occurred, not because of external pressures and tribulations, but rather from internal positioning and power plays within the organization.

Building strong relationships with customers is a key benefit of project working, developed by day-to-day interaction. It recognizes that once the contract has been signed the customer becomes part of the delivery team. The oil industry led the way in developing the use of partnerships and alliances, further integrating the value chain to build plants more cost effectively. Alliance contracting removes traditional boundaries and introduces the sharing of risks and rewards.

These multiple organizations found themselves working towards mutual objectives. In the project environment these groupings were generally established outside the individual corporate structures, thus the impacts of wider strategic approaches seldom impinged on the project. The more integrated the alliances, the more important it is to understand and manage the stresses that can build up in the same way as within a corporate structure.

From the moment a contract is placed with an external provider, or a key activity is passed to an alliance partner, success is dependent on mutual performance. Even with tight contracts, delays can never be offset against even the most rigid of penalties. With the total numbers of external people involved in a company's success, any one of whom could bring the whole process to a halt, the relationship issue is very complex. If relationships are further complicated by strategic stress there is a very good reason to consider external organizations with the same criticality as one's own.

In business, relationships build products and plants, create innovative solutions and are the foundation of sustainable development. Interdependence is a key factor in developing effective strategic approaches to a wide range of business challenges. Business processes involving external organizations are of benefit for all to capitalize on the joint use of skills, knowledge and resources. However, managing the balance in these relationships should be a key consideration and this is often neglected. Key issues in exploiting these alliances must focus on:

- Quality;
- Reliability;

- Trust;
- Communication;
- Connectivity;
- Standards; and
- Commitment.

Based on the capabilities of modern technology, future business models will be able to open up extended and flexible networks. This extended capability will enable the creation of more competitive value propositions. Underpinning these strategic alliances will need to be processes that ensure partnerships and collaborations can harness effectively their joint energy and the capabilities of networked clusters.

What I hope is very clear is the importance of relationships in this future business landscape. Despite the benefits of technology, one must recognize that the use of technology is only a catalyst for business – perhaps only 10 per cent of the equation, whereas relationships account for 90 per cent of the key ingredients for success. Developing trust between alliance partners is a crucial part of exploiting the strategic potential. As both individuals and organizations we operate in a complex world of relationships, each of which may exert an influence on the way we perform. It is in the exploitation of these relationships, whether directly or indirectly, that we both achieve and measure our success.

The issue of relationships is often lost at the strategic level, where technology is seen as the key to future business communities. This disconnection is surprising when one considers the networking and cluster communities that have grown up around the development of the technology. The impact of trust between trading partners will always remain a key ingredient for successful business strategies.

The progressive move from organizations that are founded on products and capabilities towards a network economy has its roots in the exploitation of relationships. This dependence on trust will become an even more valuable commodity, and this in turn will help to energize complementary organizations to drive strategic challenges. The less we trust, the more bureaucratic we become, which in turn drains us of time, money and enthusiasm.

The potential benefits of having the right alliance operations and in streamlining processes the significance of trust should be obvious. This is not simply one of greater openness in the external relationships; it is a factor when considering the harnessing of virtual networks.

The importance of the '50ft rule' has been recognized for many years and suggests that, outside that circle of contact, communications do not

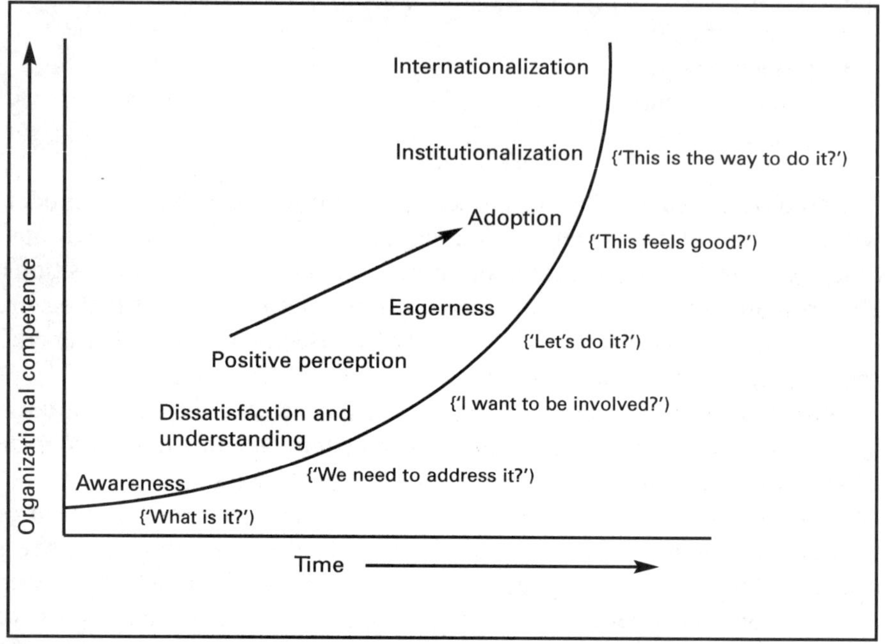

Figure 12.1   Developing trust

work well or are certainly more difficult. The problem with alliances is the difficulty in selecting the right partner and then developing an approach towards the sharing of specialist skills and avoiding people being ring-fenced in the same way as the internal corporate silo. A reducing skill base has forced organizations to consider more matrix-type operations in order to optimize resources and skills. Globalization has added a further dimension, which could not be addressed adequately with individual organizations.

Alliance teams have become accepted, but few have considered the implications of harmonizing the focus and energy of the groupings. The interdependence of teams with both customers and providers has generated the need to find more effective ways to collaborate, where not only are the processes optimized but also the strategic drivers that may on occasion pull the allies part.

Trust in a relationship is directly proportional to the effectiveness of the interface, so the stronger the relationship, the more efficient the operation. The levels of control and information requirements are damaged by a lack of trust, thus the more one improves the relationship, the lower the cost of ensuring compliance. Improving the methods of working, business processes and common strategic imperatives will help to remove the duplication that emerges from poor interfaces.

The nature of business relationships is diverse and driven by both need and a degree of interdependence. It has been interesting since the 1990s to watch the merging of ideas and concepts whereby combinations of relationship types have come together to fulfil certain market needs. The traditional supplier/customer interfaces have given way to alliances and partnerships.

Improved communications have helped this development by providing cost-effective ways of bringing together geographically separate specialist organizations. However, social relationships are also crucial in adopting change and optimizing capabilities and as shown in Figure 12.2 the emotional aspects affect the key areas of business success. The further apart people are located, the greater the need to find ways of finding a balance that supports the motivation and output of all. My experience in the world of projects suggests that generally this was a problem, but only in the early stages. Once the pressure of the objectives and goals started to consolidate, the alliance team began to pull together.

For most of the activities I have been associated with transactional processes, while crucial, only formed a small part of the cost and risk profile. The higher the graph climbs towards interdependence, the greater

Machines ⟵ Relationships ⟶ People			
Functional	Procedural	Relational	Emotional
· Transactions	· Planning	· Language	· Confidence
· Information	· Demand/supply	· Law	· Trust
· Specifications	· Evaluation	· Legislation	· Culture
· Inventory	· Budget	· Visibility	· Leverage
· Accounting	· Management	· Reporting	· Negotiations
· Payment	· Contract	· Customer	· Problem-solving
· Taxation	· Compliance	profiles	· Dispute resolution
· Security	· Performance	· Integration	· Ownership
	· Alarms	· Currency	· Motivation
			· Innovation
			· Risk management

Figure 12.2 Business complexity relationships

the emphasis on evaluation of a potential provider rests in effective relationships and trust. This may seem obvious, but many organizations try to impose a one-size-fits-all approach. Understanding the type of business relationship is critical in order to adopt the correct approach and structure between allies.

Some may suggest that too much emphasis on relationships is simply diluting age-old strategies, styles and values of trading. In fact, if one evaluates the trials and tribulations of a trading relationship it very quickly becomes clear that success results from the exploitation of interfaces. Building alliances is critical to deploying an all-encompassing approach and focusing on solutions in the wider contexts of customer needs.

In any business venture, the role of the customer is paramount, but often they can provide the greatest handicap to their own success. This is true for internal customers as well as external ones. Customer alliances are difficult to manage, since they start from the position that they have a need and usually also a fixed view of the solution to the need. Traditionalists are more apparent in the customer role as this is the nature of the power and hierarchical structures that have traditionally developed, though many of the more imaginative business models have been driven by customers who recognized opportunities. They saw improved relationships with their supply chain as a means of exploiting the potential for integration. The development of an alliance will be dependent on the profile of the customer and their interests being served is the primary goal. The more functionally structured their organization, the harder it will be to promote integration of non-aligned teams.

There are contradictions between power and influence in most organizations. Experience suggests that authority is often not the most effective route to fulfilment. Success generally comes from networking with alliance organizations where the customers' influence is stronger than their direct power. Maintaining the balance between influence and power is a crucial part of ensuring that an organization remains fluid and does not drive itself to become a rigid structure that constrains its energy.

Clearly, there are many facets of an organization where the creation of alliances can build new capabilities, and harness additional skills and energy. Certainly alliances cannot be packaged or developed based on a single approach. The type of interface will dictate the degree of influence that may be exerted or the amount of effort that should be invested. It will also be apparent that the return on investment would depend very much on the level of integration that can be exploited.

This concept may also be used to evaluate cross-functional stress factors and this would be crucial in endeavouring to exploit the full energy of the team. When the goals are clear, then the basis for establishing integrated alliances is also clear and the long-term benefits should be apparent to all the players, which in turn will ensure that a balance is maintained throughout.

Alliances and collaborative arrangements may be essential ingredients of the new digital age, but the changing nature of relationships across borders, whether organizational or geographic, must be managed to ensure that they do not deflect the focus and efforts within the associated companies. From the simplest of alliances to the most complex, the focus must be on building this trust by performance.

Relationships are a fundamental part of our business dealings and the more we wish to exploit the potential of the market the greater the emphasis we need to put on building effective alliances, which requires attention to a number of key elements. First, the need to create a business environment that accepts the premise that alternative business models are a potential solution to many issues. Second, organizations have to consider that virtual teams will need to operate in part outside traditional organization structures. This alliance approach has to be aligned to ensure effective and communicated strategies.

Shared ideas can create innovative approaches, while shared reward, whether financial or in the form of recognition, must be linked to shared risk. Achieving this while keeping the energy and balance stable means having a sound understanding of one another's capabilities.

Creating an organization to support an alliance partnership is no easy task, as in each case it will be influenced by the nature, style and history of the organizations involved. In long-established companies, the networking of individuals often operates on a level behind the formally documented lines of authority. While this allows organizations to function, in reality it means the operating focus may be diluted or even lost as a strategic imperative.

The development of alliance integration as a practical solution to the dilemmas of increasing the capabilities of organizations may be effective provided the contributors of resources accept that some degree of control may be lost. In this way, configurations can be created to suit the customer and cope with market pressures, while maintaining a recognition of the core strategic aims and without deflecting the balance of either organization.

Many companies, large and small, struggle to come to grips with the advantages and disadvantages of the various alliance models and the potential conflicts with the individual organizational strategies. The reality of these various approaches is that they generally struggle to meet the ongoing needs of a structured business that has to contend with differing pressures, whereas the alliance team can take on a specific shape to optimize resources and be successful.

The alliance solution is in response to a changing market where companies need to be more flexible and focus on customer needs. To achieve innovative solutions, and recognizing the interdependence, we must form alliances that are driven by objectives within the framework of long-term corporate strategy. This strategy will eventually encompass the virtual concept as either fully mainstream or in part. As put by Peter Drucker, 'If you want to do something new you have to stop doing something old.' A team can be structured without completely reconfiguring the current business model.

The conflict of two organizations pulling against each other may strike a note of realization both for those seeking to improve internal focus as well as the wider implications for working with allies. As we focus on trying to maximize our part of the operation we expend more energy than if we were simply to co-operate. The focus on energy and balance within relationships seeks to change this by looking horizontally at the true needs and shifting the focus towards balance.

Increased competition globally at every level has opened the way to focusing on more value-based business models, which demand greater agility, and alliances provide the framework on which to build these focused units for short periods. They may, however, require a degree of lateral thinking in terms of organizational structures by importing the necessary specialist skills as required to satisfy the demand. This is not much different from what engineering companies have done for years by using contracted labour. The difference from today's thinking is that the parties that have the requisite skills will themselves create the virtual group.

This approach may be difficult to sell inside traditional corporations, where the existing command and control structures and empire/ownership recognition approach is likely to protest at their resources being controlled at a distance. These structures are already in many cases diluting in traditionally focused organizations the need to relearn the basics of business and to change the ethos. As I have noted already, there may be a need to introduce changes to traditional control systems, which historically have had measured success.

Accounting processes are not all that must change; much of the alliance may also have to work outside current processes. Any alliance team must ensure that the players in the team have a clear understanding of what is required. In many cases today they will be part of some cyber entity, which makes it harder to maintain cross-border energy and balance.

A significant challenge, in my project experience, is the ability of virtual operations to support individual development, which in turn may divert focus from the core strategies and thus impede progress. Alliance organizations need to address this as part of the overall strategy. The challenge is not an easy one, but we shall continue to see a trend towards alliance integration via globalization and competitive markets. The world of projects provides some of the lessons that can help to integrate the use of allies without impeding the energizing of organizations, taking that focus beyond the corporate boundaries in the recognition that alliance partners are likely to have many of the same internal challenges.

CULTIVATING SYNERGY

CHAPTER 13

Corporate initiatives

Periodically, organizations look to revitalize their operations, and more importantly their employees, through the medium of initiatives. Having been exposed to many of these programmes myself it is perhaps of no surprise that to some extent we view the prospect with a degree of cynicism. This is not because these programmes are not based on real and valuable foundations but because, from experience, the true value becomes lost in the programme and the failure of executive management to put in place the right commitment to follow through.

Frequently accredited to Charles Dawin (*The Origin of Species*) that 'It's not the strongest of the species that survives, not the most intelligent either, but the one most responsive to change' highlights the need for adaptability. Unfortunately, the corporate initiative, while it can be a cause for good in terms of promoting change and evolution, it can also be the first step in creating an imbalance and the dissipation of energy.

During the last decades of the twentieth century and into the twenty-first, numerous programmes have been introduced, each of which has become fashionable for a time. Often they appear to arrive simultaneously on the market from many different gurus and consultancy organizations, and remain the key organizational development tool for a number of years – generally five – before the next wonder programme emerges to show us the way forward. Same problem, different solution:

- Total quality management (TQM);
- Just-in-time (JIT);
- Matrix;
- Restructuring;
- Re-engineering;
- Rightsizing;
- Downsizing;
- Rationalization; and
- Lean manufacturing.

It is worrying that organizations generally tend not to look proactively at improvement programmes until they are in the depressed part of their business cycle. It would clearly be much more constructive to focus on improvements and innovative activities when the organization is on a high and more able to augment these programmes.

What is often missed is that many of these programmes are built around common sense and when the hype is stripped away most contain very similar elements. It is the harnessing of internal knowledge and experience that generally delivers results. The programmes themselves often create the impetus, but frequently also get so involved with their particular gimmick that they suppress the real delivery potential. However, some do encompass innovative modelling and focusing tools, which can continue to add value long after their trendy profile, has passed. Thus retaining some of the better features without the hype may in the long-term provide a greater benefit.

It is also clear that implementing any form of innovative or motivational programme that is not properly considered or supported is likely to have more of a negative than positive impact. This is because, once people are fired up and empowered, they quickly become deflated if they are not encouraged and supported continuously to grasp the initiative and move forward. The result is often that the project drive becomes a millstone and takes the organization backwards, or develops a parallel existence that becomes detached from the real world. 'A company's blindness is due to an unwillingness or inability to look outside current experience' was Gary Hamel's rallying cry in his book, *Competing for the Future*.

Before exploring how these corporate initiatives can help to energize an organization it is perhaps worth looking at some of the reasons why these programmes fail to deliver. There is, of course, always a need to balance the degree of interaction between creating strategic plans and the handing of the reins to the people within the organization. Frequently a dynamic strategy will call for the organization to leave its comfort zone and face new challenges. In these cases, mobilizing the hearts and minds in the organization is a crucial part of the implementation.

As discussed already, the impact of strategic stress can badly undermine the strategic intent. Harnessing the energy and keeping the balance is critical if the overall strategy is to be pursued effectively at every level of the organization. The corporate programme is certainly a factor in kick-starting the integration of strategy and business operations, but if it is not handled effectively it may have a directly opposite impact. I have seen major programme investments wasted by a lack of ongoing investment and encouragement. What is perhaps even more of a concern is the common situation of the executive ignoring the results of the programmes they introduced.

One such case was that of a major Japanese company that hoped to build on the benefits of the Excellence Programme, which, as many readers will know, is based on identifying and benchmarking the key traits of successful organizations. At the same time, this programmes looks at the wider aspects of business operations, which feed or support overall performance. The approach is based on defining the ingredients that shape and produce results (see Figure 13.1).

In this case, despite their investment, management eventually buried the programme when the first results indicated that the executive was failing to deliver direction and leadership to senior management. This was not only a complete waste of effort and money; it also demonstrated that the rationale behind the programme had not been fully understood or accepted by the executive board. The result was that most who had participated felt deflated and disillusioned rather than motivated by a programme that recognized more than simply financial results.

Going back to the advent and hype of TQM in the early 1990s, this again was a programme focused on mobilizing organizations to adopt a 'right first time' approach. Many programmes were introduced and endorsed by CEOs and company presidents. The concept was simply to establish a profile of cost, waste and opportunity, and then to create multi-functional

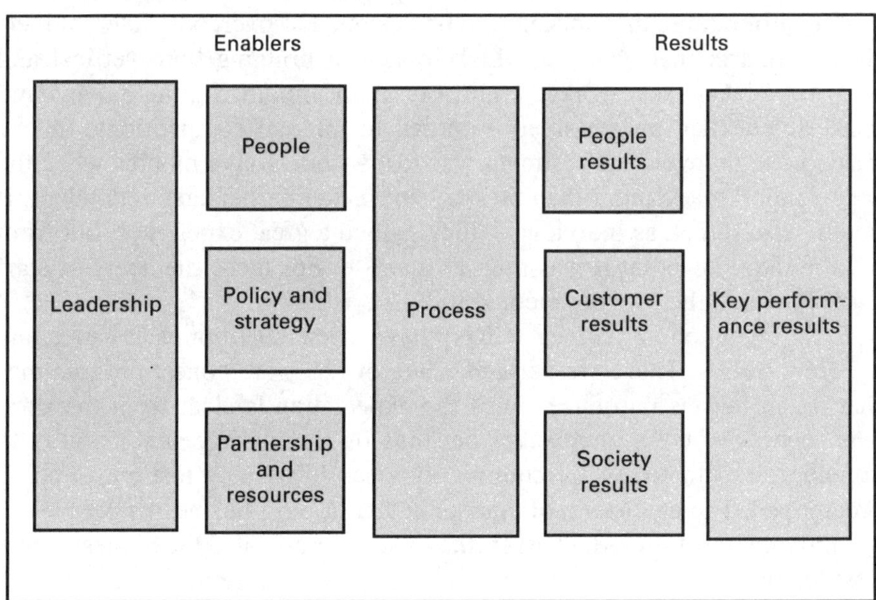

Figure 13.1 The ingredients that shape and produce results

teams to develop more effective approaches to reduce waste and increase profitability.

One such programme started with the external consultants identifying waste and opportunities for improvement that exceeded the whole operating cost of the organization: this did little to encourage support. The multinational parent then began a publicity drive that broadcast which divisions were providing the best returns, with the result that local management focus was directed towards creating more and more internal initiatives, or corrective action teams and resources were redirected to maintain image rather than obtain results. The real potentially improving programme failed to get the investment it needed, which had the effect of undermining the whole programme.

Re-engineering was one of the few programmes that sought seriously to take organizations back to their roots and reconstruct internal processes. As an advocate of business processes being the foundation of effective operations, and based on my own experience that any major mistake can generally be traced back to a process failure, I saw re-engineering as a major step forward. It required a significant level of investment from the best people in the organization. To be successful it needed the executive to be proactive in removing boundaries and barriers, along with providing supporting initiatives that focused outside the box, but the potential was often lost through vested interests and a failure to provide the 'just do it' imperative.

One programme that appeared to be designed to overcome internal inertia was matrix management, which looked at bridging both vertical and horizontal barriers. It worked well in terms of mobilizing the movers and shakers, but then progressively returned to internal competitions. In one case, the high level of investment was lost within twelve months when the organization made more than 50 per cent of the participants redundant. It could be said that, as individuals, they gained a great experience, but from a corporate viewpoint it was seen as a waste. For those members of staff that remained, the programme had lost all credibility.

Cost reduction initiatives (CRIs) have been commonplace, in many different guises. These are perhaps some of the more honest programmes that organizations introduce, since the expectation is clear from the start. The success of these approaches depends on the management's ability to convince staff that they are committed not to jobs being lost but to being redeployed. The challenge, of course, is that in most businesses people are not only the most important asset: they are generally also the highest single cost factor.

There is an inevitability that cost-down programmes mean putting people at risk. A second common impact is that functional groups seek to show their own importance and effort as a means of self-protection rather than by critical self-assessment. The focus in these programmes is perhaps the most crucial factor. Take the example of a major engineering-based organization that spent 80 per cent of its operating costs with suppliers. Internal initiatives concentrated on reducing operating costs for internal functions rather than recognizing that every effort should have been focused on reducing the external spend. The result was that considerable effort was expended but ultimately it made little or no difference.

From research and discussions with colleagues around the world, I found many examples of where sound and valuable programmes had failed to deliver. Many received a poor press because of these failures, despite the fact that, as concepts, they were based on realistic approaches. Harnessing the power within an organization requires a significant investment and commitment to people, but balancing the benefits and potential negative impacts can be an even bigger challenge.

There is no doubt that some of the more successful organizations, such as GE and its Six Sigma programme, proved that initiatives can deliver real success. So why do so many corporate programmes fail? There is apparently no common single issue. Often it is a combination of factors, the most frequent of which are:

- No clear vision and commitment at executive level;
- Fear of failure and a belief in the status quo;
- Poor preparation and targeting;
- A lack of adequate budgets and resources;
- Poor communication leading to unprepared employees;
- Lack of planning and preparation;
- Pressure from day-to day business commitments;
- Disregard of the 'domino effect';
- Goals set too high or too far into the future; and
- A legacy of previous failed programmes.

These are some of the issues that management has to face, while on the other hand employee resistance may well be driven by a reluctance to move outside the comfort zone. What is even worse is the traditional approach, which starts with an executive announcement of an improvement programme. This is followed by a half day of training, the establishment of cross-functional committees followed by resource reallocation, a cost reduction initiative, the distribution of tee shirts, and an eventual loss of focus.

The larger the organization, the more important it becomes, having recognized the need to evolve, to create a robust programme to energize the force that is the lifeblood of success. Every organization needs to keep moving forward and, as Charles Handy wrote in his book *The Age of Paradox*, 'what got you where you are won't keep you where you are', reflecting a need for continuous improvement.

Change is a process, not an event, and developing the culture of a learning organization is a challenge that must be managed well to avoid conflict and dilution of energy. Being clear on the type of change, and even clearer about the reason for change, is an important first step. Change must be planned and implemented through a change process of continuous improvement. Involving the employees and communicating the change should be complemented by short-term goals that can deliver quickly to build confidence.

The first and perhaps most important aspect when looking at a development programme is to recognize that changing an organization is not something that happens overnight. It is also unlikely to happen based on a single action but within a continuous process that builds on success and adapts to progress by raising the bar or monitoring the direction.

Whatever the initiative framework selected, and many have a similar potential, the crucial starting point is that senior executives understand the programme fully and make provision to support it with both resources and personal involvement. This has to be underpinned by a clearly defined set of goals and objectives with the rationale explained to ensure there are no hidden agendas. The most effective way of ensuring a proactive commitment is to pilot the programme on the executive. Executive sponsorship should be highly visible and ready to take down barriers to the programme at whatever level they surface.

As a long-term project, the next step is to create a well developed plan that is linked to measures of success. It is important that everyone understands what is being sought and how outcomes will be assessed. Supplementing the plan must be an appropriate budget and resources to maintain the impetus.

The core requirements in any initiative should be to focus on the key ingredients for energizing the organization and ensuring that the balance within the operation can be maintained within the context of the business strategic imperatives. Here, I will remind readers of the key drivers in the second section of the book:

- Awakening the knowledge
- Cultivating synergy
- Harnessing the power

These three elements capture the essence of what every organization seeks to achieve when implementing an organizational initiative. These programmes have as their prime ingredients the need to capture and exploit the skills and experience of the people. It is this input that delivers 90 per cent of the success in any initiative. The recognition across the organization that functional operations and a silo mentality will hold back the progress of the overall operation. The third factor is clearly to mobilize the collective power that exists in all organizations but is often suppressed by structures and management styles.

CHAPTER 14

Strategic sustainability

Every organization, and more importantly the individuals within them, will today be aware of the focus on a wide range of corporate social responsibility (CSR) and sustainability agendas. It is unlikely that, as inhabitants of this fragile globe, we do not take seriously the implications of environmental exploitation. Recent studies have shown that the positioning of companies in this regard has a significant impact on recruiting programmes. It is also suggested that while people may feel obliged to their employers many, who cannot take comfort from an effective sustainability agenda, will be less focused. One can therefore see that building a strategic programme that encompasses a sustainability profile can contribute to the maintenance of balance within the organization.

The business world has been challenged to address the widening of the focus of CSR and recognize the wider implications of sustainability in the global marketplace. Responsibility for environmental issues is a major consideration for the business community, but with the increasing impact of globalization this aspect becomes a crucial part of business strategy. In addition, increased awareness through communication has far-reaching implications. The developing of sustainable business models within extended supply chains runs in parallel with the external pressures on strategic development (see Figure 14.1).

Strategic initiatives must consider the integration of supply chains and outsourcing operations, not simply react to the implications of public opinion on issues of Third-World exploitation but in the development of sustainable propositions. The balance between corporate competitiveness, shareholder value and the practical implications of ignoring the sustainability implications of investing in overseas operations, either directly or indirectly, is a difficult challenge.

Business relationships are a crucial factor both in the exploitation of the potential of extended supply chains and in terms of supporting sustainable objectives. The business landscape is complex and volatile, so leaders of business today (and tomorrow) must make sustainable strategies wider than

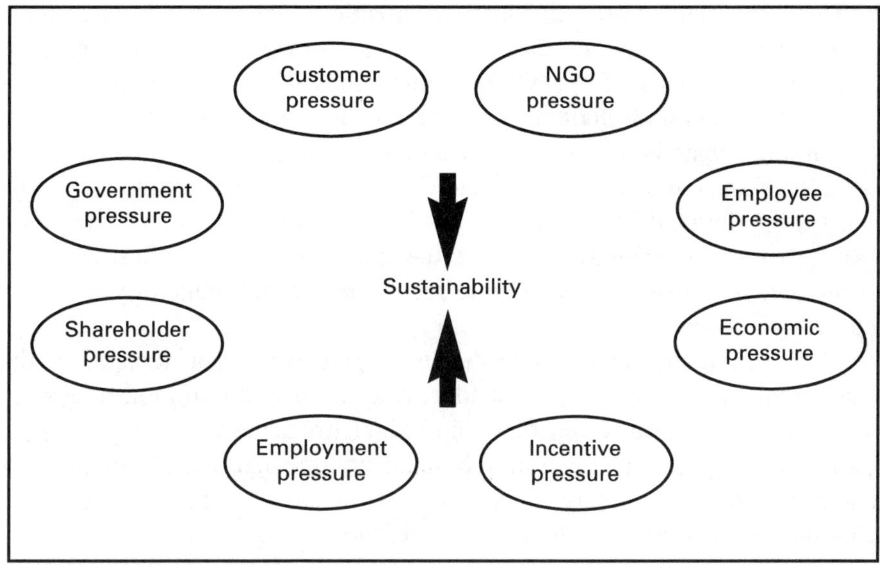

Figure 14.1   Pressures of sustainability

market sector competitiveness. At the same time, events such as the Enron crisis have seriously undermined the credibility of corporate leaders and their advisers, and have increased the focus on and demand for corporate responsibility. Global competition means considering many factors outside simply the traditional product or customer relationship. Changes in demand increase pressure on planning processes to meet the shareholders' search for return on investment, while satisfying customer demands for greater innovation and lower costs reflective of a global market place.

While political and environmentalist powers grow, the market wants ever more competitive products. This means expanding the supply chain or extending the enterprise to satisfy demand. The planning cycles of organizations and the implications for long-term environmental investments are often far from that compatible, which means corporate executives have to walk a difficult line. It is a challenge to reach new markets for sales, or supply, and in doing so to embrace the implications these opportunities afford with regard to shareholders and customers. Within these business cultures the pressures and standards that are accepted traditionally may be in direct conflict with those expected or accepted in more traditional markets. The sustainability agenda may be viewed as being restrictive in the short term, but the integration of business aims and objectives could provide opportunities for long-term value creation.

There are many views of what sustainable development is, and this is generally because there are many different sectors of the global community addressing elements of the whole picture. It is often this complexity that creates conflicts and challenges in the business arena. What is often lost within this debate is that, in most cases (if not all, long-term) the end-game objectives are the same. The difficulty for the business community is the short-term demand to maximize profitability and return on investment (ROI) for the shareholders, while the customer, whether individual or corporate, is focused on best value for money, which generally translates into lowest price.

This complexity becomes further entangled when one recognizes that each organization must not only address a number of common issues, but the spectrum of issues and their individual impact also creates a unique profile for every organization. There is no one-size-fits-all model, and therefore every company must look at these sustainability issues in conjunction with its own drivers and pressures.

Sustainability, then, needs to be integrated into the business strategy along with the implications of maintaining balance and progress against a background of strategic stress that an integrated strategic profile can create. In the main, from a business perspective, the subject of sustainability is related to maintaining business positioning and growth. This environment is often categorized as three dimensions – financial, social and environmental – within which businesses have to operate.

In a wider context, it is an integrated process, which helps people to improve their quality of life while protecting the environment. The difficulty is that these multiple agendas develop along different parallels and at alternative speeds and often fail to recognize the rights and wrongs of each other's priorities. These conflicts can seriously impede an organization's development. The pressures on business strategy coming from many different directions often force organizations to adopt an avoidance agenda rather than look to the long-term potential advantages. It is not realistic simply to place the responsibility on the business community through regulation, or at the other extreme for that community to try to maintain the status quo in the face of change. For the business strategy the way it does business should be key considerations, including:

- Working conditions
- Ethical investors
- Ethical consumers
- Email and Internet abuse
- Domino effect of supply chains

- Bribery and gifts
- Equal opportunities
- Moral dilemma
- Corruption
- Cultural diversity

The interrelationship between business and the ramifications of the sustainability agenda are very closely intertwined. All business operations seek a long-term plan that underpins the business objectives, but the pressure may be in the short term, driving organizations to seek relief from regulatory demands and the depth of public opinion that can be invoked when the issues are not fully appreciated or exploited for initial gains. The development of sustainable programmes within strategic planning requires the integration of multiple business relationships focused on building long-term operations that recognize the global implications and the furthering of local agendas that support growing economies and add value to an organization's business profile.

While the business environment comes under continuous and growing competitive pressure, the manner in which business is conducted may itself have significant impacts on the ultimate perceptions of the marketplace, which is seldom a level playing field. These pressures move into the corporate ethos through the personal agendas of staff, which in turn can introduce strategic stress. People generally want to work for companies that they can feel proud of and to which they can relate. It is often easy for those outside the active business arena to demand standards of practice that are in direct conflict with the realities of local cultures and diversity.

Whether in the local business field or in the wider global context, there are many factors that reach beyond traditional trading relationships. The higher the degree of interdependence, the greater the opportunity for many of these issues to be overlooked in the short-term drive for commercial advantage. Focusing on the mutual benefit of trading parties can open the way to looking at business strategies and processes alongside the long-term integrated objectives to meet competitive market demands, sharing knowledge to build more robust commercial structures.

Sustainability must be seen as a focus to create more effective and efficient business operations that can adapt to the market, with programmes that will benefit wider society. The sustainability agenda offers many challenges and building a business strategy that addresses these issues in an environment where many diverse organizations may be involved in the value chain demands a high level of focus on the relationships that bridge the organizational boundaries. The challenge for business leadership is to develop the ethos within their respective operations to consider the competitive opportunities and to build into the processes a regard for sharing responsibility for the sustainable objectives.

The expansion of globalization creates pressure that often impedes the development towards national and global government sustainability targets. The growth of global trading and the increasing drive for competitiveness is a fact of life. This pressure tends to subjugate the individual feelings of business people and organizations and to recognize the long-term impacts of short-term commercial actions. These, while being a direct objective in relation to business growth targets and market expansion objectives, are often viewed as being in conflict with the public image of fostering a green agenda or defending the developing environments that are being exploited.

In many cases, these result from a lack of balance. The current perception in many sectors of industry is that sustainability in green terms is a factor of compliance rather than a focus for long-term commitment. Inducing a reactive approach that focuses on compliance to or accommodating national and global sustainability and environmental objectives or regulation can be negative, as opposed to considering innovative approaches that may satisfy these objectives while improving the efficiency of the business operations and reducing internal conflicts.

For the many stakeholders, the drivers are focused not on potential second- and third-generation environmental impacts, but on the deliverables for today's marketplace demand. This is not to suggest that individuals or many organizations are not concerned with the long-term global impacts of their actions, but they do operate on a far from level playing field globally. As a result of these imbalances they are forced to meet the competitive drivers of today. The reality for companies, in the short term at least, is that they must balance the demands of the market and the social community. The sustainability agenda must recognize the need to support the short-term business communities' challenges. The by-product of this improved approach to commercial enterprises is that, in reducing waste, power consumption, packaging, transport needs and resources in general there is a natural contribution and satisfaction at every level to sustainability leading to confidence in the strategic direction.

When considering the challenges of integrating overseas partners and the potential to benefit from low-cost labour, the development of long-term training or support-programmes will underpin immediate production needs, while creating a longer-term platform for future development. Better conditions improve output and a stronger, more educated workforce provides the catalyst for further innovative and competitive propositions. Programmes focusing on worker improvements also have the benefit of creating an answer to those who see simple exploitation.

Far from being an impediment to competitiveness, sustainability programmes can open the way to an alternative and beneficial approach to eco-efficiency. Adopting sustainable influences in strategy must be holistic. The traditional linkages between organizations through arm's-length contracting fails to recognize the potential reactions to sustainable issues flowing negatively through trading relationships. This may be more clearly apparent in the context of global trading but should not be ignored even in the more localized and traditional market.

The investment profile of any business needs to exploit the longest possible optimum return that will provide the highest return on investment. Short-term exploitation of any resource will not only limit the robustness of the proposition, but it will be likely to increase exposure to elements of non-governmental organization (NGO) and regulatory demands. As with any business initiative, the first major step has to come from the corporate leadership. This is key to combining sustainable programmes within the wider strategy and is crucial to success. The goals of the shareholders and regulatory demands must be uppermost in the profile of the corporate direction, and these must be reflected externally as well as down through the whole organization, thus empowering the front-line staff to recognize the strategic objectives of the organization. Collaboration offers the opportunity for cross-training to build stronger long-term foundations that meet both commercial and environmental objectives, underpinning corporate responsibility and relieving the stresses of internal balance.

Relationships have always been the foundation of business activities, but in more recent times the stresses of increasingly complex trading have in many ways diluted the traditional values of performance and trust. The progressive development of more conflict-based trading has built up barriers to exploiting the integration of knowledge, skills, resources and technology. In the context of integrating a strategy of corporate responsibility and building towards sustainable objectives, the strengthening of relationships internally and externally is crucial. Relationships are the key ingredient that must be expanded to achieve meaningful results. These relationships will be across internal factions of a single organization or between partners, suppliers or service providers. Customers, whether corporate or at a consumer level, also have a significant role to play in the development of cost-effective operations and even more in supporting the social and environmental implications of sustainability. In the longer term, the development of integrated strategies provides a significant advantage to all parties, by creating alternative and innovative approaches to address key pressures from sustainability and contribute towards social responsibility.

For many in the business environment the issue of risk management is a natural part of their corporate and management operations. What are not, perhaps, given as much consideration in this regard are the implications of sustainability. Sustainability is a subject that at an individual level either inspires people to be strongly proactive or engenders apathy in terms of it being someone else's problem. In addressing the implications of strategic stress and the negative impacts of a lack of balance, success comes from a joint commitment to a set of common goals and objectives. The structuring of incentive programmes can often be diametrically opposed to the idea of building a sustainable future, focusing simply on short-term exploitation. Often the potential commercial benefits of adopting a sustainable approach are ignored in favour of short-term profits.

In the wider aspects of social responsibility and sustainability, the objectives may not be separate and can be integrated but it is important that the organization fully appreciates the big picture and does not undermine the programme for localized improvements. People, as has been emphasized a number of times already, are the most important resource in the business environment and their ownership of the strategy is paramount if it is to be driven towards success.

There are many who view the issues of sustainability as being mainly negative for the business community, thus creating an idea that compliance and public image are the only factors to be considered. The reality is that many of the factors that are raised as issues of sustainability are also key facets of business-process improvement. Eco-efficiency is focused on exploiting the potential benefits from capturing cost savings and passing these to the bottom line, while contributing simultaneously to long-term sustainable returns.

These elements of eco-efficiency (Figure 14.2) and other aspects of business each contribute to the overall framework of CSR, both in terms of business process development and the market perception of organizations through badly-managed exploitation. The exploitation of this approach to sustainability builds on direct and meaningful commercial benefits, while providing contributions to overall sustainability goals. In fact sustainability, social responsibility and profitability are all linked, as well as being complementary. Developing value propositions is a basic element of organizations, and to build effective approaches it is important that the partners share goals and objectives. In terms of sustainability, the definition of value may be viewed as being less commercial but in reality if business is to prosper and help developing areas, then commercial

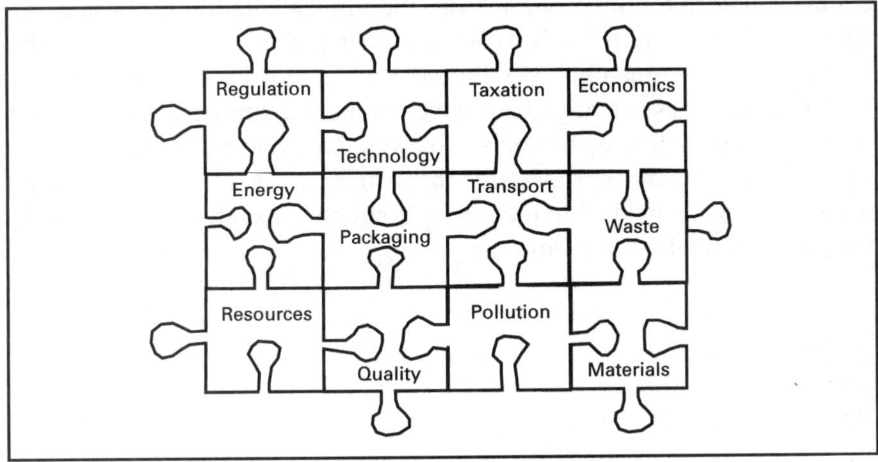

Figure 14.2 Eco-efficiency focus

concerns, market demands and profitability have to be viewed as being interdependent.

Whatever the aims of the business or social partnership, the value creation process still needs to address the fundamental facets of the operations. In each of the three key points of focus, there will be opportunities across the business agenda to concentrate on improvements that will bring cost or time savings, and at the same time deliver contributions to sustainable targets, whether governmental or those that the organizations themselves promote as part of their business approach.

The extended enterprise or outsourcing model can also benefit from using this or similar approaches to set targets across organizational boundaries. Social responsibility, and thus many aspects of the sustainability drivers, is integrated into the model, providing a valid basis for setting performance targets and addressing the key aspects of CSR. The mutual focus on the future will inevitably lead to organizations having greater knowledge of each other and appreciating more fully the benefits that can derive from joint development rather than short-term exploitation.

The future holds increasing challenges and therefore organizations must consider in their long-term strategies how to deal with the changes and maintain their business profiles and profitability. Sustainability is not simply about ethical development or environmental considerations and pressures; it also has a significant impact on profitability and growth. Business ventures are seldom established for short-term targets and as such the long-term perspective is an important factor.

Sustainability is in fact itself a valid catalyst on which to draw on the common objectives and benefit from the implementation of an integrated approach. The future is likely to demand even greater attention to the whole spectrum of sustainability issues and focus on corporate responsibility. Organizations may see this as intrusive, but in real terms the potential benefits that can be delivered through a structured approach can satisfy many of the challenges within a programme that is focused primarily on commercial advantages while balancing the strategic stresses that emerge from individuals or groups within the business.

CHAPTER 15

Finance management

As the foundation of all business ventures is making money, this clearly has a great deal of influence on the way that organizations operate, and the way this is managed can have a significant impact on the balance of an organization. There can be few of us who do not recognize that the key driver behind any business is the need to generate profits for the many stakeholders involved. From experience, the drive to create value and profits can often get overshadowed within organizations when the focus becomes based more on considerations of allocation rather than generation.

Historically, the two key challenges for business are to acquire resources that are better than those of the competition, and then to deploy those resources better than the competition. The harder organizations strive to optimize these two key drivers, the more risks they have to face and the more conflict that can be generated internally. Profit may be the lifeblood of business but it has to be recognized that, if not managed effectively, not only can financial advantage be dissipated but it can also engender the worse type of friction, with the result that more energy its expended on chasing internal conflicts than is directed towards generation.

In earlier chapters I outlined the potential divisionary impact of incentive schemes and functional performance assessment through financial reporting. There will probably always be battles between various parts of an organization in terms of budget creation and allocation against committed resources. When major operations or market developments cross internal and national boundaries, the issue of financial management becomes more complex. When adding the complications of external economic influences it is easy to envisage even more potential conflict.

Many would perhaps share the traditional view of the finance world, which is often coloured by the perspective that number-crunching is deemed to be an exact science of black and white (or red), whereas most organizations in practical terms operate in a grey world with increasingly fuzzy trading boundaries. It is often said that a bad accountant tells you what you can't do, a good one says what you can do, and a great one advises what you can get away with.

I would generally agree that in a global market with all its complexities, the need for sound financial management is crucial. Defining budget responsibility and distribution of profits and incentives clearly is critical if the organization is to focus on real tasks and objectives, and avoid the negative impacts that everyone has witnessed to some extent, from a media headline regarding 'fat cat' payments through to compatibility of salary scales within in a local functional unit.

The many faces of financial management and accountancy reflect the complexity of how these activities interface and impact at every level of the business operations. These growing pressures on organizations may explain the increasing numbers of accountants that are appearing. It has been said that the number of people handling accounts is directly proportional to how badly a company is doing. The stresses between the demands of the customer paying the bill and the expectations and demands of the chief financial officer (CFO) are generally balanced by those in operations trying to keep everyone happy in a difficult juggling act.

In reality, sound financial management can add greatly to effectiveness and profitability. It has been our experience that, in major projects, having financial managers inside the team gave everyone a focal point for advice and actions that often seemed insoluble to those who don't talk that special financial language.

Financial management that is not in tune with the business objectives can, however, have a significantly detrimental effect on relationships across the operation, since what may make good sense in terms of improving profitability or cash flow may have a significant impact on the interfaces between customers, partners or suppliers. The implications for any financial programme must be balanced to ensure the uniform application of business strategy. Any imbalance of pressure will not only affect external relationships with the organization, it may also create friction internally across the organization.

This is not to suggest that organizations can ignore the financial impacts of their operations, since this would be counter to the business objective. It is, however, clearly an area where the efforts and energies of those within the organization can be influenced and barriers created, to the overall detriment of all. When customers receive a bill they should be looking to appreciate the value, and when suppliers complete their tasks timely payment is a recognition of their efforts. This integration of activities allows all participants to take credit for financial stability and effectiveness without losing the drive to maintain and foster effective relationships. Planning and managing the financial aspects of any business is crucial to keeping relationships focused.

Major factors in today's marketplace are the indirect financial implications of how a business venture operates and delivers on its promise. Traditionally, companies had assets and liabilities balanced against costs and revenue, but today the market tends to look deeper into the structure and approach of a business. Market value is now being derived from a more complex analysis, which is still reflected in financial terms but is developed by considering the wider assessment of value. The progressive move from purely asset-based valuations towards a more knowledge- and skill-structured value has led to a number of high profile initial public offerings (IPOs), particularly in the middle of the dot.com boom.

The change in valuation is perhaps what many of us would consider to be the reality behind an organization's true value: that of its people, skills and knowledge. The financial results of a company have in the past been viewed as the only measure of its success, but the problem with this is that with financial measures, frequently it is only the results that get measured, whereas the success of an organization is more likely to be reflected in trends and traits. Thus these reflections have led to many acquisitions and investments being slanted more towards high levels of goodwill and less focused on solid assets. It also means that in the future the stock value of an organization will be driven increasingly by the way that organizations operate and manage their people assets, in contrast to their investments in hardware and real estate.

The new thinking opens the way for greater entrepreneurship, which is essential to progress. Entrepreneurs think the unthinkable; then they do it. It is entrepreneurs who have made most of the major advances in commerce, industry and science. A key factor in successful competition is the innovation that an entrepreneur's vision can provide, and this certainly offers a challenge to the financial community to manage and maintain integrity. Certainly, the Enron and WorldCom situations have led to increased needs for financial propriety, but this should not become so stringent that it hampers health development within organizations.

This change in the basis of market appraisal has pushed the role of financial managers much deeper into the operational side of organizations. The auditing and presentation of organizations in the wider financial measurement profile provides an even greater challenge to those who traditionally have looked simply at the bottom line, fixed assets, loan gearing and growth potential. These now also have to be configured to satisfy the complications of stock market value being assessed against factors of sustainability and CSR.

These far-reaching changes in value assessment have given the financial sector and business management a major challenge to blend traditional accounting processes with the more subjective trading environment. At the same time, the regulatory implications of global business is an increasing minefield for the practitioner who wants to get on with the job of developing new and profitable business. If one considers only the issues of taxation and currency within multinational organizations, the challenges and pitfalls are many.

Building business relationships and integrated teams is a difficult task, but creating the financial infrastructure that will support rather than hinder development and progress is a challenge on its own. The distribution of responsibilities and rewards, together with the relative risks for the parties, need to be in balance to avoid creating a negative impact and stress between groups. Ensuring that effort and reward also remain in tune with the investment and development effort of each is also important.

What we do and how we are rewarded are fundamental aspects of the business culture. Thus at every level the financial implications of effective management are critical to maintaining the energy and balance across business operating units. So while historically the accountant has been seen as a necessary evil in most organizations, the effectiveness of the role is now crucial to managing the strategy of the organization at large. These issues of financial management are relatively well understood within the environment of a single business. At the multinational level, major corporations have teams of people focused on the cross-border implications, such as addressing investment and taxation responsibilities and opportunities.

Those organizations that have significant outsourcing or procurement operations within the world market will understand the wider implications of cross-border commerce and the stresses that can be created when these relationships are not synchronized with the overall financial programmes. The pressures on financial management increase as they endeavour to maintain a balance between spending and revenue as the organizations' operations become more global. When considering an extended enterprise that has cross-boundary processes but wants to optimize the value chain, the accounting rules, both legal and organizational, can add a whole new layer of complexity.

Building specialist teams from across organizations will generally be found to harness their common personal interests and professionalism. However, as we saw earlier, they face the challenges that will develop from the corporate silo, but perhaps the even greater challenges they will encounter are likely to come from the accountants and financial managers. The financial management of every business operation touches on all aspects of delivery. Alongside any business venture, development must be a parallel process that recognizes the objectives of the approach while satisfying the legalities of financial reporting.

Added to the basic interfaces of financial functional needs (see Figure 15.1) which themselves can create tension within an organization, there are the ever-increasing demands of taxation and duties. Government treasury departments have no interest in the complexities of business; their role is merely to maximize the revenues due under their rules. Thus, when organizations seek to simplify cross-border processes there is a matrix of issues that must be addressed to keep everyone happy. At the same time, tax offsetting or avoidance is a major business opportunity in a highly competitive world. For all these reasons, and many more, the tendency has been to create ever more complex contracting arrangements, which are often promoted by the financial management within organizations to protect the interests of the individual company. The downside of this is that this very protectionism, though understandable, inhibits the growth of innovation.

I do not want to be seen as promoting an anti accountant viewpoint – it would be very dangerous for any of us in the business world to alienate that sector of the community. My purpose is to raise awareness of the implications of financial management not being considered as an integral part of the building of teams and organizations. Like good lawyers, if one only involves them when one is in trouble, they can generally be of less help, but

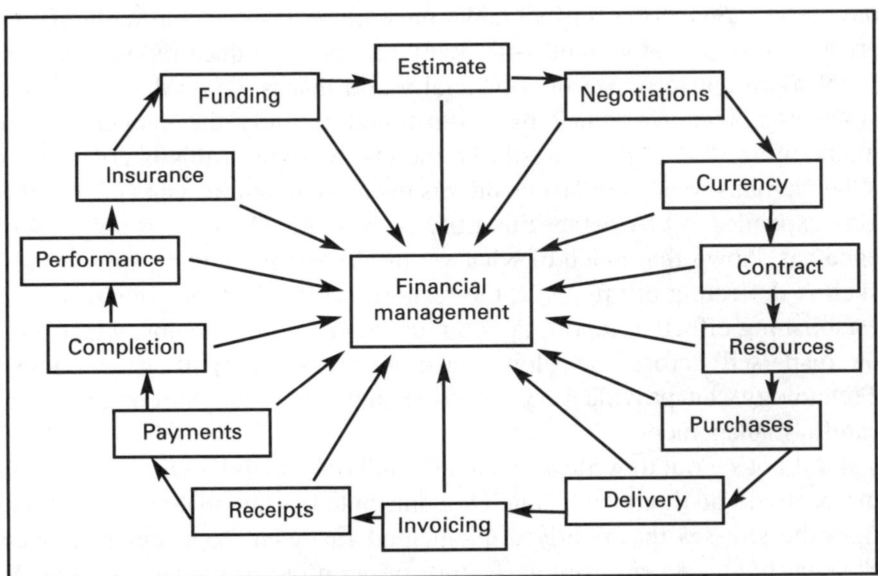

Figure 15.1 Interfaces of financial management

if they understand the proposition they may well be able to add significant value. On the other side of the coin, the complexity of modern financial demands is such that organizations should be looking to blend sound financial management with the wider business profile in order to promote growth and meet investors' and regulators' expectations.

In all of this, the key factor is that a strategy must be established for the organization and its objectives validated. Considering that the true value of cross-border organizations is to optimize the process, these can be established around any number of integrated activities in the enterprise. When task planning, the financial management must work with the operators to create a model in terms of who does what and when they get paid. I mentioned the importance of financial planning, and optimization of resources and cash flow are key to enabling organizations to work effectively together. Therefore, once each group, function or team understands the implications for themselves they can debate the options for relieving pressure or improving overall returns.

Maintaining investor approval for a venture is only one part of the financial management activity. Keeping the balance right between internal and external partners can be a challenge, as well as keeping all parties informed and comfortable. In my experiences I have found that it was never the project itself that was the challenge, but the amount of reporting that was required to keep those outside the operation informed. We frequently produce far more than is useful or understandable without detailed day-to-day knowledge of the business. We have all probably spent a significant amount of time and worked with many others to produce reports that one felt seldom got read. Yet the financial world insists we do this, and given some organizations, which have illustrated recently the dangers of not maintaining visibility, we would be the last to suggest this is not needed. What perhaps we should all consider is the amount of effort and energy that gets expended, and whether this truly adds value. Over the years, experience has shown that much of what we produce is not adding value and as such is deflecting efforts, with the result of creating stress. Investment in establishing effective reporting is a must to ensure that teams, which may be dispersed across the globe, also appreciate how they are doing. Technology can provide very effective platforms, but the content needs careful management.

I did not set out to write a financial handbook, so those with an accounting bent will no doubt have much to contribute but my objective is to highlight the stresses that poorly implemented financial management induce. Finance is no longer a simple feature of counting beans and scoring the results in debits and credits. It has a significant role to play in efficient operations and is often a major contributor to overall profitability. More important is the proactive role it can play in removing boundaries and restraints within an organization. The success of relationships, whether internal or external, depends on how a team delivers results and how it is viewed from outside. The financial implications will reflect on the levels of contribution and support, so reliable and effective management is crucial.

The future is likely to see even greater involvement and responsibility directed towards the financial management of organizations. The implications of globalization and the complexity of the marketplace valuation will continue to place growing pressure on the integration of finance and operations. These two elements will become more entwined than ever before. What must not be allowed to happen, though, is that they develop as parallel functions rather than fully integrated activities. The key drivers for global development take financial management to the core of growth and risk management. The creation of development strategies and market positioning will lean more and more on the financial sector to maintain integrity and growth potential.

Every part of a business operation needs to understand and appreciate the role that financial management plays in the wider picture, recognizing the interrelationship between both financial numbers and the operational value of an organization in creating a value proposition for investors. Those in financial management teams need to understand that they have to consider their much wider role in monitoring and presenting the organization's values and growth potential. In this position they have the ability to contribute significantly to growth and development, or to drive innovation to the wall by failing to recognize the wider implications of their demands.

Financial management is obviously seen as being the custodian of fiscal responsibility, but it is perhaps less appreciated for the role it has to play in helping to facilitate the delivery of strategy and maintaining the balance of energy within an organization, which in turn will help to deliver those strategic goals.π

HARNESSING THE POWER

CHAPTER 16

Goals and objectives

Harnessing the energy and power of an organization requires goals and objectives that are well understood and supported. We are all driven by personal or collective goals, which in turn enables us to define objectives against which to measure progress and performance. Every organization needs challenges that stretch its capabilities, while helping it grow and expand. Generally, organizations that do not grow will eventually contract and fade away. These stretched goals, however, have to be set at levels that will pull the organization forward but not offer a mountain to scale that is so high that people are defeated before they begin. Balancing these forces is a major challenge for the effective management of organizations, since they need to respond to the drivers of markets and expectations of shareholders, while retaining the recognition of what is realistic.

Many times in my career I have seen the focus of organizations set by the executive level without any recognition of the implications. There are many who will say the role of the executive is to set the objectives and then leave it to the troops to find a way forward. Frequently, however, this devolves not simply by setting, say, projected profit a margins, but also dictating cost reduction goals to underpin these margins, while at the same time not only establishing the focus going forward but also simultaneously creating a stress that may well undermine the prime objective.

It must also be recognized that the main goals for any organization are only part of a wider matrix of interconnected pressures and that optimizing energy requires recognition of other pressures (see Figure 16.1). There is a clear understanding of the corporate positioning, but this can be affected by the interactions at both a social and personal level. Organizations, like virtually all of us, are part of a community, and thus the objectives of each organization will need to mesh with those at the community level. Recognizing these implications when setting goals for the organization is the first step in removing many of the strategic stresses that can be created, since it should also be remembered that the people who will strive to deliver those objectives are part of these communities as well.

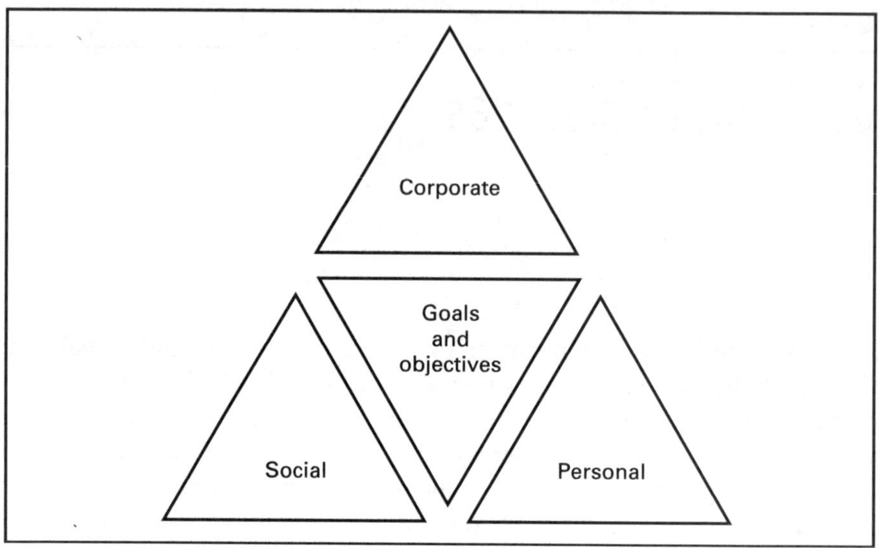

Figure 16.1   Optimizing goals and objectives

It is also true that individuals have their own objectives and goals in life, and while the organization may be the means of delivering these it may also be the in conflict and thus perhaps not draw the fullest of support. It is clearly not realistic for executive management to design its strategies and business plans around the collective considerations of every employee, but it is important that each employee feels committed to the overall objectives of the organization and feels empowered to push for the goals that are cascaded down through the organization.

There is a balance in all things, and since it is the objectives of the organization that set the drive to move forward it requires that careful consideration be given to establishing and publicizing these. It may be easy to demand a 10 per cent rise in profit every year, but as we all appreciate, reaching these targets can be a very different picture. It is also true that to achieve such an objective in the short term might mean resource reductions, which in the longer term will make the challenge even harder. These subtleties will not go unrecognized at the working level, and as a result often act as an anchor to progress.

Thus every objective is always constrained within a framework of complementary but often conflicting pressures and influences (Figure 16.2). It is within this framework that each has to be evaluated individually and then balanced collectively to ensure that, by default, they are not diluting each other. This evaluating process also allows the executive manage-

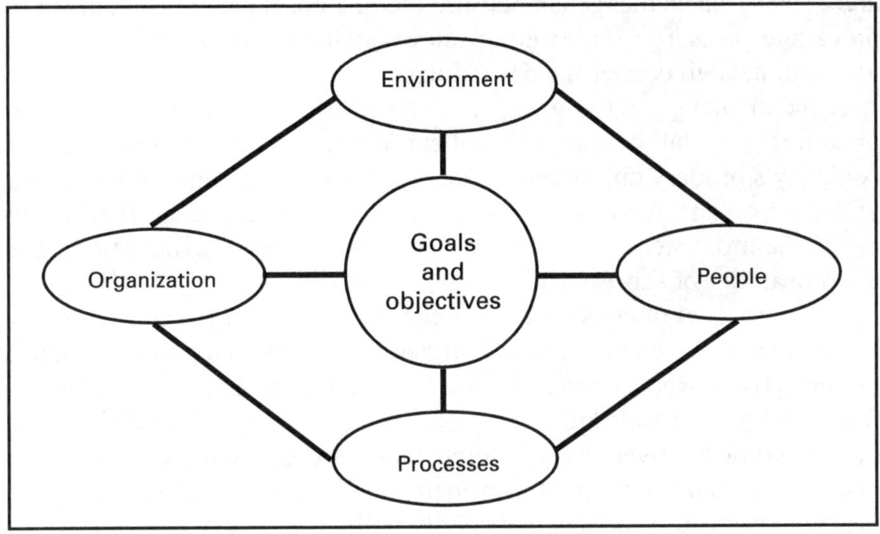

Figure 16.2　Complementary framework influences

ment to challenge their own thinking and perhaps recognize the need to temper some goals with the realities of the situation.

The first of these pressures is the environment, and by this I mean the business landscape within which the organization operates. We discussed in Phase One of the book, 'Decoding the force', the implications for strategy of the business environment and it would not be realistic to consider setting objectives that flew in the face of current trends. Unless, of course, the organization has developed, or is considering developing, an alternative approach to the market that flouts these trends. This could be a new product or an extended proposition, an entry into a new market sector or a complete change in direction.

Certainly, within this context one cannot ignore the implications of political change and the demands of regulatory control. It is not realistic to set agendas that confront the demands of the public and what more recently some are calling the 'green' or 'grey' shareholders, whose investment pressure is focused on how organizations behave as much as how well they perform financially. Indeed, some organizations have taken the initiative in promoting their socially responsible objectives.

This redirection of the organization obviously opens up a much wider strategic evaluation. In the context of this chapter we are focusing mainly on the traditional structured approach to existing market activities and the implications for managing goals and objectives in that context. In this arena, then, the challenge is to ensure that the goals are realistic, given the prevailing pressure from external sources, which will be evident to those who will have to deliver the desired outcomes.

If the challenge is too great, then the probability will be that internal pressures will build that will deflect resources and energy from the company's primary objectives. As has been said many times, it is the force within an organization that is its real strength and key asset. If this force cannot be motivated, or worse is deflated by excessive expectations, then the probability of success will clearly be reduced.

The next level of consideration is the organizational structure itself and the manner in which the various components are expected to contribute to the objectives. Recognizing that every organization is a configuration of functional groups and skills, every part needs to be synchronized in terms of delivering the overall goals. Frequently, the cascading of information and objectives is not properly considered and as a result the various groupings are out of step and thus potentially pulling against one other.

This is totally different from creating internal competition, which is an alternative approach where often separate divisions or production units are set against each other to act as a spur. What is crucial in the optimizing of focus it that the corporate silo syndrome is not introduced by the disjointed application and goal-setting process. The business processes provide the third element of the framework, which is perhaps the least obvious of the constraints that impinge on the successful delivery of objectives. Most of us would see that, in the case of meeting goals, processes could be circumvented or changed should they create any obstacles. The reality, of course, is that in today's world the development of ICT systems and globalization, interactions can be a lot less easy to adapt than we might think. As a result, when setting objectives these must consider the ability of the existing processes to meet the demands.

This may seem obvious, but those who watched the dot.com boom will recognize the difference between the goals and expectations of many of the propositions and their physical ability to deliver on those promises. The other implication of ignoring business processes is that those who are charged with delivery will clearly see the limitations of the existing systems. Failing to recognize potential constraints would clearly have a negative impact on the perceptions of those trying to meet their goals.

Clearly, of the four primary influences the major factor is people. Objectives are not delivered by systems or machines. However automated a process might be, it will be people that will be charged with the responsibility and criticized for not meeting objectives. It therefore follows that the biggest positive or negative influence will come from people. This is not simply a question of their skills being sufficient to meet the challenge, it is about their commitment, focus and energy that creates the force within organizations. If this force is not charged, then resources will be deflected and performance will drop, with the end result of goals not being achieved.

Unlike machines, which can be driven beyond their performance windows, sometimes resulting in complete failure, in general people tend to pull back if they are deflated or unconvinced of the way forward. It is always a challenge for the armed forces to create a lateral-thinking soldier with the ability to follow orders unquestioningly. In the corporate world the challenge is even more difficult because innovative thinking and entrepreneurial development are the cornerstone of future development. Thus blind obedience is not either likely or desired by most organizations.

It therefore follows that the development and communication of corporate goals has to be both logical and realistic within the commonly understood environment of the business. Failure to address these issues will probably fail to motivate the workforce to stretch themselves and deliver. Again, we are not suggesting collective or communal agreement, which would in any event be unworkable, since there has to be a focus that is set by the senior management on behalf or as result of shareholders.

The aim is to create goals that are achievable within the current marketplace and within the capacity of the organization to deliver. It is also important to ensure that the objectives themselves are not likely to pull against one other, as in the case of, say, increasing market share, while reducing the cost base and resources. It does not take a rocket scientist to see that conflicting objectives will dilute the focus and distract those who need to concentrate on delivering the objectives.

It is equally important to ensure that corporate objectives do not invoke the wrath of the community or set challenges that employees will find unacceptable. We are all members of the community and as such generally want to work for organizations that in the main support a responsible approach. The issues of corporate social responsibility and sustainability locally, nationally and internationally are major factors of corporate governance. Therefore when setting objectives for the organization there must be due consideration for the governance implications within the wider community.

These CSR issues are a major concern for many organizations that are looking to relocate manufacturing or outsourcing offshore, to exploit low-cost markets or address environmental problems. This environment then creates a wide range of issue to be balanced against significant objectives being set for the organization. Thus developing goals for the operation is not simply a case of setting new profit levels or market directions and throwing that challenge to the operation in the hope that it will blossom into reality. In most cases there will be some degree of success but it should be obvious that ill-considered objectives can fail to capture the total force of the organization and thus it will not deliver its full potential. At the same time, if these objectives disturb the balance of the organization, then rather than moving things forward they could at the worst be detrimental overall.

The process of developing corporate goals and objectives then plays a crucial role in the wider issues of strategic development, as do the implications of strategic stress the operation. These objectives are clearly the catalyst for energizing the force within organizations if developed effectively, or the reverse if not managed well. There has to be synergy across the organization and thus the process cannot be handled in isolation or devolved purely by edict. Moving forward requires a structured approach that enables operations to consider the implications and realities of goals and objectives before launching them on the organization.

The goal for every organization is to achieve operational excellence, which delivers optimal performance. However, to reach this point many first have to progress through the other phases of development that start with a realization of the need for change. This leads to a rationalization and equalization of the force that can then be exploited through standardization, co-operation and optimization. The challenge is then to maintain this devel-

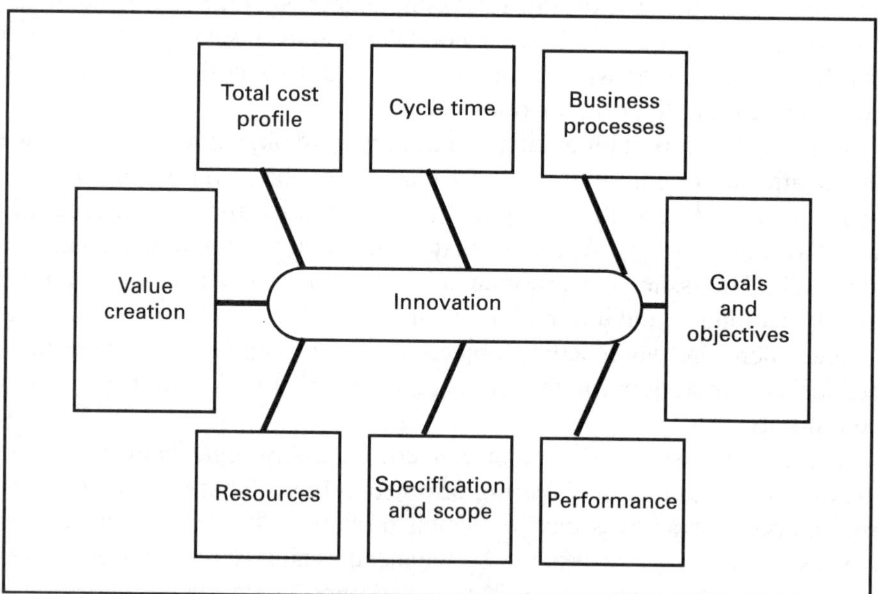

Figure 16.3   Innovation framework

opment growth and be able to set short and medium-term goals that do not detract from the long-term objectives.

The prime objective of any organization is to create value, whether for shareholders or stakeholders. The key to any process of setting objectives for any organization is to understand fully the definition of value in relation to the operation. This concept of value can be very different in, for example, a major multinational corporation and a not-for-profit charitable organization. Therefore defining an organization's concept of value will establish the direction in which to define goals and objectives. The innovation framework (Figure 16.3) provides a structure to focus activities.

Objectives should not be far off target; they need to be measurable in the short and medium term in order to establish that consistent progress is being made towards the final objective. These goals must also be deployable at the working level so that people understand where their contribution fits in, and how they can establish ways of gauging their own performance. This model was developed to establish a starting point for organizations to look at their definition of values and then be able to drive this towards key goals and objectives. The advantage of working from a common framework is that various parts of the organization can develop their own elements within a consistent structure.

I have used this model in many different situations, but it is interesting that it focuses on most if not all of the challenges in any organization. In the context of strategic stress it is clearly important to ensure that the organization is focused on common approaches that enable the easy exchange of views and ideas. In almost all organizational environments, each goal or objective will include a number of aspects and frequently multiple groups within the organization. To this end the common model works well in focusing attention on the issues and not the differences.

Certainly, the total cost of operations is a major factor for any organization, but often it is one that becomes disjointed because of organization structures, budgeting and functional barriers. Thus setting objectives for the organization as a whole will frequently create pressures and competition between groups that ideally should be working together. This becomes even more critical when one looks at alliances outside the organization where much of the cost and spend could in fact be generated or managed.

For most organizations, cycle time is an issue that more often than not causes a great deal of internal conflict. Those who have any background in organization process development know that resolving or improving on challenges rests with the many inputs to the process. Again, if one is looking to set objectives that focus on any form of time reduction, high levels of interaction and co-operation will be needed.

This leads to the next element of the model: the business processes for whatever organizations do to develop or improve their operations will surely have an impact on current approaches. Process re-engineering has long been one of the development concepts for organizations but many fail to recognize that, at every level, when they establish goals they will probably need to address some of the processes that thread thorough the operations.

These first three factors then drive one to look at the others – namely resources, specifications and performance. Whatever organizations set as goals they invariably focus on optimizing resources or transferring activities outside their own operations. As I noted earlier, we frequently see challenges between increasing performance on the one hand and the reduction in resources on the other. The obvious impact of this is that efforts are focused more on self-preservation or lack of confidence through lack of resources. This is clearly where people issues come to a head, and where organizations, and particularly executives, need to consider the wider implications of conflicting objectives being defined.

The next in line is the specification or scope of work. Increasing market offerings or changing the selling proposition has a direct impact on every aspect of the business operation and it is likely to be where compromise has to be driven into the objectives and goals. Unless there is some significant innovative approach, the operation will simply be reprocessing the resources it already has, with the effect that most will look at the objectives and back away.

The final element is performance, which frequently is the prime target for organizations, whether this is product performance, production output, or increased service provision. Meeting increased performance standards may require the organization to look at different aspects of the business in order to achieve goals. Too often the decision to offer increased performance is made without taking into account the internal and external risk that could result from pushing the envelope.

Performance is often the easy target, since it is assumed that people working harder can simply improve performance. This may in a few cases be true, but more often than not there is much more that needs to be addressed to support improved performance, though this is clearly an area for any organization to differentiate itself from the general market and therefore a key area for attention. Enhancing performance value also involves exploiting risk, and again this needs to be supported across the organization.

What becomes clear when using this simplified model to help organizations to understand their drivers and set objectives is that the six elements are interconnected. It is not some magical formula but pure logic that most if not every organization understands but frequently fails to consider when declaring goals and objectives. The result of ignoring the obvious is that most of the employees understand these linkages and then focus the goals with a negative perspective.

The failure to appreciate the connectivity in the model highlights the potential for creating strategic stress when setting goals and objectives for the organization at large, because for whatever aspect of the business operation you seek to improve or change, there will inevitably be a knock-on effect. Every action has a reaction, which then leads back through the business processes, and this in turn is likely to cross boundaries within the organization. The net result is that whenever an objective is set it will impinge on many different aspect of the business, which must be addressed if the goals are to be achieved. Recognizing this interaction helps to focus on the key issues and objectives, and to provide some rigour to the decision-making process. It is often too easy to declare operational objectives without appreciating the implications across the organization.

The business process sits at the centre of any development and is likely to be a major area of conflict when changes are considered. Adopting some form of evaluation process means that, again, each part of the organization can utilize an identical approach and eventually bring together their inputs

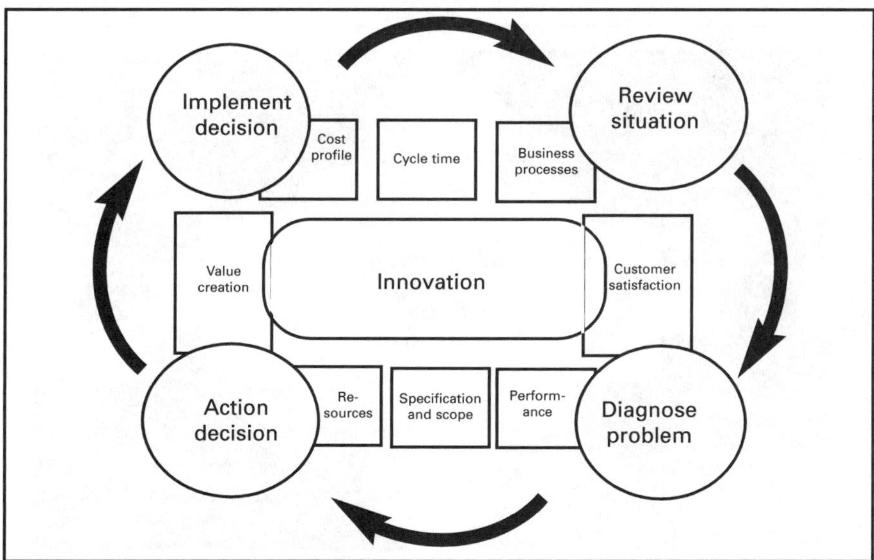

Figure 16.4   Validating innovation

for consolidation. When objectives call for changes, or where organizations are looking to be innovative in order to meet new objectives, it is also important to put a validation approach in place.

Introducing this four-stage validation approach (Figure 16.4) provides the organization with a benchmarking system that avoids simply introducing objectives and then either failing to meet them, or worse, deflecting other challenges through strategic stress. Building on the basic six-element model, organizations can evaluate innovative approaches.

It is clearly important that every significant objective should be reviewed to evaluate its overall benefit to the organization. Too frequently, organizations create so many objectives and goals that they lose the real focus and often end up with internal conflict as groups address their own areas without considering the bigger picture. What is also quite common is that while a patchwork of objectives may initially be put in place, progressively they become disconnected. This in turn often means that some goals are missed because of the failure of others to deliver.

Understanding the problems and challenges that an organization faces and then establishing actions should clearly be followed by effective implementation. It is crucial to avoid disconnections between objectives if efforts and resources are not to be wasted. Therefore, the interactions of corporate goals are a question of ensuring effective balance across the organization, which in turn will help to maintain the force and energy at every level.

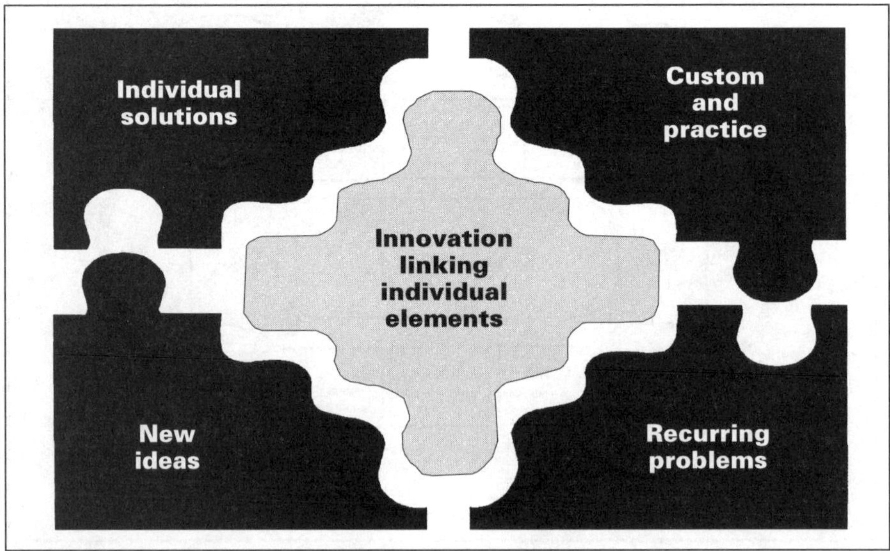

Figure 16.5 Connecting innovation

Objectives and goals are frequently linked to elements of innovation or problem solving and this is an arena where the organization can become internally focused rather than concentrating the drive towards customers' challenges and requirements. Product enhancement and improved performance can be implemented without validating the needs of the market, so the objective of developing a new product base must be grounded in understanding what the market wants. Increasing service performance may be acceptable to the customer but the company needs to ask whether they would be prepared to pay a premium or should the organization streamline its processes in order to provide the improvement with a cost consideration.

In the main, it is probable that every objective will have a downside for some part of the organization, and it is important to identify these issues and address them up front. These may involve individuals or groups whose own position may be at risk, based on success in achieving the goals that have been set. For example, exploiting offshore opportunities as a key objective may in fact depend on certain key staff undertaking the knowledge transfer.

Any objective that cannot be linked to delivering customer satisfaction should be re-evaluated, since it is likely that this is being pursued at the risk of not supporting an objective that is customer-centred. Customer needs and expectations should be the foundation of every development within the organization. This should ensure that the energy and focus is maintained where it will support the long-term market positioning. The customer is the most important constituent of any organization but is frequently ignored when setting objectives.

Increasing market share relies on the customer base being able to generate demand. Increasing margins means internal reductions or premium pricing, which will clearly reflect on customers. Improving customer satisfaction may be laudable, but can it be measured against current data or should a new matrix be introduced? At the same time, it is also important to consider the implications of risk management within the objective setting process. When the organization sees goals that are inherently risky and do not recognize that the appropriate checks and balances are in place, then they will pull back. Risk is a factor we shall discuss in more detail later, but it is a tradable commodity and meeting some objectives may be a question of exploiting risk. On the other hand, meeting certain objectives in isolation may not only create internal stresses, but it may very well also, create additional overall risk.

All corporate objectives therefore have a direct impact on internal stress points and pressures. Each objective will sit within the strategic framework and contribute in some way to the overall success of the organization. At the same time, the failure to integrate objectives across the organization will probably introduce even more pressure into the operations.

Objectives should be achievable but limited, to maintain the maximum focus without creating an imbalance in the forces across the organization. The creation of meaningful goals sits at the core of stimulating an organization to reach for the stretching challenge. Effective goal setting will underpin the management drive to exploit the potential of the organization and aid in the harnessing of knowledge and synergy to concentrate the power of the operation.

Counter to this, *ad hoc* objectives that are not synchronized or fully evaluated will probably dilute the energy of the organization and lead to the failure to achieve desired results. It is crucial to identify the processes affected by the target goal, then evaluate the implications, testing and consolidating changes clearly so that the organization is able to see the logical approach. Also, regularly monitor progress to ensure that efforts and connectivity are not compromised.

We all need a goal to aim for, but too often organizations fail to recognize the risks they run by not managing the goal-setting process effectively and monitoring progress to maintain a synchronized approach.

CHAPTER 17

Planning and process

In some way or another every organization utilizes planning to co-ordinate activities, measure progress and highlight areas where progress may be falling behind schedule. Clearly, at the same time the business processes have a significant impact on the planning profile, since time and activity are closely linked. Action without planning is chaos, while planning without action is futile. Therefore, it is not surprising that, in the context of looking at organizational pressures and in particular the implications of ignoring strategic stress, we should look at planning and process together. These two key functions are closely connected and can often be the cause of disputes and conflicts within organizations.

Process addresses the sequence of events, and planning relates these sequences to time and resources. In the adoption of corporate objectives, goals and initiatives clearly the linkage between process and planning is quite crucial to the seamless integration of ideas and developments. If you change one, then inevitably you must adjust the other, but frequently I have found that this logic is not always apparent. As a result of not balancing these two key functions there will certainly be stresses developing across the organization when processes become constrained because there is insufficient time to function normally. It is therefore import for organizations to understand the potential impacts of these conflicts and to address the stress limits.

When organizations develop a strategic programme they quickly – often too quickly – revert to converting the concept to a plan. I say too quickly because often the move from the strategic to the planning stage means that strategic thinking stops and hard planning and tactics take over. The problem is that strategic thinking should not be constrained by the necessary but rigid formality of the planning process. Strategy is about considering every known parameter then looking for or thinking the unthinkable to produce ideas that are outside current standard thinking. When the planning process starts, the 'out of the box' thinking tends to stop, often resulting in limiting the reach of the overall strategy.

The impact of making the transition from strategy to planning too soon is that while initial objectives may be clear, the way to implement them is often constrained. The implication is that the strategic imperatives are put under pressure within the confines of a structured plan before the widest possible thinking has been developed from a strategic perspective.

Planning is, of course, an important element of the overall strategic programme, and once it has been decided to progress into the detail it is crucial to capture the broadest of views across the organization. As in any situation where an approach is force-fed into the group, it will be received with caution and resistance. The likely result is that the plan will not be given full consideration or support. It is also common for the plan to be viewed as an immovable platform, which then fails to recognize the changes that occur in the natural evolution of any business venture. Again, the implication of the view is that, as life moves on, the planning baseline does not reflect reality and soon becomes neutralized, from which point the stresses within the organization will increase.

Clearly, when we talk of a plan we recognize that in most organizations this will be a number of plans that are, one hopes, integrated at their key points. How often this integration in fact occurs is left to experience, but from my own experience of many organizations, the focus on such integration is often missing. As one might suspect, the impact of this is to accentuate the pressures between functional groups and divisions within the operation.

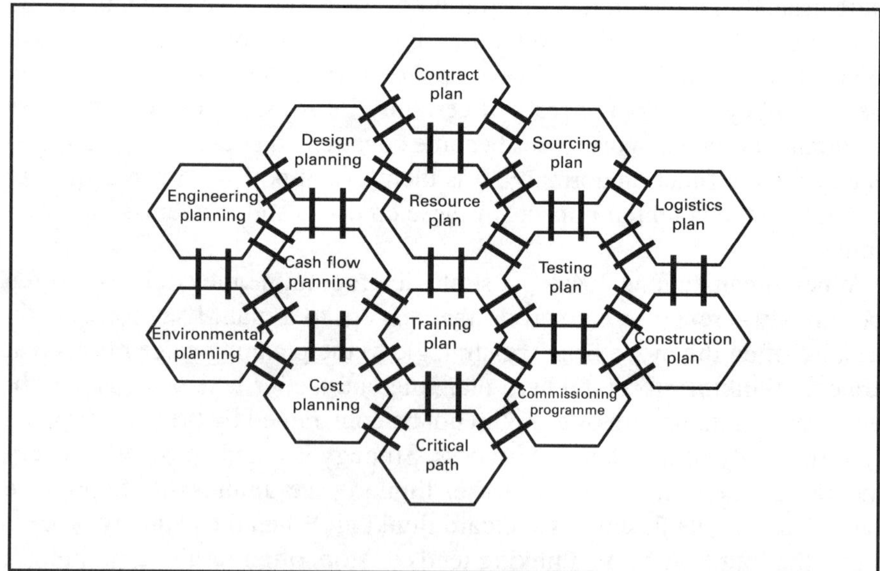

Figure 17.1   Integrated planning

There will be many who suggest that modern ICT capabilities allow organizations to maintain much better integration between functions, but in many cases these strategic plans do not readily fit into the rigid structures of systems-driven planning. What can be done is to ensure that planning-based reports will alert everyone when things do go out of sequence or are delayed. What tends to happen then is that the various groups involved look to pass responsibility down the line. Clearly, if a strategic approach is to be implemented effectively, planning needs to consider all the players and recognize that adaptation will be necessary over time.

The key element in any planning activity is to understand what is really critical and then be able to monitor those issues to ensure that no one loses sight of the prime goals. As business operations become more complex and fragmented in terms of locations around the world, the importance of maintaining a robust planning process is crucial to success. Surprisingly, many consider that critical path analysis has only limited value when trying to maintain overall business operations but from my experience it has proved time and again to be the mainstay of key business activities. In many cases the effort that goes into tracking and monitoring non-core activities considerably outweighs the effort that should be directed towards the critical elements of the plan.

Fire-fighting is a waste of resources and frequently fails to recover the situation after delays and rework through claims, loss of profits and potential loss of customers. Thus a robust planning approach is an important constituent of any strategic programme, while at the same time it must be seen as a tool and not a rigid and inflexible framework that does not respond to the needs of the day.

Meeting the demands of the modern business environment means ensuring the close integration of business operations. Optimizing these operations and moving strategic developments forward also means that planning must avoid creating conflicts within the organization. When activities get out of step the probability is that this will generate considerable internal stress, diverting resources and energy from the mainstream focus. To complicate matters further, planning is not simply about a delivery process: it reaches into every aspect of the business. Financial planning, environmental impacts and resource management link into the strategic plans, evaluation and implementation. This multiplies the potential complications, criss-crossing every aspect of both internal and external operations.

The '5 P's' ('proper planning prevents poor performance') should be the mantra for every business venture. A major concern is that, while planning should support the effective integration of the operation, it must not become a stick to beat people with, or for them to beat each other. It is only part of the strategic process and should be recognized as the reporting platform that identifies problems. The planning process will not solve problems; on its own it is only one of the tools used to help organizations maintain visibility and co-ordinate multiple functions and activities.

As was highlighted in the previous chapter, business performance is derived from a combination of inputs and resources, so there is not just one element that dictates success. Planning only adds time to the sequences of events, but if one wants to reduce time then either one must reduce the scope or change the process. So in the wider context of developing a strategic approach, the evaluation of business process becomes a crucial part of the overall programme.

What is also certain from personal experience is that once one enters the arena of changing established business processes or methodologies, one will certainly enter a field of conflict. The more traditional the organization, the greater the challenge to make changes to the way things have been done. Most organizations have developed their operating approaches over a long period of time, and many of the processes are embedded in the habits of the longer-serving employees. As a result, when change comes into play the barriers quickly go up, and this can drain the energy from an operation in trying to find a solution.

It is therefore important that, when considering strategic change, effort is invested at the start to establish the basis of why change is necessary and to obtain buy-in from the organization before starting the re-engineering process. A similar situation arises when introducing alternative ICT systems which challenge the status quo, though in this case the problems are often compounded by the lack of defined business processes in the first place.

It is my experience that most organizations fail to recognize the damage that can be done by force-feeding changes that affect individuals or functional groups without first convincing them of the need for change. Many do not appreciate that, as the business world moves on, so must business approaches keep pace and remain competitive.

Developing effective processes is critical to having an organization that is able to meet the volatility of today's market as well as being adaptable for tomorrow's interventions. Frequently, when discussing the subject of business processes one is met with blank looks, often because this approach is seen as something new and divorced from their experienced world. In time, people come to realize that this is not the case, and they start to recognize the opportunities that can be exploited.

My support for process mapping in the context of harnessing the power of an organization stems from three very clear drivers. First, whenever one evaluates why things went wrong invariably the failure was related directly to a lack of 'joined-up-thinking'. In one dramatic case, the organization involved suddenly found a massive hole in its finances based on advanced profit-taking and recalculation of margins. The review showed that across various divisions everyone had been doing the right things but the information was not being linked. The result was a major conflict between directors to shift responsibility instead of looking to address the problems.

The second reason is that when business processes are mapped, the complexity of what is in fact being done often becomes very graphic. Many times, this engenders a major debate taking place based around comments such as:

'Why do we do that?'
'That adds no value.'
'Why can't we simplify the steps?'
'I didn't know we did that.'

Each comment is valid and shows that even in the closest of organizations there is often no one who understands the full picture. This indicates clearly the potential risks or wasted capacity, but certainly means that organizational stresses are deflecting energy away from the primary focus of the business. Reputedly Albert Einstein once commented 'Things should be made as simple as possible, but not any simpler', and for most organizations the truth is they have generally overcomplicated their processes and built in conflicts and stresses without appreciating the implications.

Readers will therefore I hope appreciate that when considering the effective balance of energy across any enterprise and particularly where the process crosses geographical, organizational and cultural boundaries, a clear understanding of what each person has to do is essential. When considering the creation of novel strategic approaches and propositions a common road map is crucial.

The changing business landscape demands that all organizations at least consider their business process and approach to the market. I certainly share the view that in the next decade or so we shall see vastly different business models emerging to maintain a competitive edge. Companies will have to change strategically and develop new value propositions or be left behind in the wake of globalization and technology. The centre of this repositioning must be focused at driving new value for the customer (Figure 17.2).

These new propositions will in themselves require alternative organizational structures and a multiplicity of players creating flexible options. The ability of organizations to meet this demand will clearly put pressure on the

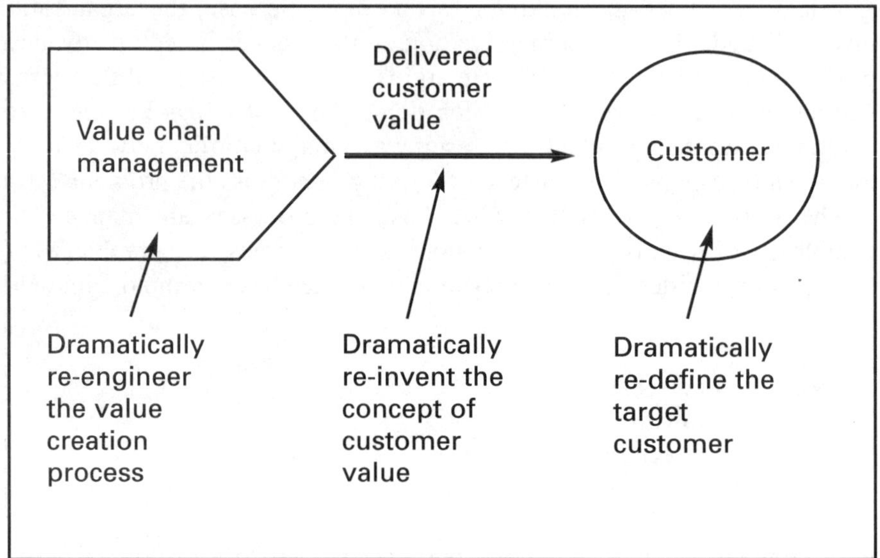

Figure 17.2 Driving new customer value

baseline processes that link them and will necessitate business processes often developed for one specific solution. This progression and development needs to be seen against an understanding of where one is and where one hopes to be.

This may seem somewhat obvious, but I am often surprised at the number of occasions when people talk of partnerships and alliances, but in isolation. Another point is the complications that occur when other divisions or external organizations do not support the prime goals. If teams are to be energized to offer new potential, then the resource providers and business processes must be assessed, adapted and focused.

While it is possible to create generic business processes, the likelihood will be, and the goal should be, to focus these against customers' valid requirements. There is no one-size-fits-all solution, and this is where project experiences showed the benefits of customer-centred operations. It must also not be assumed that the process will never change, even in a single proposition case, since external influences will drive this, as should the quest for continuous improvement.

The innovation of business propositions is linked directly to the imagination of the provider and the strength of the customer relationship. It is therefore important not simply to consider the business process in terms of integrated delivery, but also integrated innovation, and the closer this is to the customers' initial challenge, the greater the opportunity for success.

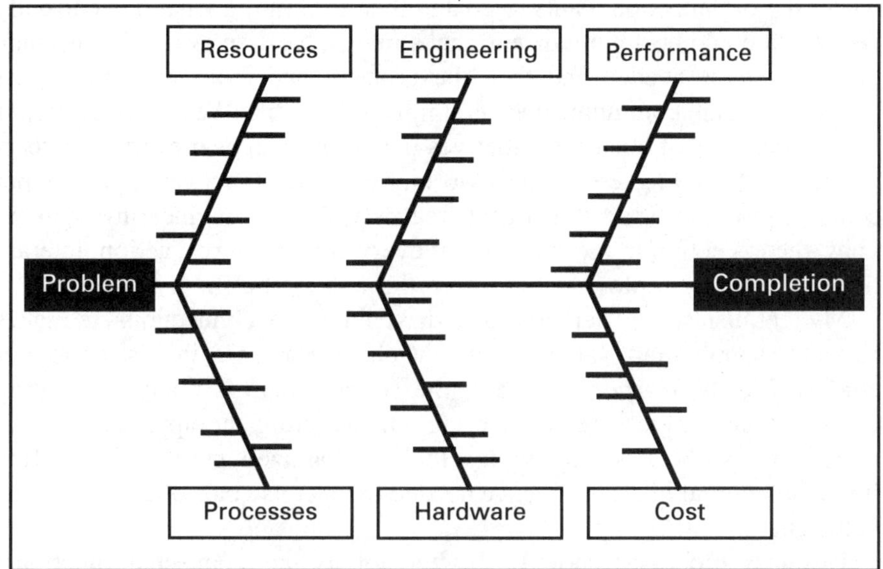

Figure 17.3 Focus on the joint objectives

I frequently use this caption since the greater the interdependence of the various organizational constituents the greater the opportunity to improve the overall proposition. We all know this but it is strange how often in discussions that the functional ownerships created boundaries. I would recommend a book called *No Boundaries* by James Tompkins and pass on one quote: 'The more boundaries we encounter in today's business world, the greater the limits on ability to move to the next level of performance excellence.' There are certainly enough challenges in the competitiveness of the market without creating more of our own through a lack of integration.

Earlier I suggested three drivers for using the process mapping approach but I did not mention another crucial ingredient, that of the business strategy. I have read many corporate and project procedures and often been charged with writing these. I wonder how often these are in fact referred to in the day-to-day cut and thrust of business.

The problem is easy to understand, in that these are mainly rules based on administration but do little to support the daily interfaces. They also seldom show any connection to business strategies or investment plans. So, in most organizations around the world there will be vast volumes gathering dust or hidden in some electronic vault. Yet these are the platform for all interactions across the company.

Process re-engineering takes an alternative approach by first establishing where the organization wants to go and then examining what it is currently doing that could be a hindrance to that strategy. Next an evaluation is made of the changes needed and then the process, and more importantly the connectivity, are communicated as simply as possible. We discussed earlier the implications of business initiatives that seem to appear every five years or so, each heralding a brave new world. Many are 40 per cent hype, 30 per cent common sense and 30 per cent creativity. Process engineering is, in my view, the exception to the rule, in that every cost, resource, action, interaction and strategy deployment is linked through the business process.

My enthusiasm is perhaps also driven by the connections it makes between supply and value chains. Michael Hammer in his book *Re-engineering the Corporation* said 'the supply chain is really the cutting edge of contemporary re-engineering'. In adopting the approach several organizations I have worked with actually recognized, perhaps for the first time, the internal interdependence needed to meet its goals of exploiting the value chain.

Business processes should be seen not as interconnected functional groups but as distinct process chains that require a concerted input from specialist functions. It also presents a framework for external contributors to be recognized as essential ingredients to success. It therefore creates a higher platform on which to explore the potential that to a large extent had been locked inside corporate structures, contracts and procedures. More than anything it should be a true reflection of work-flow patterns.

There are many mapping tools available on the market and in the main it does not matter which one organizations utilize as long as they are readily available through an electronic medium, such as the Internet. This is a must if the tool is to be used effectively across organizational and geographical boundaries. As it should be live and dynamic it should not be paper-based.

Establishing the overall model is, surprisingly, not difficult, whether working in a single location, inter-company or with external organizations. The basics steps taken each day are not rocket science, since mapping is based on what we do or should do, the stages are generally common to all. As with any development, the devil is in the detailed workflows and in the procedures, forms and instructions that support the process, but, as in any debate, the first step is to identify the differences, whether real or perceived, then proceed to define responsibilities for resolving these.

In the context of multifunctional teams or virtual networks, the hurdles will be more complex in terms of who is responsible for which operation. Success in this area is more dependent on the leadership of the organizations to look forward in terms of overall goals rather than ownership.

Again, the map is how one wants to operate, so it has to be jointly owned and honoured.

One of the interesting by-products of process mapping across organizational boundaries is the ability to collect, evaluate and adopt best practice. Those of us lucky enough to work with many organizations will have been able to accumulate reference points on what we think each did best. In more stable business areas this cross-fertilization of ideas is more difficult. In the context of awakening knowledge and cultivating synergy the process mapping approach can provide a value forum for innovation. The ethos should be to allow the custom and practice of the participants to share what they know and learn from each other. The mapping process has often been used in merger operations to find the best aggregate approach to blend resources. The foundation maps for the organization should then enjoy significant enhancements from knowledge-sharing which may on occasion be drawn back into the mother companies.

After the initial mapping is in place this is not the end, as each new challenge creates the need for new solutions to be evaluated and, where they are seen to be effective, incorporated. The premise of a knowledge-based organization is to achieve more with less, or expand without investment growth, so the improvement approach is a process and not an event.

Once the concept and working models have been introduced, like any other business venture the company must monitor whether it is meeting its goals. 'If you can't measure it you can't control it' was always the maxim. It is generally easy to monitor limited-duration projects as they have objects that can be validated, but those spanning years prove much more difficult. The more basic project and business management tools, particularly schedules and financial reporting, provide an indication of how things are proceeding and must be maintained.

The introduction of the Business Excellence Model and its incorporation into the ISO 2000 quality programme has provided an additional framework to focus on the success formulas of organizations. The business process sits at the core of the programme, which also recognizes the principal elements of good management and corporate responsibility. The nine criteria of the model focus on those factors that have been shown to influence business results and enable organizations both large and small to develop monitors or key performance indicators (KPIs) to gauge performance and improvement. These are not prescriptive inasmuch as it is the organization's structure, its drivers and methodology. It is, however, a good starting point for an organization to set some measures of how it wants to measure success.

Planning and process are key facilitators in the exploitation of an organization's energy, and they may also contribute towards maintaining the balance of the organization and ensuring focus on strategic objectives. The counter is also true – that if the business processes are not validated, owned and developed, then they present a significant opportunity to induce stress and pressure into the organization at the core of its delivery programmes.

CHAPTER 18

Risk management

In any business venture there is always an element of risk, but it is the skill in managing this risk that generally distinguishes between those organizations that are successful and those that are not. In the development of any business strategy risk factors are a key consideration, and the robustness of risk management programmes is a crucial element in maintaining the balance of an organization. How organizations address risk, and more importantly the ethos of the organizations towards risk, can have a significant impact on how the people within those organizations react to and handle the implications of risk.

Many organizations have a tendency to be risk averse, but as those in business understand, there is a direct correlation between the amount of risk taken on and the premiums that can be attached to well-managed risk. Understanding the impacts of a negative culture towards risk, and even worse, operating within a blame culture that is ready to focus responsibility for problems, will clearly have an impact on the manner in which organizations respond to any strategy that carries a high level of risk.

Risk is the potential variability in the future outcome of a stated situation caused by uncertainty. It is a common factor in the business landscape, and how that risk is managed within the business process and relationships will indicate how successful ventures might be: the highter the level of risk, the greater the potential reward. On the negative side, those who try to eliminate all risk may create such rigidity that they produce stagnation, which is in itself a form of risk. Risk is therefore both an opportunity and a challenge to the business community.

To enable organizations to harness and stretch their capabilities, the management of risk must be high on the agenda. Clearly, failure to identify the risk element of a strategy may ultimately undermine the programme and thus in turn build up increased risk. Developing a robust and highly visible risk management programme as part of the business process is a crucial factor in being able to build a responsive and flexible operation. Calculating risk means clearly identifying the potential impacts

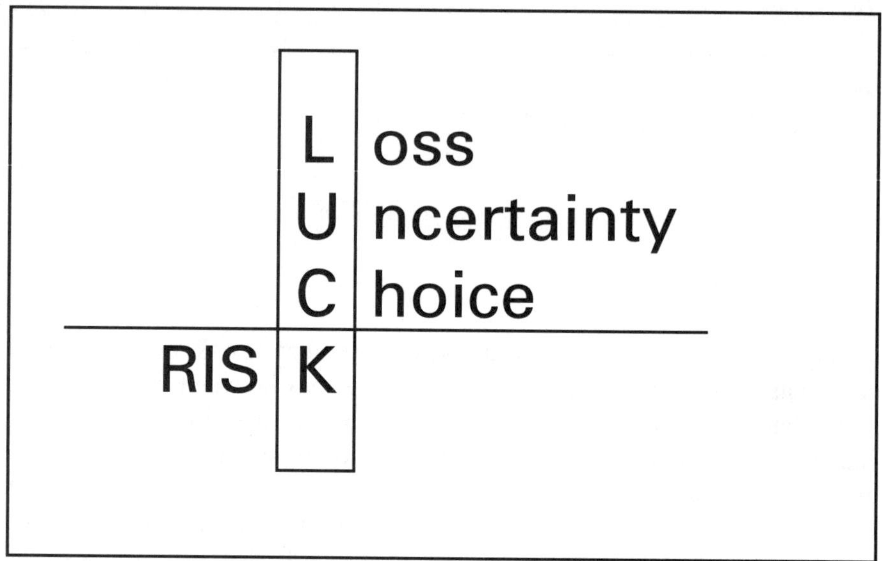

Figure 18.1   Calculating risk

(Figure 18.1). This may be true in many respects, but it would be dangerous to assume that once a strategy is in place the risk will disappear.

The essence of managing risk effectively is the ability to distinguish between assumption and reality. This challenge is amplified when the parties involved are focusing from within their separate functions. In many cases, competitive edge is lost through the cumulative impact of risk contingencies throughout the delivery process, and thus the perception of risk may in itself be a significant risk factor. The more confidence there is that risk is being recognized and managed effectively, the greater the probability that individuals and groups will focus on the application rather than on their own concerns.

The key activity that must be introduced into any organization is the development of risk profiling as part of the business strategy process. The earlier a risk is identified, the more opportunity there will be to manage the situation, and certainly the less costly it will be to mitigate or eliminate. What cannot be seen is unlikely to be managed effectively, and the more integrated organizations become the more important it is to ensure that all those involved both understand the risks being faced and, more importantly, allocate responsibility for action.

Developing a risk profile starts with analysing the many areas of risk that might be likely to affect future development. The profile will differ for any given strategy, and the objective is to optimize the approach to the market and distribute risk to those best suited to manage that risk. This risk management process can often highlight opportunities that not only eliminate risk that had previously been based on assumptions within the organization, but also elevate situations that would normally be passed over and managed poorly, or opportunities being totally ignored based on poor information.

The management of risk within an organization has to be established to ensure the widest appreciation and assessment of risk. What is often more difficult to establish is the risk management culture that accepts the principle that risk is a joint responsibility and does not simply ignore risk on the basis that it is another's problem.

The advantage that can be derived from a more integrated approach is that many risks are a result of the interfaces between organizations, and once these are open to joint assessment are often seen to be unfounded. Effective risk management offers considerable advantage in a marketplace that is becoming more volatile in many aspects of its business culture. In most organizations, risk represents a significant cost consideration and by developing an appropriate approach, organizations can gain a competitive edge. More important, in the context of strategic stress and maintaining the balance of an organization, realization and visibility will engender greater confidence and focus.

Risk can be classified in many ways, and this process is the first step in establishing a risk management strategy. The key challenge for business is to acquire resources that are better than those of the competition, and then deploy them more effectively. The harder organizations try, the higher the levels of risk they encounter. The management of risk depends on the nature of the situation, and in many cases the answer is simply a case of insuring the risk. Most risk can be segmented into the following categories:

- loss;
- liability;
- interruption;
- waste;
- technology;
- social impacts;
- political impacts; and
- environmental impacts.

The more sensitive issues are those that relate to improving the management of the business process, such removing potential risk. These offer the greatest opportunity, but will often mean changing traditional working methods. Areas such as poor planning or waste management are risks to the business profile, but are often only manageable once the organizations have opened the debate and structure that manages these processes.

The wider aspects of risk involve the social impacts of extended enterprises where the performance of a partner or a supplier can have an immediate backlash on the organization. Managing the risks of outsourcing can often be mitigated through greater integration and ensuring that the aims of both partners are shared and projected through their business dealings. The concentration of joined-up thinking and energy across the organization will aid the process.

Classifying risk enables an organization to evaluate the most suitable strategy, whether this is a formal system between the parties to ensure effective control, or economic steps such as insurance or contingencies to absorb impacts, at the same time as identifying who is the most suitably placed to manage that particular issue. Without a risk management programme the decision-making process is hindered in moving forward by a lack of data. Focusing on the drivers and impacts of risk helps in delivering solutions or mitigation:

- cost;
- demand;
- performance;
- production;
- completion;
- liabilities;
- competition; and
- customer.

All risk has an impact in terms of cost, time and profitability. To establish an effective approach it is important to analyse what the potential risks are, and more importantly what are the potential effects. This analysis may be focused into three main areas for attention. First, those issues that can be identified by source in terms of where the risk comes from. In many cases, this might provide the ability to reduce some risks by changing, say, supply options. Others may be natural risks, which generally are subject to insurance cover, or in certain cases the need for design adjustments.

Second, the risks that come from the operations themselves, whether an internal function or an external source of supply. They may result from production processes and in many cases can be neutralized through re-engineering. In this case, the ability of organizations to share working knowledge can often provide a wider range of solutions. This operational analysis should also focus on the environmental and social implications of the operations. In today's marketplace, the regulatory and investment impacts of poorly managed operations may bring major risks to the fore.

The third area is the effect in terms of being clear what the repercussions may be. These would generally subdivide into effects on people, property or earnings. In each case the risk manager is seeking the most cost-effective mitigation and then being able to balance future actions to reduce the profile to acceptable levels. Risk may not simply be an issue of cost against business today; it can also be an influence on tomorrow's potential business. The biggest risk to any business is to lose customers through poorly managed processes.

The range of risk issues that confront any business venture is extensive, and the need for organizations to consider and develop effective approaches is crucial. Some of these are outlined and expanded below. However, it is important for every organization to recognize that while many risk issues may have common bases across all commercial ventures, others will be specific to a given industry sector, location, customer or contract requirement. The creation and deployment of a corporate strategy must define these situations clearly and promote a culture within the organization to grasp the challenge. Ignoring them will most probably generate negativity and reduce efforts towards solutions.

Risk management is by its nature a dynamic process, should be approached with a clear programme that recognizes the need for constant validation, and be adaptable to change. The risks that each organization identifies for itself may well be dispelled or reduced by greater visibility and openness. In a counter-position, some strategies may have their own inherent risks and these too must be addressed.

In the majority of business operations the level of external expenditure is at least 50 per cent of the operating cost. It is therefore not surprising that one should consider the supply chain as a major potential area of risk in terms of every aspect of the business profile, from profitability to long-term reputation. Since many within the organization will have their own perspectives on the outside world, this in itself may create friction and challenges that must be addressed.

The supply chain is the most underrated facet of the business landscape, and the potential it can introduce into organizations to improve performance and reduce cost is significant. However, the greater the level of exploitation, the higher the risk potential, thus high on the risk management agenda must be the development of strategic procurement approaches. Key elements such as complexity, criticality and hazard evaluations are normal parts of most selection processes, but wider issues such as customer acceptability can be a major deciding factor.

The issue of risk is not simply a question for the buyer; it also has a major impact on the profile of the supplier. How a supplier is perceived in the market is a critical part of their marketing profile and a key element of how they present themselves to customers. The evaluation of potential supply partners is a crucial part of the risk management activity. There can be few business ventures today that are not influenced directly by the spread of globalization. The multi-dimensional nature of the global landscape creates an environment that generates an ever-increasing profile of risk that for many is a major cause for concern, either its impact on their personal positions or as an unknown that they are concerned will fall back on them. Integration in the risk management process not only makes sense in terms of collective thinking, but it also aids the confidence of all involved.

The quest to exploit the opportunities of the global market and the volatility of the many factors that can change the platform of a business deal engenders a need to focus on managing risk. Together with the growing risk of facing new competition, it means that there is a dynamic culture against which to develop a flexible strategy. Technology has further complicated this business environment by providing faster communications and raised the expectation of customers, who now anticipate the benefits of global pricing while still focusing on traditional quality and performance.

The pressures of regulation and environmental liabilities, together with the wider and more indirect ramifications of global trading, are factors that every organization must recognize. The political and cultural challenges of working outside the comfort zone of traditional business networks are complex and developing a structured risk approach helps to direct the energies of the operations towards solutions. The implications for organizations are far reaching and necessitate an increase in focus on risk mitigation and management to ensure successful ventures. The attraction of low-cost resources and manufacturing is certainly a potential opportunity for all organizations, but the implications and risks should not be underestimated. The challenge, then, is for organizations to adopt a more flexible perspective that enables the maximization of potential but retaining effective management of process and performance.

Outsourcing has become an accepted methodology to capture competitive advantage, but this extended enterprise approach brings its own level of risk through interdependence and reputation risk. The need to ensure that external suppliers share a common focus on business objectives is crucial to long-term sustainability and maintaining a perspective on corporate social responsibility. In any business venture, the key ingredient for success is the development and exploitation of the relationships that govern the interfaces between organizations. The more complex a venture, the greater the possibility that the relationships will generate their own arenas of risk.

In today's business world, the importance of relationships is often secondary to improved technology and communications links. These interfaces are the foundation of sound business dealings and if not considered in the overall risk profile will lead to pressure points, which may undermine the venture. As has already been noted, people are the biggest asset in an organization, and the ways in which they work or even appreciate their role, are key factors in the overall success of the business. Those who may see the venture as eroding their own future security often challenge approaches aimed at exploiting the potential of extended resources and capabilities. This facet of risk management is one that requires firm leadership and a programme of integration to ensure that potential is achieved. The view of each individual has to be considered and managed to avoid conflicts or the simple abdication of responsibility, which in turn may allow more conventional risks to be uncontrolled.

The risk to any organization of failing to recognize the impacts of its people can be significant, and in cases where the business strategy is being developed within the concepts of widening the enterprise, can be significant. At the same time, dealing with people in different business cultures is also a risk factor that can damage the overall possibility of success. There can be few in the business world who are not constantly aware of the many pressures from the environmental objectives of individuals, NGOs and governments. In many cases these are not simply the impacts of regulatory change but also an ever-growing desire to adopt a long-term perspective on our business activities.

The thrust for business organizations is often to focus only on the legislation and compliance with this. Unfortunately the playing field is seldom a level one and the temptation to export problems is high in the short term. The danger is that, while seeking suppliers who may be prepared to take risks within their own national regulatory frameworks, this is likely still to have potentially negative implications. Communications now put very effective and speedy pressure on organizations, resulting from the failings of their supply network. Just ask sports equipment producers Nike and perhaps their employees who have had to share the public focus negativity resulting from reported exploitation of sweatshops.

Managing the risks associated with environmental pollution and social exploitation is a major factor for most businesses. What are often missed in the quest to maintain competitive headway are the potential benefits that may be derived from a proactive approach to integration that exploits the savings from waste and energy conservation. Improvements in training and education will in the longer term provide more effective supply opportunities.

An environmental strategy is a significant element of implementing effective risk management, and operating the programme through a wider collaborative network may provide new opportunities. In many cases, risks are not just related to the obligations and penalties that can be imposed, wider implications can be in the effect of delays to the venture that ultimately may be even more costly.

The implications of developing an approach that defers the addressing of risk can be significant. Most people will appreciate that the longer a problem is left, the harder and more costly it is to resolve. The problem often results from a lack of real communication whereby the problem is not fully understood until it has gone beyond a simple solution.

Risk profiling is not a one-off exercise – it has to be a focused approach through the entire programme, and one needs to consider the mitigation against long-term cost implications. Risk management is a process that must be developed over the operating life-cycle. This is often ignored, on the basis that risk only arises once a contract has been put in place. The reality is that in many cases risk issues are generated in the pre-contract stages, through either error or lack of knowledge. Developing an effective risk management approach has to be integrated into every facet of the business venture. Life-cycle management is now a major factor in business development strategy, both in terms of customers extending their requirements and investment analysis, and the marketing profiles of businesses seeking to extend their range of products and services.

The primary objective of every commercial venture is to generate an acceptable level of return on the investment made and the risk carried. As I have said already, the higher the risk, the higher the probability that the rewards will be proportionally greater. Thus it would not be practical to consider a risk management programme that was not focused on financial risks. In a more linear, structured organization the traditional approach has been to concentrate on passing risk down the hierarchy. The potential downside of this approach is that those asked or coerced into accepting the risks are often not the most capable of managing them.

Many areas of the execution process have a direct effect on financial management but are often overlooked against a background of the implications resting with others. In fact, a more holistic perspective would perhaps suggest that a more integrated analysis would shift responsibility and management to those best able to maximize control and optimize results, for the benefit of all the players.

Most commercial ventures do implement forward planning, at least at the start of an activity, but the biggest risk to all organizations comes from changes that arise after the contract is signed. This risk may come from outside the venture – for example, in the form of unexpected political or legislative change for which the parties could not have planned. Others come from customer or internal changes as a result of development. The major risk is not so much in the changes themselves, but in the manner in which these changes are handled and the way the impacts are apportioned. In any organization, the amount of effort expended in managing change and assigning responsibility is often disproportionate to the change itself. The key focus should be towards identifying:

1 Who pays?
2 What is the benefit?
3 What are the alternatives?
4 What is the impact?
5 Why change?

Change is generally viewed in a negative light, but often changes can be introduce to improve performance or to add value to the operation. However, the impact of such positive changes may well have a negative effect at other points in the process or on the activities of others. Thus any change is a risk and needs to be evaluated before it is introduced. Where change is imposed from outside the operation, the widest possible assessment should be made to identify the potential ramifications that might arise. Failure to make adequate adjustments could result in the impact being much greater than planned.

A more open approach to change may introduce alternatives that could be mutually beneficial and create less of a significant impact. Change is the number one risk arena in any business, but the way in which it is processed and incorporated can provide a major bonus for future business opportunities. Each case needs proper evaluation and appropriate risk assessment.

The perception of risks that might emerge from a partnering relationship are in the main driven by those who failed to understand or appreciate the full benefits to be exploited. The concern often comes from a traditional background where there is a background of deferring risk to others, while in reality these are often only superficial transfers of liability in overall terms. For partnering relationships to develop, the parties must profile the risk to the operations from both an internal and a market perspective, then implement an approach that addresses the major issues.

In any business venture there is always a concern when trading outside one's own organization that information exchange may dilute market positioning and release intellectual property into the public arena. The higher the level of interdependency, the greater the probability that, in order to exploit the relationship, it will become necessary to export data. The challenge for organizations is to balance the potential benefits against the risks of giving away the companies' product secrets. However, in many cases, the information provided is either necessarily transferred or formed data that was in real terms already available in the public domain.

Information may be viewed as a corporate asset but in many cases the truth is that this competitive edge is one that has only a short life-span and despite attempts at control will eventually be dispersed. An alternative approach may be to focus on taking the short-term advantage and maintaining a development programme that secures a future edge, at the same time ensuring that the commercial advantage to any external organization is such that exploiting the current information is of little long-term value in comparison to an extended relationship.

Having identified the various areas of risk, it is then important to develop a strategy to find the most suitable approach towards mitigating or managing the issues. This process should start from the implementation of an internal assessment focusing first on the risk elements within the control of each party. This provides a platform on which to consider solutions or alternative approaches that would exploit the risk, to support a more competitive proposition.

Optimizing mitigation is a significant stage that must be processed as part of the overall development. It is possible to build such a negative risk profile that doing business of any sort is viewed very negatively. Risk must be assessed and balanced to ensure that provisions, contingencies and resources are not loaded into the proposition to such an extent that it becomes non-competitive. The application of risk management and mitigation strategies must be assessed to focus on the market value of the risk profile, and the potential for winning and executing business successfully. The full extent of risk can only be assessed and managed against a background of the total business relationship, whether this is with customers or supply chains. How the elements fit together and interact will have major impact on overall success.

Often risk strategies are implemented without the impacts being acknowledged fully across all parts of the organization, with the result that implementation may be flawed and fail to meet the full objectives. The deployment of risk management strategies can often include many facets of the overall operation, and therefore any strategy that ignores the impact on other areas may ultimately dilute the solution or waste effort by not taking into account the domino effects of other actions.

Finding the right balance is an important part of developing any business strategy, and the extending of this to consider external contributors to the delivery process provides a sound basis for the development of risk and reward contracts. The overall aim should be to reduce the levels of risk, or to implement programmes that take a measured approach to exploit the advantage of absorbing greater levels of risk than the competition.

It is often easier to identify potential risks outside the organization, when in many cases there can be risks that in fact are the result of internal practices and culture. The initial stages of developing an effective risk management strategy should proceed from a baseline of understanding the internal issues and then prioritizing actions related to these and the external issues.

The targeting of risk issues is an important part of being able to take appropriate action. Addressing what may be considered as top issues can lead to expending effort without having an impact on the overall programme. It also enables the risk manager to identify where external influences might have a significant impact. Often, because of financial pressures, the focus is directed towards high-cost areas, but these can in many cases be relatively simple challenges that have a lower contribution to the real risk profile.

Assessing internal impacts on risk is often related to the nature of the organization's ability to work in an integrated manner. This aspect of risk management is one that many organizations prefer not to address, but as many will appreciate the internal boundaries to overall success can often be greater than those that may be considered external to the operation. Larger organizations may have many divisions or functional departments, each with its separate targets and objectives. These might be considered as having a common focus, but in reality might be risk barriers. Many organizations will place high levels of expectation on external companies, which they would not normally place on themselves, with the net result that risks are built up internally while efforts are being focused outside.

It will probably not be a surprise to many in the business world that, when considering the complexities and variables that can be faced, even the simplest of interlinked events presents a low probability of success, but it is in the management of these events that success can be created. It should also be apparent that the risks involved in these complex ventures are largely found at the interfaces between various operations, whether these are internal boundaries or with external organizations.

Mitigating the potential risks of poorly interconnected events not only provides a basis for improving the probability of success; it also opens up opportunities to improve the overall efficiency of the activity. The greater the number of interdependent operations that are involved, the higher the degree of challenge to find mitigating approaches that manage the risk profile while meeting the aspirations of both customers and the market-place.

The traditional business model which promoted the concept of one orga-nization owning all the requisite functions, resources and facilities has been in many ways neutralized by increasing evolution towards a global approach, creating for the business world the need to find alternative oper-ating models that can provide the degree of flexibility required by address-ing the multiple variables involved. The risk created by the dynamics of the changing environment can in many respects be overcome by the deploy-ment of collaborative ventures and the move towards partnering, providing a basis upon which to evaluate and apportion risks to those best qualified to manage them effectively.

Since there is never likely to be a totally risk-free business environment, the concept that risk can simply be deployed fails to recognize the greater risk that will be inherent in a relationship that does not enjoy shared values, objectives and a fair apportionment of rewards. The major risk in relation-ships is the failure to consider the traditional concepts of power within organizations and across operating boundaries, which, if left unchecked, will introduce conflicts and stresses.

The risks to any business venture can often be deflected by the timely application of specialist resources with the combining of expert and profes-sional knowledge. Failure to share appropriate information and accept the input of others may provide a short-term influence but ultimately generate higher levels of risk further down the line. Understanding the capabilities of partners and being prepared to share information, authority and resources can provide significant risk mitigation. Risk can often be identi-fied and mitigated simply by addressing the points at which disparate oper-ations interface. The major element of this process often falls simply into the action of developing integrated planning.

What generally consumes resources, and thus time and money, is the inability of organizations to recognize the relative impacts of their internal scheduling needs. Failure to address simple supply and demand require-ments creates an environment where efforts are focused not on the first-time processing but on the corrective actions of poorly co-ordinated activities. This then leads to over-consumption of resources and ultimately the risk profile is worsened by a desire to recover lost ground. Further advantages can be gained through this process by assessing future needs, which allows appropriate forward planning and, in areas such as external supply, advantages from economies of scale.

Risk is seldom, if ever, a single point of reference and can be addressed from several directions to evolve a suitable solution or implement safeguards and strategies based on a wider range of knowledge and understanding. One aspect of risk that creates a great deal of activity is the assumption of risk based on a background of unrealistic expectations. This may seem a strange concept in the whole picture of establishing a risk mitigation strategy, but in many cases the effort is expended in order to prevent losses or potential risks that have no real basis.

Every risk strategy is built up from a legacy of history within organizations and the perceptions of the current position and expected outcomes. Establishing what an organization expects from a given commercial undertaking is a crucial part of developing a risk mitigation approach, since appreciating where one expects to be in the end defines in many ways the course of events that must be experienced in order to meet the objectives. The level of expectation will promote internal focus and thus concentrate on the key elements of the strategy to be accomplished, but if those objectives are not realistic, the effort will be centred on meeting internal goals rather than addressing the real risk. Risk management is not simply about responding to external influences; it is about ensuring that the objectives are achieved within given parameters.

The impacts of risk may be seen at the execution stage, but the creation of risk situations is often a factor of the pre-contract activity. Therefore, to establish an effective risk strategy and mitigation approach, the groundwork must be completed before signing on the bottom line, thus ensuring that programmes of actions are transferred properly into the operations arena. The implementation of isolated mitigation approaches being undertaken without considering the wider perspective of the whole risk profile, may result in the use of resources to counter a specific circumstance, while failing to recognize the bigger problems just around the corner.

Risk profiling is a multi-layered activity and must be approached and analysed from every possible viewpoint before defining a course of action, since what may seem to be a high priority for one part of the organization may in fact be only a small element of the main game. The role of the risk manager or team must be to capture all identified potential, then evaluate and optimize the approach to encompass all aspects. This process must take into account short-term opportunities and roll-on effects into the medium and long-term situation.

The concept of risk and reward is not new; it was a factor of the business world long before the idea of formal alliances was expounded as a possible alternative business model. The essence of developing an effective approach has to be a sound balance between the risks envisaged and the potential to gain from the operation. Any risk assessment and the implementation of a risk management strategy must be a considered evaluation of the impacts of such risks as are identified, and the projected cost in time and resources to mitigate the potential reality of those risks. The contractual structure that is defined will need to detail how the reward can be realized.

Organizations build up many times the initial structure within an environment that is reflective of a comfortable pre-engagement stance. However, when the realties of the day emerge, the parties fail to agree on recognizing these arrangements, which may in hindsight appear unfavourable. Careful consideration should be given to developing a number of 'what if' scenarios that present the arrangement under different circumstances to ensure that all parties have a clear understanding of the structure. Failure to play through these different potential outcomes might at a later date produce conflict and thus introduce new risks to the overall programme while the dispute is being resolved.

Clearly, certain situations may be subject to later developments or outcomes from earlier actions, and therefore establishing a structure that identifies these specific issues and provides a decision-making process will enable progress to continue in the main areas of activity. Risk is an opportunity that can be exploited, but at the same time any challenge that is accepted must be driven by suitable recognition.

Proceeding to the development of a risk profile requires a structured approach, and many organizations will already have their own risk management teams and processes. But what is often ignored in the quantification of risk is the imbalance that can be generated within an organization based on different perceptions of risk. These, in turn, lead to conflict and friction in operation, and ultimately to even more risk to the organization.

Liberating the force

When one visits organizations around the world and interacts with their employees it is not difficult to build up a profile of what should be done differently, or what is clearly not being done well. It is this platform that often provides opportunities that can be exploited by consultants. But when it comes to making changes to an organization, while it may be the external facilitator who claims the credit, it is the mobilization of internal energy that actually delivers the results. Phase Three looks at the key factors that are necessary to create the ethos and focus that is required to support any strategic programme.

The internal conflicts and stresses within organizations do not emanate in the main from lack of capabilities, but from the way that leadership and strategic programmes are rolled out across the operation. Ignoring the natural balance will certainly increase internal pressures, while harnessing this balance and energy can turn an organization into a more integrated and focused operation.

The most difficult part of any programme, and in particular when it comes to significant strategic changes, is in removing the internal barriers created by comfort zones within various functional groups and operating divisions. Changes in direction or increased performance demands raise the vista of strategic stress but in fact it is more frequently the perceived challenge rather than the reality that is the cause of the friction. The major challenge for the organization is in **breaking the pain barriers** that are holding the organization back. Clearly, the first stage of this process, as already outlined, comes from establishing what the specific issues are; but information has no value unless it is used.

As has been mentioned several times, the majority of organizations have the ingredients they need to be successful, though some can lose their edge over time through complacency, and refocusing or revitalizing an organization is no easy task. It is important to look at the issues and approaches that will help in **mobilizing for action** the knowledge, skills and resources that are often constrained within current thinking.

Building on the realization that change is a necessary part of today's business world, it is crucial to focus on ensuring the widest practical visibility for all involved. Change is a process, not an event, and organizations need to adopt a more flexible perspective and develop new and alternative relationships that complement the wider demands of the market and look towards optimizing strategic plans. The crux of this strategic approach and the core requirements are to ensure that the organization is capable of **gaining illumination** in terms of the market and the future.

The changes that have taken place since the 1970s have changed the business landscape significantly and thus the profile for creating strategic developments has also changed dramatically. Capturing these developments and harnessing the organizations' focus against this background of volatility necessitates strategic change, and maintaining the balance of energy in this and future programmes offers a complexity that many will not have seen before and will certainly foster opportunities for strategic stresses to build in conflict with the strategic focus to build the destiny of the organization.

BREAKING THE PAIN BARRIERS

CHAPTER 19

Leadership

There can be little doubt in anyone's mind that one of the most important elements of success in any organization is the nature, style and visionary capability of its leadership. Many organizations invest in leadership development programmes in the belief that it will improve the performance of their managers. Frequently, however, these programmes fail to connect with the organizational change programmes.

The interesting dilemma is whether developing competences will be enough, or whether they are only attributes that underpin leadership characteristics that are core skills of the individual. Most people would agree, I think, that if leadership is lacking, the potential for success is reduced. Thus in terms of liberating the force of an organization there must be a strong focus on the practice of leadership rather than on its competencies.

The demands of the modern business world are complex and volatile, and require agility and vision to adapt and develop. Future business models will probably be even more diverse and dispersed through technology, creating than environment that opens the way for more virtual integration across organizational and geographical boundaries. Looking to this brave new world, the question one must ask is, 'Do we have the leaders capable of taking us there?' It would be presumptuous of me to suggest that we do not, but I suspect that there are few that can. Leadership is the crucial capability for focusing organizations on the capacity to translate a vision into reality.

Yet despite those high profile business leaders who stand head and shoulders above the rest, one sees limited investment generally in cultivating leaders to take up the banner. In a recent survey that addressed over 400 companies across Europe, only 16 per cent had any effective training plan and 30 per cent had no plans at all, though 86 per cent said that management training should be part of an organization's goals. One must ask the question as to whether management is disconnected from business needs, and thus one should not be surprised that strategic stress builds right from the core of leadership.

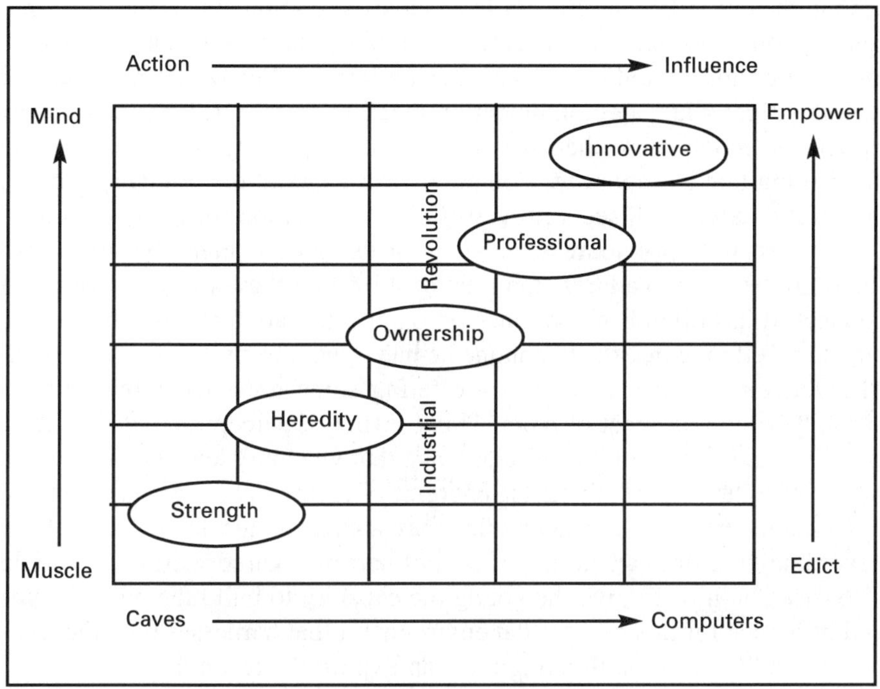

Figure 19.1   How has the concept of leadership developed over time?

What I have been interested in trying to evaluate has been the change in recognition that has accompanied the development of the knowledge-based environment. The more we move towards a business community that places a greater value on knowledge than on assets, so the nature of leadership changes. The adaptable organization of the future will depend more on the individual and collective intellect rather than on the traditional command and control structures that emerged with the Industrial Revolution. As such, the style of leadership will also have to adapt.

I have found that the terms 'management' and 'leadership' are often confused in people's minds, and while to many this may seem to be of no consequence, in fact the two are clearly different. Management is about providing direction and administrative control, while leadership is about empowerment, vision and strategic thinking. Others may argue with these definitions but the debate is not that important. What is clear is that the future business environment, and specifically the advent of agile organizations, will require a special breed of leadership to be successful that operates more through influence and empowerment.

Consider this need against the background of the changes that have been seen in the development process from caves to computers. Younger people see the computer and its connectivity as being the new business environment. I certainly would not challenge its impact, but would promote the idea that this is just a communication medium. While ICT has enabled us to achieve much more than was previously physically possible, it is the application that is important. Computers can take out the drudgery but it is doubtful that we shall see a fully artificial imagination for many decades.

We must not only address the skills of using computers, but must also focus on the need to address the relationships that these bits and bytes will connect. It has often been commented on at seminars that when Alexander Graham Bell invented the telephone he had to wait to find some one to call. The dot.com boom was similar – offering some great ideas but with no capacity to deliver most of them. This conflict of perception between relationships and technology is the challenge that visionary leaders will have to bridge in order to consolidate the energies of their respective organizations.

Certainly the younger generation has an advantage in that they have never known a time when they were not part of a wired world. We should also focus on how to give the young the capacity to build the relationships and influence for this new virtual environment that harnesses both the technology and the futurist thinking that can exploit the technology.

The leader for today's diverse environment has to be much more than an effective manager, since he or she has to inspire and capitalize on the knowledge platforms that they lead. Traditionalists may see this as just fluffy talk, but if they take the time to think about the nature of business values today, based on innovative thinking and inventiveness, these must by their very nature derive power from free-thinking individuals. Exploiting this capability at every level of the organization means creating an environment and focus that allows the new ideas to blossom while remaining within a strategic business focus.

So what capabilities do we look for in a leader, and how many of the leaders we currently follow do in fact demonstrate many (or any) of these attributes. I prepared a list in just to be provocative, but in truth we as individuals probably expect our more successful leaders to be many or most of these. What we probably want more than anything else of a leader is for them to be a winner and, as acknowledged by Napoleon, they also need to be lucky.

We look for many attributes in leadership, from mentor to street fighter, and clearly every organization needs certain aspects more than others for the emphasis to be effective. In the virtual world that one sees as a distinct possibility there will be more of a holistic structure. To lead such a venture effectively will mean a greater deployment of authority and thus more

- Champion
- Motivator
- Arbitrator
- Mentor
- Strategist
- Planner
- Tactician
- People manager
- Risk manager
- Salesperson
- Relationship manager
- Customer-focused operator
- Negotiator
- Innovator
- Clairvoyant
- Business manager
- Street fighter
- Social worker
- Futurist
- Business manager

Figure 19.2 The capabilities we look for in a leader

focus on communication as opposed to edict. Often, many of the players will be from external organizations with second-tier responsibility to their own management, and probably from multicultural backgrounds where a single style of leadership would fail to draw their proactive support.

It is wonderful when people believe in their leader; but it is even more wonderful when the leader believes in the people. This issue of leadership is one that has always fascinated me and in seminars I often ask people to identify the great leaders of our time. You will probably not be surprised that at the top almost everyone's list are Adolf Hitler and Winston Churchill. What is also predictable is that, when asked which leader they would prefer to follow, Winston wins every time. Conversely, however, based on reports, Hitler was the better boss to work for.

Clearly, the impact of effective leadership is recognized through corporate success but perhaps what lie behind that success are the issues that leadership influences. In most cases this will be reflected in business environment in higher profits and a greater market share, which in turn often attracts market and investor support. Dig a little deeper and what you find are high levels of innovation and motivation, which more often than not are found to generate high levels of satisfaction throughout the organization, and this in turn stimulates the other results.

The financial marketplace is beginning to recognize the potential for different business models, and shareholders already place great store by the charisma and profile of business leaders. It is therefore reasonable to assume that if the future knowledge-based organization is to be accepted then the standing of business leaders must also reflect confidence back to the market. In any event, we are looking here at liberating the force within organizations, and this needs a strong and effective leadership. We must therefore develop a new breed that can deliver on the promise.

There are many interfaces that these leaders have to satisfy and support, starting with the customer and corporate owners and shareholders. But this cascades down through financial institutions, internal divisional managers, and more and more external partners and suppliers.

No management role has ever been an easy ride, but now we are talking of raising the stakes and alongside this the traditional style of relationship management by diktat will fall short. Leadership skills, starting with vision and strategic thinking, will need to be merged with inspiration and communication as never before, since much of the future organization may need to function without daily or hourly direction but must share and support project goals from afar.

It is interesting that the army has a very strict command and control structure but promotes leadership through its officers on the setting of 'what' and leaving the lower ranks to establish the 'how'. So the nature of leadership is both command and inspire, which many will see as a contradiction. I have no problem with this idea, since leadership must be positive at all times and give approval when necessary; the art is perhaps in understanding when approval is really necessary.

An old adage to consider is that he who wants to lead the orchestra must sometimes turn his back on the crowd, or to put it another way, a good leader can step on your toes without messing up the shine. Leadership is about maintaining the balance between transactional management and transformational thinking that will provide the level of competitive edge. Organizations will in future be forced to operate in a more diverse and flexible way to meet the challenges of an increasingly volatile marketplace. Thus in this new era of virtual integration, the leadership needs to focus on maintaining a balance between control and innovation. The global complexity of business is, in my view, already beyond traditional structures and in time must become more complex as the boundaries between organizations become blurred.

We should also consider those that are to be led in this quest to understand the nature of the new leaders we need. What is now emerging as a potential business model is outside the reference of most of the working population. The concept of being part of a virtual organization is tearing at the fabric of their comfort zones. They need to understand and appreciate the drivers in order to function, and yet people seldom challenge themselves in terms of understanding their own perspective on the world. The organization must be educated at every level to understand how employees interface with and respond to the challenges that face the business leadership.

Good leaders must take note of the background against which each organization or individual player is assessing the direction they see being taken, or which they are being asked to follow. The drivers can be very diverse and often conflicting, and leaders need to adjust their style and communicate differently in each case. Individuals must also rationalize their position, since where we position ourselves reflects on the way we interpret the performance of the leaders.

Understanding people power is about how each individual is placed on the line between traditional and transactional performance through the high-level innovative and strategic approach. There are many people within organizations who quite clearly sit in the comfort zone and ask *why* they need to change. There are many who sit passively within the organizations who wait to be told *what*, *who* and *where*. Some will be more progressive in their thinking, and they generally ask *how*. Then we find the visionaries, who simply ask *when*.

It is this diversity that organizations, and in particular the leadership, use to fashion strategies and approaches that can blend these internal cultures towards a common business objective. There are, and will continue to be, doubters who see change only in terms of their position and crave the status quo but we have already seen that volatility in the global marketplace is fired by influences outside our control. The more we adapt to promote flexibility of response, the greater the challenge for the individual to be proactive.

It is difficult to measure leadership except through results. The connection between leadership and performance is an indirect one but intuitively we believe that leadership is a major contributing factor. Management development does not have a direct impact on behaviour; it is seen through a sequence of changes from theory to awareness, to skill enhancement and then on to behaviour. Leadership training will influence management capability, which will affect implementation skills and thus performance. In this evolving business world we are looking to stretch the envelope of business relationships, so leadership has to be futurist.

The three key elements shown in Figure 19.3 capture the essence of the balanced approach to leadership. They set the nature of what I believe are the cornerstones of dynamic virtual operations. Leadership sets the pace, but this must be underpinned by the ability to develop partnerships, both internally and externally. At the people level, effective leaders need to generate the fellowship that allows people to benefit themselves but still contribute to the bigger picture. This skills profile is what we should be encouraging for the future leaders in this changing landscape we are trying to exploit. The challenge for most organizations is where to find these hybrid beings, or to develop them from existing management pools. I do not profess to have the answer, or even to guess whether it is possible to

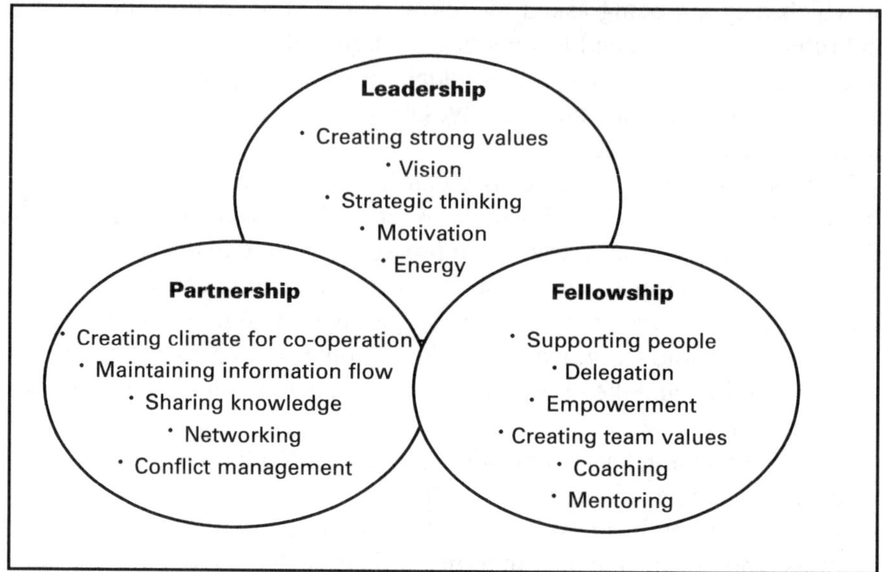

Figure 19.3   Leadership, partnership and fellowship

develop such leaders but the further we progress into the new millennium, the greater the urgency, in my view, to recognize the need to try.

Amongst many challenging assessments of the nature of leadership I have seen is the analysis shown in Figure 19.4. This suggests that there are four different types of leader and each carries with it certain traits, which may or may not be appropriate. It may strike the reader in the same way as it did me, that we may be able to recognize in ourselves certain styles, but it is more likely that we share a number of the traits across the spectrum. Which takes precedence at any given time, and how we manage that transition, may be related to good leadership: as good negotiators know, when to fold and when to hold is crucial.

For those leading the charge they must consider the nature of leadership power and assess where they are in relation to what may be necessary to meet up-coming challenges. **Resource power** is a common traditional trait within organizations since authority is derived from command and thus fails to use persuasion. **Professional power** comes from knowledge and experience but is often very traditional and works by collective assessment. **Position power** is based on authority and seldom uses any form of consultative perspective. **Expert power** is derived from experience and knowledge. These four power subsets are easy to recognize but when reflecting on the strategic proposition perhaps none fits the required profile directly.

Effective leadership is about more than identifying traits and applying

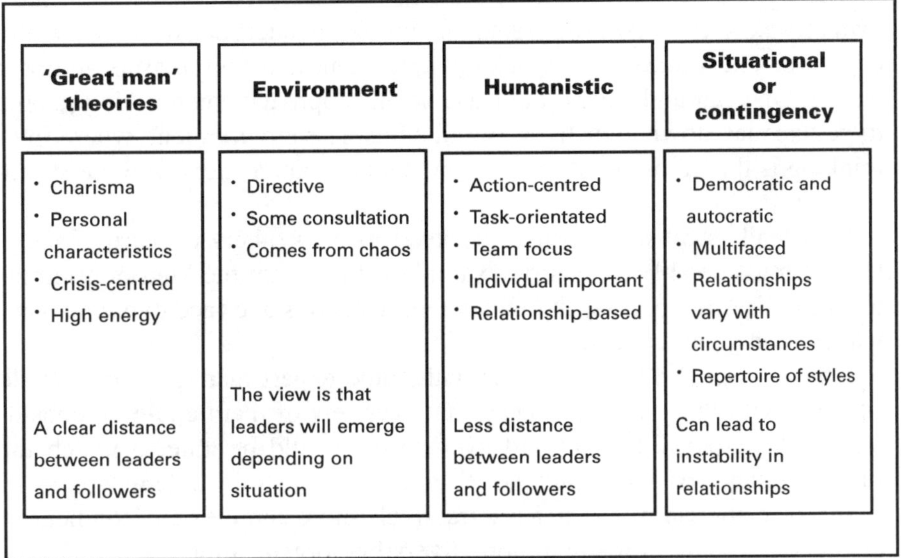

'Great man' theories	Environment	Humanistic	Situational or contingency
• Charisma • Personal characteristics • Crisis-centred • High energy	• Directive • Some consultation • Comes from chaos	• Action-centred • Task-orientated • Team focus • Individual important • Relationship-based	• Democratic and autocratic • Multifaced • Relationships vary with circumstances • Repertoire of styles
A clear distance between leaders and followers	The view is that leaders will emerge depending on situation	Less distance between leaders and followers	Can lead to instability in relationships

Figure 19.4 Assessments of the nature of leadership

checklists of tactics, however. It is the difference between theory and being straightforward in one's dealings with the team. Good leaders believe in what they are doing, constantly cross-check events against these ideas and involve their teams on a regular basis. This may become more difficult as we progress more towards 'follow-the-sun' working. One has to be to some extent an entrepreneur if one is to take full advantage of the new thinking and exploit the rapidly developing virtual network. At the same time, leaders must be adaptable to change and focused on drawing out the best from their team.

Many readers may see this chapter as somewhat philosophical and perhaps even fluffy. In response, I would suggest that they have yet to understand the changes that are taking place in the market and that have still to emerge. If meeting these demands and trials is a focus for sustaining business in a global environment then in my view we need special leaders to take us there. What emerges from my thinking is that there are five key themes that should be the focus of leadership development. The first of these is the desire for personal development in whatever guise. The core to challenging others is to have goals of your own that need to be satisfied. The next is that there must be a strong linkage between theory and practice. Effective leaders need to instil confidence in those who follow. Many managers may have read all the books but unless they have the practical background and a record of success they will not inspire others to follow.

There must be a willingness to learn, both from others and from their own mistakes. It is often suggested that military leaders can never show any degree of uncertainty or any acknowledgement that they may have got it wrong. One can understand the basis of this approach when asking people to perhaps lay down their lives, but in a business environment, where free-thinking is the lifeblood of innovation, people want leaders who are strong but honest.

And leaders must recognize the need to help others to learn. Finally, leaders must be able to lead by example if they want the kind of commitment that is often necessary to take hard decisions and face dynamic challenges in the marketplace.

I have worked over my career with some expert managers, but would suggest, with the greatest respect, that very few of them could be considered real visionary leaders and even fewer would be able to match the future demands of organizations. We need to harness a whole new facet of business relationships and in a progressively more complex environment be able to harness the force in a more diversified organization.

CHAPTER 20

Tactics

As we move forward in the process of liberating the forces within an organization, the issue of tactics comes to the fore. All too frequently, when discussing strategy development with corporate leaders and managers, the flow of the debate leaps rapidly from strategic thinking to tactics and implementation. Clearly, strategy must be created around the practical implications of implementation but for leaders of industry it often seems that they skip directly to constraints. The whole issue of strategic stress perhaps centres on this point of transition. The weakness in strategic thinking is that it is constrained by historical custom and practice, while the development of effective tactics and capabilities is often disconnected from the strategic vision. The result is clear: the organization fails to make the links and as a result underperforms.

The danger in many organizations is that traditional approaches to business operations create a rigid structure of thinking. This in turn means that the tactical approach is in essence dictating strategy development. In many ways this may be less of a conflict generator and certainly addresses many of the strategic stress issues, but it is unlikely to support innovative strategic development. On the other hand, the practical and tactical issues should provide a valid testing input for adapting the strategic focus. The two aspects of development strategy and tactics are, of course, interlinked, but the challenge is to ensure that while tactics are developed to support strategic thinking they should not be used to develop that thinking.

A more lateral-thinking leadership will address strategy from a perspective that, whether the resources or capabilities exist or not, should not detract from the validity of the strategic objective. If the strategy is the right one, then part of the tactical planning development process is in establishing where those necessary skills and resources can be identified and harnessed. Certainly, with the increasing development of the extended enterprise and alliance or partnering thinking, the limitations are only a question of finding the right partner. As a strategic thinker, I suggest that if the strategy is right then the tactical requirements will follow and the reverse is also true – if the tactical needs cannot be solved then the strategy is wrong. The dilemma, then, is to open the mind and harness all the knowledge and experience that is available, but avoid allowing these to constrain, dictate or limit the strategic vision.

Given this potential conflict, it is perhaps no wonder that strategic stresses creep into organizations. But if one is to breakdown the pain barriers and mobilize the organization, then the transition from strategy to tactical implementation is crucial, and taking the organization with you is fundamental to success. The key is in the level of visibility that is provided to ensure that the team understands the rationale that that has been developed, and that the main issues have been resolved or at least addressed. Acknowledging a challenge after having validated the end-game objective will often be enough to take the organization forward. What frequently happens is that the strategy is set but fails to understand or recognize the limitations and concerns of the organization. The result then is negativity, which engenders additional risk in the business process.

Risk management is certainly a major factor when looking at the tactical implementation of any strategy. Failing to recognize and adapt to mitigate the risks will in itself create even more risks for the venture. The whole essence of an effective tactical approach is that it addresses the risk profile presented, and where necessary evaluates optional approaches. The risk management process has to reflect not only those issues that the strategic approach has identified but also those that flow from the tactics themselves. It is perhaps these more than the strategic issues that tend to dilute or diffuse the workforce, because it is at this stage that they are directly involved. It will also be their experience and capability that is being put to the test. Thus one should not be surprised that they prove less effective where the tactical approach is less than sound based on their knowledge.

The tactical approach, then, should be focused on the weaknesses of others, while recognizing their strengths where appropriate. There is also a view that if we ignore history, we undermine the future. This, however, needs to be balanced by the view that, if we only look backwards we shall never move forward. Being strategically innovative creates the challenging environment where past practice may no longer be applicable. It is therefore crucial in the volatile global marketplace that we consider the tactical approach outside the comfort zones of the past. This is easy to say, but for today's managers the challenge of finding the right balance should not be underestimated.

Since the 1980s the business world has changed dramatically: with old political boundaries being removed, the traditional business model is proving not to be agile enough to meet the market. Advances in technology and communication have created a new marketplace that is operating in a virtual environment. Economic war has to some extent replaced traditional conflict that was at least easier to predict. It is against this background that we now have to consider and develop tactical approaches to support the strategies for tomorrow. Clearly, we should learn from the past but integrating these traditional benchmarks with a wider vision must be a crucial part of the process of moving forward.

Moving outside the comfort zone will certainly add to the potential for internal conflict and stress. The evolving marketplace is creating an environment that is less structured, more unpredictable and not so dependent on the traditional business model. The virtual organization is a reality that is capable of expanding, contracting or reconfiguring itself to provide customer-facing delivery that is agile and flexible. It must therefore follow that the key to developing a tactical approach is that it must reflect the new marketplace and be equally agile and flexible.

Protectionism is perhaps the biggest barrier in this new business environment, at both corporate and individual levels. Many Western organizations, particularly those in traditional manufacturing, expect to go on fighting the traditional battles. This ignores all the evidence that low-cost labour markets are raising quality and performance, which means that they will remain highly competitive but gain greater acceptability. So unless traditional businesses change their approach they must eventually fail. The alternative may be to form alliances across these markets and exploit the established companies' historical knowledge and positioning. This will require alternative thinking. It may be that they will choose to change their market position, moving, as many are, towards service provision higher up the hierarchy or expanding the product or market positioning. The tactics are clear for those that have made the move: 'if you can't win with the existing rules, then change the rules'. It is this lateral thinking that will come from the strategic level but which must be supported tactically.

Many, however, will also recognize that protectionism also exists at the individual level. Changing the rules means creating vulnerability that is likely to contribute to the lack of performance. The perception that organizations will eventually move their operations away from their traditional base establishes a platform of concern, stress and discontent that will undermine any strategy, so it is important that the tactical steps that need to be taken are understood. Take, for example, the training of overseas workers and the natural first reaction of 'Why should I train them to take my job?' The failure to communicate the wider picture and the potential for the future is crucial if the training is to be delivered effectively.

Understanding the level of information to divulge is often a major challenge, particularly where the end result could be the workers' worst fears being part of the long-term strategy. What happens in many organizations is that the strategy and tactical demands are presented without considering employees' reactions, and this could perhaps result in the failure of the strategy. Perception in a tactical sense can be both a powerful ally and a dangerous enemy. Understanding how to use it or address it is a skill that many would seek to exploit.

In testing the perceptions of others it is necessary to expose certain aspects of the strategy but it will provide an opportunity to validate the assumptions that helped to shape the strategy in the first place. Tactical opportunities or constraints should be tested and evaluated where practical. As we have noted before, modern knowledge-based organizations are built on the intellect of their employees, and it should therefore not be surprising that these free thinkers will be able to evaluate and challenge many strategic approaches where they affect employees directly. The problem with employing the best thinkers, though, is that they can often out-think the management.

When developing tactics, irrespective of whether the focus is on internal organizational developments or external markets, it should always be remembered that what is obvious is available to everyone. The more successful tactics are those that look to be innovative and thus surprise or out-manoeuvre those that they are focused towards. It is the alternative thinking that differentiates between those organizations that are predictable and thus generally in decline, and those that are innovative and clearly growing.

The tactical watchword is adaptability, which is focused on providing multiple solutions and options at varying stages of tactical development and implementation. As highlighted earlier, the global marketplace is anything but stable, and for any organization to survive and exploit these opportunities, traditional linear profiles have to become broader and more agile, not only when starting the process but also along the way as the initial assessments and knowledge will probably change as the strategy unfolds. Too rigid an approach will certainly impede the ability of the organization to react and respond to changes, whether internal or externally introduced.

Perhaps the other important aspect to recognize when developing tactics to move forward are the implications for current business processes and procedures. If strategic thinking is unconstrained and the deployment of innovative and adaptable tactics flows directly from these strategies, then for many organizations the stumbling blocks will be current custom and practice. The more traditional the organization, the harder it will be to introduce a tactical approach that steps outside 'the way we have always done it'. Over the years I have seen many strategic initiatives and innovative approaches founder against established, even ingrained, practices.

It is crucial to ensure that there is a rationalization process in place that can be allowed to challenge existing approaches and balance these against the strategic objectives and tactical demands. It is not enough to say 'Just do it', since in many organizations the structures may require multi-functional support, and where a degree of collaboration crucial. This is not to suggest the organizations should tear up the their own rule books, but it is important to recognize that the external changes that take place and the development strategies these invite may well require internal changes.

When it comes to the subject of tactical disposition I am drawn back to the writings of Sun Tzu, an ancient Chinese strategist. He attributed success to a simple process that is defined in Figure 20.1. After 2,500 years this seems an equally valid background for today's manager. The crucial route to success in any tactical disposition is, first, to undertake a detailed measurement or assessment of the situation. Such a review has to consider all the implications and influences, both internal and external, and included in this must be the effects on people and processes within the organization. Failing to recognize all the issues will only leave gaps in the implementation and include potential risks in not fully understanding the challenge or in execution.

From the assessment, one moves to estimating the required resources, timescale, costs and benefits. This provides the background against which the third phase of the process is focused: evaluating the overall risk and reward or cost–benefit analysis. We often over-complicate the business process and ignore the basics of common sense that is not very common today. Every action has a reaction and until you fully assess, estimate and evaluate it, success is never certain.

The modern business world also has to consider the implications of

---

- **In respect of military method, we have, firstly, Measurement; secondly, Estimation of quantity; thirdly, Calculation; fourthly, Balancing of chances; fifthly, Victory.**

Measurement owes its existence to the Earth;
Estimation on quantity to measurement;
Calculation to estimation of quantity;
Balancing of chances to calculation; and
Victory to the balancing of chances.

Figure 20.1 Extracts from the writings of Sun Tzu

sustainability and corporate social responsibility (CSR), which should be a major consideration in the development and implementation of tactics. For whereas a strategy provides the objectives and ideas, it will be the tactical approach that potentially exposes the organization through aspects of CSR. Operational rationalization, cost-reduction programmes, offshoring and outsourcing, among other tactical issues will clearly create the potential for CSR risks, not to mention the normal implications of global trading.

The people involved fundamentally create successful tactical approaches, and all organizations need to recognize this in the transition from strategy to tactics. What is often a challenge is to identify the level of information that needs to be released in order to provide people with the background to the tactical direction. The more knowledge-focused the company, the more information people need to function effectively. The golden rule is to provide just a little more information than is necessary, but not enough to open up a larger arena of debate. CEO's frequently profess that their employees are their greatest asset, but fail to play to the strengths of their workers, developing strategy and outlining tactical demands without considering the people involved.

Successful tactics do not just happen; the more focus that goes into the process, the greater the potential to exploit any opportunities that arise. Having spent time and effort on establishing the strategy and identifying the issues, the next step is to look at the approach towards executing the plan and playing the game (see Figure 20.2). The degree of success is directly proportional to the amount of careful orchestration that goes into the tactics and the focus on making the venture a team effort. One indiscretion, however innocent, can totally undermine the programme.

The choice of referring to these activites as a 'game' is deliberate: the right tactical approach can be mirrored in the sporting arena as a combination of knowledge; strategy; skill; and application. It could be said these are the main constituents of any competitive sport that matches one team against another, and I would defy anyone to suggest that the business world is not a competitive environment. The primary importance must focus on how one uses these attributes to one's advantage.

In a trading environment there are no rules, since rigid thinking limits the capability of exploring alternative routes to success. There are, however, perhaps four key points that should be considered in the development and implementation of tactics. When buying, if the supplier knows what one's drivers are they will play to one's needs and one will lose control. When selling, if one knows what the customer really needs, one can play to one's own advantage. When trading, straw issues are the makeweights that enable one to maintain the timing and direction of discussions: pushing the things

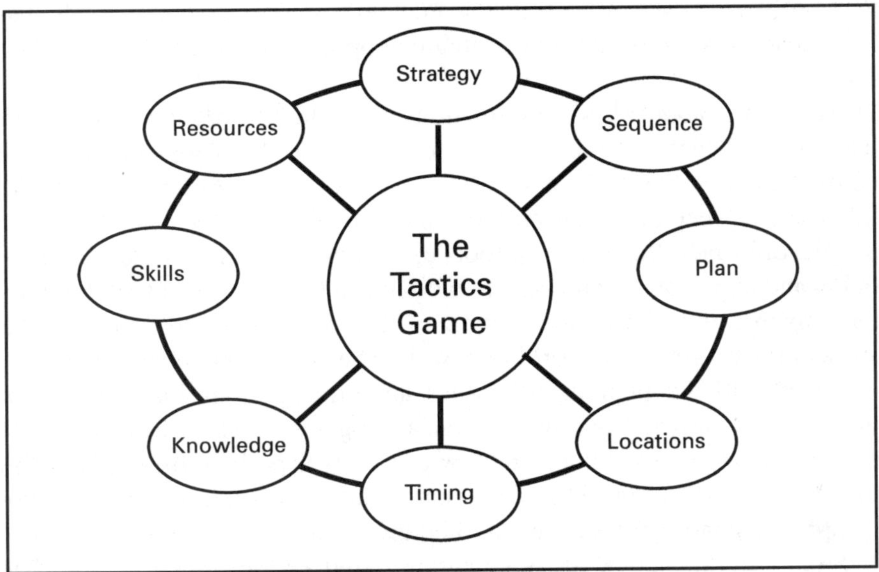

Figure 20.2 The Tactics Game

that do not matter then conceding, while targeting the things that *do* matter and sliding them through, keeps the opposition off balance. Finally, confidentiality – the less you say, the more you learn.

The sequence is one's game plan: the more detail that is developed the more comfortable one will feel as it progresses. On the other hand, the publicized position should be as limited as possible in order to avoid providing others with too much information. This includes time factors for events; this will keep others focused productively, while the actual flow and use of time will be dependent on how one wants to play.

Clearly, for complex strategies and dependent on the scope of developments one may need many different people to participate to cover the depth of issues, but the principle should be established that one only involves those that are really necessary.

Timing is major factor in putting the game plan into action. First, to ensure that one keeps the organization focused on deadlines, while it is important to make sure there is enough time to reach the overall objective. In negotiations, for example, it is common practice to call meetings just before a the weekend or a holiday, thus adding additional pressure. One problem here is that, if the meeting drags on and needs to reconvene later the impetus is lost. Time is also a significant risk. All organizations try to use time to their advantage and often apply pressure by manipulating the use of time. This is a key issue for the business manager and one that must be managed within the tactical approaches being evaluated. Real deadlines may cause the strategic approach to fail if there is no flexibility.

Business is about managing relationships, which is often why the better leaders are those who have an interest in people. People-watching is considered by many to be a science but even those who treat it as just an interest will recognize the amount one can discover by analysing body language. In fact, the strongest tools can be tone of voice, style of presentation and appearance. The use of emotion is a very powerful tool, but must be tempered with an understanding of the local style and culture. What works in one part of the world may well have the reverse effect in another.

Despite all the planning of issues and strategy it is likely to be the unscripted comments that are the most dangerous in terms of letting the tactical approach out of the bag. Confidentiality is perhaps the hardest thing to manage in any organization, and particularly where, in order to develop an approach, large numbers need to be involved.

Strategy and tactical deployment is based on accumulating the best possible body of knowledge around the plan. This building of the knowledge base is where most organizations lose control of confidentiality. Every piece of information is useful and so is every question. Those who know their marketplace can disseminate questions and predict the approaches under consideration. From knowledge one starts to define the skills required, which will in turn identify the resources required to execute the programme effectively. If the organization fails to understand these key factors or fails to operate in a structured way, then stress will build and the tactical planning process will be wasted. The greater the level of understanding, the higher the buy-in will be to deploy the right approach.

It is important to set objectives that are within the capabilities of the organization, but not too comfortable: setting the bar too high will ultimately lead to failure. Those challenges that are understood but force a stretch in current experience will probably provide the stimulus for liberating the energy within the organization. When these objectives can be related to the tactical approaches being defined, then the operational people will be more likely to rise to the challenge.

On the other hand, the tactical approach to the external world has to be completely the reverse. The market and competition should be shown what they expect, while the organization concentrates on positioning alternative approaches that will capture new ground. It is easy to see where organizations unwittingly expose their tactical approach and where the sharp external observer can determine the overall strategy, through a failure to safeguard the internal planning.

The tactical process is based on how organizations handle interactions internally and how they present themselves externally. Nothing they do or say should be directed to any other outcome than the strategic objectives they set out to achieve. If this is in the back of everyone's mind, it will be conveyed through performance. To optimize the power of an organization there is a need to empower the people and educate them to understand where they fit into the overall strategy.

Finally, tactical approaches need to recognize that the marketplace and the political environment will not stand still. It is therefore important to have in hand alternatives that can be brought into play, and to have contingency plans where practical. Some programmes will need to progress before they can be fully defined or adopted; and an understanding of where the fire-break points are is equally important, particularly since for many people the overall plan may be unknown and therefore they see only short-term targets. However, their commitment to meeting these intermediate challenges is crucial to the long-term objectives.

Flexibility and adaptability are the cornerstones of effective tactical approaches, and focusing and organization to deliver tactical advantage is founded on the ability of the leadership and management structure to recognize the implications of the actions they propose by their strategic thinking. Meeting the demands of translating strategy into tactical operations is perhaps the crux of the bending moment within most organizations. The hardest challenge is to maintain the balance between information and instruction. The more people understand this, the more effectively they can generally be able to operate. There is, though, a down side where the strategy may have an effect on their future, which can be distracting.

CHAPTER 21

Change management

In recent years, the focus on change has been reflective of the marketplace and the political and economic changes that influence that market. Technology changes have also created new dynamics which have in many cases forced the traditional organization to rethink its business model and strategic business operations. Yet while there have been many change programmes promoted and initiatives created there still remains an interesting gulf between the concept of change management and change control. This conflict is perhaps part of the dilemma that faces both individuals within organizations and the leadership that recognizes the need for change but frequently fails to deliver on the promise of one scheme or another.

This lack of balance is to some extent understandable, in that on the one hand we tend to view organizational change management as being a positive and good thing, or at least that is how it is generally promoted. On the other side, the focus on change control is more often than not viewed in a negative way, being the policing policy that monitors and apportions responsibility for operational or product changes. The reality, of course, is that both can be good or bad depending on the eventual impact of the change.

To influence the direction of an organization and to remove the conflicts and stresses that impede progress it is important to establish the concept that change management processes should not differentiate between the organizational and operational. The same philosophies and approaches should be applied equally to both, recognizing that the fundamentals of change management should be applied to every aspect of the business. Change control at the operating level is generally focused on error detection but, as most people will appreciate, errors are usually reflective of poor processes, equipment or training. Organization restructuring can in the main be effective only when it focuses on improving the operating processes, tools or resources.

It is also not a given that change is bad when affecting operations and delivery processes. Since there are clear linkages between performance and processes, changing a product to correct a deficiency could be part of evolutional improvement. Organization change, unless properly orchestrated and developed, may be sold as being for the greater good but often has a negative impact. Thus, in my view, change is change no matter what, and management approaches established within organizations should not differentiate. This avoids confusion and conflict, and at the same time sets an ethos in place that is certainly crucial for today's volatile business environment.

There can be little doubt that, if one looks at any operation, there is room for improvement in the way it operates. In most cases it would be surprising if the operating efficiency were greater than 80 per cent. In the same vein, it is hard to conceive of a market where change is not part of daily business life, whether driven by politics, economics, nature, technology or the demands of the customer.

Given this background, it is little wonder that strategic decisions permeate every aspect of the organization and engender change that must be managed effectively to keep the balance right. And if change is inevitable, we must ensure that organizations incorporate effective management systems and, more importantly, cultural attitudes that underpin the development process. The business environment of today is perhaps more volatile than ever and thus change is a factor in almost every trading situation. The customer profile is becoming more demanding and the rising profile of competitors demands that organizations push the limits of their expertise and capabilities continuously, while looking for innovative approaches that provide some form of competitive edge. The more global the business world becomes, the more opportunities (but also the more competitors) that come into the game.

The pressure from stakeholders to maximize return on investment means that an organization cannot sit still even for a short time, which strategically is a hard position to be in, particularly in the more traditional industries. Yet the stretch between investment return, regulatory pressures and long-term sustainable agendas creates a change profile that demands careful attention and certainly does not need knee-jerk reactions that undermine operational efficiency.

The first step in terms of managing change is to understand the origins of any given change. This is import in terms of ensuring that subsequent actions are reflective of the cause and not the effect. There have been many programmes introduced to help organizations to identify change and implement corrective actions, which assumes an error by someone. There have also been many focused on continuous improvement, which assumes that there is a need to keep improving when perhaps the reality is that the market needs a paradigm shift rather than incremental change. Therefore, understanding the drivers for change is a crucial part of putting an effective programme in place. In my experience there is certainly no one-size-fits-all solution and anchoring the change process means evaluating what is generating the need. Understanding these influences and drivers thus provides the basis not only for introducing the innovation necessary to effect the change, but also for creating the right appreciation and ethos around the change culture to implement it most efficiently.

When people understand the need for change then frequently they will be the people to develop the solutions, whereas if they consider the change is not appropriate they may be the cause, directly or indirectly, of resisting the introduction of effective change. The more traditional the organization or industry, the more crucial it is to find the core of the issue and establish the justification for change in order to overcome resistance. Innovation that challenges tradition is the hardest of the change programmes, so building the right foundations is critical to mobilizing the organization.

For the majority, change can be classified simply in order to understand the reason for it as well as to position the impact, which should be part of the evaluation and cost–benefit analysis prior to implementation. The 'XY' axis provides on the one side the structure of change from a clear need to

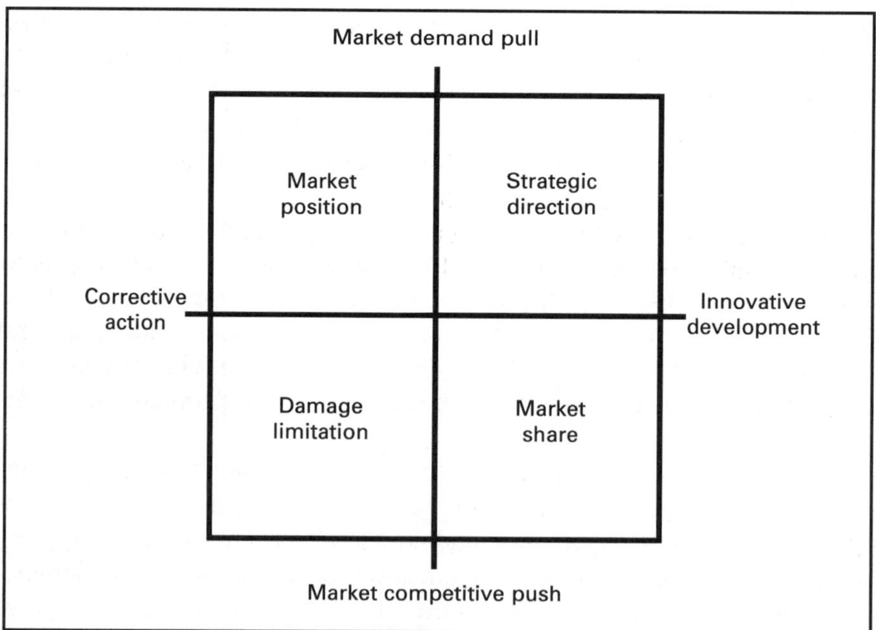

Figure 21.1　Positioning change

undertake some corrective action to investment in innovative developments that may put the product or service ahead of the competition. The other aspect comes from the pressures behind the change. The market push encompasses competition, regulatory demands and third-party influences such as NGOs. Market pull comes largely from the customer profile, looking for greater value in terms of cost or performance.

By positioning a change within this simple framework it becomes easier to understand where the change is being driven from, and why (or if) action is appropriate. I say 'if' because in some cases the short-term solution may often be to do nothing, particularly if there are other, more strategic, developments in progress. The bottom left quadrant in Figure 21.1 reflects the damage limitation zone where product failure and competitive pressure may stimulate a need for action. On the bottom right, organizations would be looking to maintain market share by incremental improvements in the product matching competitor outputs. Top left, one sees the customer pulling the product performance up and thus creating the drive for improvement. Strategically developing a new product offering should provide its own pull. This structure provides the background to positioning change appropriately in order to move the required changes through the organization. Recognizing that if the change is to be implemented effectively, then the organization has to understand the need and the focus.

The next issue to consider is why does change fail, whether this is organizational- or production-based, or even both, as in many cases I have encountered. The biggest obstacle of all is the concept, 'we have always done it this way'.

There are certain management philosophies that suggest every organization should replace at least 10 per cent of its staff every year to ensure that there is no opportunity for complacency or conservatism to establish itself within the ethos of the operation. This is in my view a negative concept, suggesting that the leadership is not able to stimulate innovation except through fear. In fact, one might consider that the whole thrust of this approach is more likely to induce protectionism and prevent people sticking their heads above the parapet and simply follow the corporate line.

Fear of failure and a misunderstanding of change create a fundamental block to getting organizations to think outside the box. This is frequently followed by a lack of communication and a disregard for the knock-on effects of changes. An equally prominent factor is often the concept that the problem is someone else's to resolve and if it is not viewed as a high priority is left for tomorrow to solve. And, of course, tomorrow never comes, so seldom does the real issue ever get properly addressed. In an integrated organization, of course, the interdependency is often such that it can never be someone else's problem and eventually every challenge has to be addressed. This lack of vision is one issue that I find undermines most strategic imperatives, and when the ideas and needs are not adequately conveyed to the organization, failure frequently follows. We are all used to management by objective (MBO), which has driven most organizations for many years and often fosters the protectionism that permeates many business ventures.

The introduction of external consultants very often engenders another philosophy that can be equally diverse and by this we mean the GBO (or glaringly blooming obvious). Everyone at the working level knows the issues that need to be addressed but when external parties highlight it the reaction is often to ignore it. More recently we have seen the emergence of management by vision (MBV), which tends to float concepts without the requisite support or tactics being introduced to effect the change.

The most important part of any change programme is to measure the benefits of change and quantify the added value. Certainly, there are many cases where the quick fix is necessary, but for more fundamental changes the cost–benefit analysis is crucial if the organization is to take a focused view of change at all levels. Challenging the way organizations work, and evaluating whether the change adds value is crucial to implementing change. What is even more de-motivating is the attitude that the staff cannot be trusted to get on with what is needed.

Change, then, is often a cultural shock, and if that change is part of some wider strategic agenda, then overcoming the shock factor is the key to optimizing the process. This should sit at the core of any change management programme. Ensuring that while the comfort zone may be attacked there is a clear process in place to meet these issues, defuse any possible resistance and bring the challenges to the fore. However, it is important not to undertake change merely for its own sake.

Change is about learning to think differently about the things we do every day; taking a fresh look at problems, however these arise, and adapting the processes and approaches to meet the challenges. It is never easy, for all the reasons we have already outlined, to see why change fails. It is often about challenging conventional wisdom or simply recognizing that to maintain a market position, or even a more forward one, means a change in the rules of engagement.

Correcting flaws in the system or making a paradigm shift towards a new business model, the starting point is to understand the nature of the change and then develop innovative solutions. The situational review must not seek to apportion responsibility but to delve into the root cause of the problem. Too often the approach is focused on apportioning blame, or worse, shifting blame to avoid responsibility. In this process, the real issues frequently become blurred by self-interest.

Diagnosing the problem should equally be approached from a perspective of identifying from where the problems emanate, which more often than not is a process or training failure. Analysing the situation effectively provides a foundation for evaluating and developing an informed decision as to the actions necessary. Finally, the decision being made, it has to be protected and implemented without trying to influence the process through protectionism. An organization which cannot accept that errors will occur is likely to be weak in terms of being able to adapt to the market drivers. Certainly, a company that apportions blame will fail to harness the full potential of the capabilities it encompasses.

What should always be at the forefront in any change management programme is the concept of delivering value. Whether this is product improvement or market positioning, organizations need to focus on the value they deliver to customers and stakeholders. Failing to recognize these contributors to the business venture will ultimately result in the failure of the organization. This does not mean that, in some cases, changes to product delivery automatically necessitate change. Some changes, though desirable, may prove to be uneconomic or 'out of sync' with the overall strategy of the business. What is important is that the process of evaluation is undertaken, and that change is not implemented without a consideration of the implications, both positive and negative. We come back to the point that change may be good or bad, and that its value must be understood

Many times when organizations are challenged to define value they gravitate immediately towards direct cash impacts on the bottom line. With more thought, however, they begin to recognize that value is a much wider issue than profit and share dividends. Value for many organizations outside the mainstream business community can be defined in a multiplicity of ways depending on the motivation of the organization. Those working within the social sector, including the medical world, often stumble between 'good works' value and commercial practicality. What is equally interesting is that in the business world the bottom line frequently reflects the delivery of value at a higher level: still profit-motivated, but customer satisfaction and reputation can often outweigh the immediate cost analysis. On the other side of the coin, my experiences in the world of engineering have shown many cases of change being introduced to improve a product where there was no real need in terms of meeting customer requirements.

The management of change runs, or should run, in parallel with a focus on improving quality and productivity. The harnessing of people power means moving them from being linear thinkers through being reactive, responsive, proactive and, finally, to recognize their interdependence. The driver for this is about the need for cost effectiveness and depends on the depth of employee participation.

Where there is a need for organizational change, the more open and trusting the ethos of the organization, the more likely it will be to react positively to the dynamics that external change can dictate. How organizations deliver value is what differentiates those that are successful. Putting a fresh face on customers' perception of value can be a major driver for innovation, and building an environment that takes this to the forefront of thinking is crucial to the change development process.

As I have emphasized so many times before, people are at the core of every organization and as such they need to understand their roles and responsibilities. At the same time, they need to appreciate fully the need for change and how this links to their personnel success factors. These in turn should be linked to the organization's critical success factors (CSF). This linkage is crucial, to ensure an integrated approach to any development. These are often founded on quality expectations, both internal and external, but are often only monitored against criteria such as levels of rework or quality failures. When incentives are also connected to these outputs, the culture of effective and proactive change will be less positive.

Most organizations today utilize some form of key performance indicators (KPIs) to monitor progress and performance. This approach is certainly one I would support in that if something cannot be measured, then you cannot change it. Visibility is the heading of my next chapter but for now it is important to recognize that KPIs can be both positive and negative. Where they reflect the implementation of change or trigger the need for change they must be transparent and meaningful, while at the same time being clinical and not susceptible to manipulation.

It is equally important to recognize that, in meeting CSF targets, the right tools need to be available. I often find that when looking into the problems that organizations have suffered, one of the main causes stems from the lack of appropriate tools to meet the challenges. In the field of change management this is an area that gets left behind in the euphoria of driving change forward. These tools may include the necessary skills to meet the proposed challenges.

In the main, however, the core issues mainly come down to the operation processes, many of which may not have been changed for years despite a recognition that markets and service delivery demands have outstripped the current business profile. There is a simple change checklist that can be applied to most situations:

- Process validation;
- Plan;
- Re-engineer;
- Train;
- Implement and control;
- Monitor; and
- Continuous improvement.

There are many techniques available to map and develop the business process including process re-engineering, process modelling, process diagrams and flowcharting. They all in essence focus on the same principle, which is to document the delivery process through every step and then evaluate where the process can be improved. What is often ignored is validating whether what is documented is in fact being done. The other key stage in this process is peer review across functional boundaries to validate the steps and eliminate those that no longer add value.

Often even a simple Pareto analysis is all that is necessary to identify the high priority issues. For most, the rule that 80 per cent of problems result from 20 per cent of the activity is a common norm, but frequently organizations focus on what they sense needs to change rather than what will in fact deliver benefit. Cause and effect charts can provide similar targeting, along with SWOT analysis and even the simple Boston Square. Whichever is used (and it can also be a combination), what is important is to get collective agreement and then concentrate on delivering added value from the process of change.

Many times in my experience even these simple processes are ignored when it comes to organizational change, which becomes focused on strategic perceptions. Clearly, changing the structure of an organization or the nature of the delivery chain without evaluating the impacts on the process makes little sense. Operational cost reductions that do not reflect organizational or process changes will generally lead to even less efficiency than was originally being targeted.

All change requires some investment in people, and the more radical the change the more importance there is in ensuring that the people within the organization are prepared for the new dimensions of the business. Then come the really hard questions such as whether the company has the required skills to take the strategy forward, or the more difficult question as to whether to contract in, outsource or train. There is no simple solution, and as I said at the beginning of this chapter, there is no single solution either.

What should be considered is that knowledge is the most important asset that any business has, and this sits within its people rather than in filing cabinets or data banks. So the first stage of evaluation should always be to train internally. With the growth in outsourcing and offshoring this may well be a contradiction of many strategic plans, but even in these cases the impact of when and how to transfer that knowledge base is likely to be critical to overall success.

Change is with us and will become an ever-increasing pressure on organizations. The global market will not go away, though some of the short-term advantages in many cases may prove not to deliver on their promise. Customer demands will continue to force a change in culture, where product loyalty will be less dependable, and sustainable business models will of necessity require greater flexibility and agility. These drivers for change will bring more complex dynamics to the strategic thinking of organizations, and within these organizations the culture of change must become a critical success factor.

Failure to build the recognition of a robust change management process will perhaps be the most significant strategic stress factor. Sustaining the balance and focus of the organization's energy through this continuously changing environment, while ensuring that change is grasped and implemented effectively, will be the major challenge for business leaders in the coming decades.

MOBILIZING FOR ACTION

CHAPTER 22

Visibility

Without a doubt, when you ask any employee how the organization can improve its operations, the answer will include better communication. This may be true but from experience I would suggest it is often a reflection of the reality. To some extent poor communication is a weak excuse for those who choose not to find the answers they desire. In the many cases it is likely that poor communications both vertically and horizontally in organizations is responsible for some problems.

However, when one digs a little deeper, the challenge to improve communications from the top is often a symptom of a much wider issue within the business. Frequently this stems from a lack of confidence on the part of the individual, and then a lack of trust in the leadership. Even with those managers who operate an 'open door' policy it is seldom possible to ensure that everyone knows everything. The best one can hope for is that people know what they have to do and receive all the information they need to enable them to do it.

But this may not always be the case. With more secretive managers a complaint or request for more information is valid. There is a traditional view that knowledge is power, and the less information you share the more power you retain. This may be true to some extent but it certainly does not provide a formula for success. This is particularly relevant with respect to the developing virtual world that is being created through globalization and technology.

There is, of course, another side to this easy way of crystallizing the problems of an organization being caused by poor communication. Individuals can often find what they think they need simply by making enquiries themselves. If they are then told they cannot have the information it is likely that the answer they seek either does not exist or is currently still be considered at a higher level.

Visibility and communication are clearly important to any organization, and the more diverse the operation the more crucial it becomes. Being able to see where one is going is critical when moving in any direction. What most of us will have experienced at one time or another are the problems that can arise when the organization creates its own answers. What we don't know we perceive or assume, and internal networks, the office grapevine and the 'Chinese whispers effect' percolate these ideas throughout the organization and more often than not it is misdirection. The negative impact on performance and development can be significant, as people debate and evaluate against false information. The likely trend for most is to assume the worst but anticipate the best, and as such seldom does the reality of any situation deliver satisfaction. When this relates to the employees' perception of where the organization is (or is not) going, then the impact can be felt quickly in terms of productivity.

It has always been the dream of business leaders to be able to see into the future, but the best we can ever hope for is to use the knowledge we have to predict likely trends. At the same time, we try to develop sufficient flexibility and alternatives to be able to react to change and mitigate negative influences along the way. The challenge is to ensure that the organization understands that not all the answers may be available but still remains focused on delivering strategic direction.

The key to any vision or strategy is to ensure that those who will be required to execute and deliver it can in fact understand it. Clear visibility is a crucial part of considering not only what the strategic direction should be, but also how this will be disseminated to the organization. In many respects, technology has opened up visibility now on a global scale and provides the concept or illusion that information is a free and open commodity.

This is, of course, not true, since the information we receive is totally dependent on what those delivering it want us to have. Whether this control is based on protecting intellectual property rights, misdirecting competition or specifically withheld to manipulate the internal focus of the organization, what we are told is always balanced against how reliable we consider the delivery channel to be. It is worth remembering that providing information is only part of the equation; the other aspect is that people need to have confidence in that information. Thus the desire to provide information on strategic direction can often be diluted by the level of trust that people have in the leadership.

Looking forward either as an individual or as an organization is often a reflection of history. How we see the future is dependent on what we know; what we can learn or are told; and then how we interpret that information based on past experience. Trend analysis is a key part of many organizations' strategic thinking and development, but what frequently happens is that the true trends are interpreted through the filter that is the individual's historical road map.

To some extent, both individuals and organizations see what they want to see. This then becomes a strategic direction, which others viewing the same data fail to interpret in the same way and thus challenge or limit commitment. Visibility, then, is not only about providing information; it is about ensuring the appropriate level of transparency that enables others to share that information effectively.

In more recent times developments in computer technology have provided us with the ability to focus increasingly on specific detailed analyses of any given situation. Some may say that in some respects we have built a rod for our own backs, and in many organizations death by analysis is suppressing innovation and development. However, on the plus side the levels of detail that can now be evaluated enable organizations to look much more closely at the world today and thus are better able to predict the world of tomorrow. Demand forecasting, for example, has moved from generic groupings by region, type and so on to a situation where, with the historical database in place, it is possible to predict almost by individuals. As a further example, at the leading edge of technology in the health sector, the development of personalized medicine will in time bring us to a point where every prescription is individually configured based on an individual's unique profile. Thus the more we know, the more we have the ability to focus, target and develop more accurate strategies.

Reliance on these technical solutions is, however, only part of the analytical process; there is still a need for flair, imagination and innovation to create differentiation. The creation of effective business strategy is about differentiation and positioning in the market, having a clear view of the market and being able to model its impacts remains within the creative and often abstract knowledge base. It is this aspect that is much harder to build into a corporate vision and a strategy that can be disseminated easily throughout an organization.

The ability of organizations to assess how things are, and then to make the leap to how they might be in the future is the domain of very few leaders. It is this vision and proactive leadership that enables organizations to balance knowledge and trust, and then move forward with confidence. Target-setting quite often has the reverse effect, particularly if the organization has not adopted fully the depth of information that has gone to form the strategic approach. All objectives have to be SMART – for example,

- **S**pecific;
- **M**easurable;
- **A**chievable;
- **R**ealistic;
- **T**ime bound.

The trend since the 1990s has been to use key performance indicators (KPIs) at every possible opportunity. There is no doubt that establishing effective indicators of progress and setting improvement targets is a valuable way to maintain visibility at every level, and helps to promote a focus on continuous improvement. Unfortunately, as many will recognize, this trend has resulted in a plethora of programmes. Even worse, in many aspects of both the public and private sectors, these myriad of measurements demand huge amounts of administration time and frequently provide very little real opportunity to take forward the process of improvement.

A side-effect of this wasted and often mis-focused effort is that performance incentives are linked to these programmes, and these distract people from the real focus. One should not be totally negative about the value of having a visible and measurable benchmarking programme in place to reflect the aims and successes of the business, however. Certainly, the more success you create, the greater the appetite for more at every level.

Not being misguided by KPIs can also be dangerous in terms of operating processes, rules and procedures. In many organizations one finds vast tomes focused on providing the detailed rules of operation. These have frequently been built up over a long period and seldom reflect the current position of the organization. It is easy for management to say that all individuals have a clear idea of how to operate, and of their roles, responsibilities and authority. The reality is that these tomes are seldom referred to on a day-to-day basis, and as they frequently do not reflect adaptations that have evolved they become in many cases worthless. Thus what should be providing a clear visibility and focus is often only propping open a door.

Business processes have long been recognized as the fundamental backbone of an organization's operating approach. Therefore, changing the direction of the business or adapting the approach automatically requires these processes to be assessed, amended and then made clearly visible to everyone who needs to know. The problem is that in many cases organizations have failed to appreciate the importance of defining and understanding business processes, and as a result, in many organizations the processes are documented but not followed up or passed on through custom and practice.

Process mapping provides a very valuable tool in first evaluating and then documenting how organizations operate. The approach heightens visibility and as a result frequently leads to a greater focus on improvements in performance. As organizations move towards the globalization of their operations and integration with external organizations, the process maps provide a platform against which to assess how best to incorporate the interfaces to best effect. The additional benefit is that, once established, any changes can easily be recognized and made visible, addressing the communication challenges (see Figure 22.1).

Perhaps the biggest obstacle to providing visibility within organizations is the failure of the leadership to 'walk the talk', and as a result vision and strategy are devalued and diluted. While it is clearly important to manage and control external visibility, the danger is that this lack of openness in fact undermines the internal focus. Maintaining the balance is crucial if the strategic imperatives are to be consolidated and delivered.

As any experienced negotiator will confirm, the less the opposition knows, the more opportunity one has to bend and blend the situation. The more dynamic and innovative the strategic direction of the organization, the more important it becomes to maintain the leading edge, and thus a commercial advantage, through minimizing the amount of data disseminated. The challenge in this is that, to move the strategy forward, the wider organization needs to be informed and involved in the development. This dilemma is one that faces every business leader and is also often complicated further by the external media running their own 'what if' scenarios and frequently undermining the leadership or forcing them to come earlier to the market in order to control speculation.

The subject of visibility has become much more of an issue in more recent times when it is entangled in the whole spectrum of corporate social

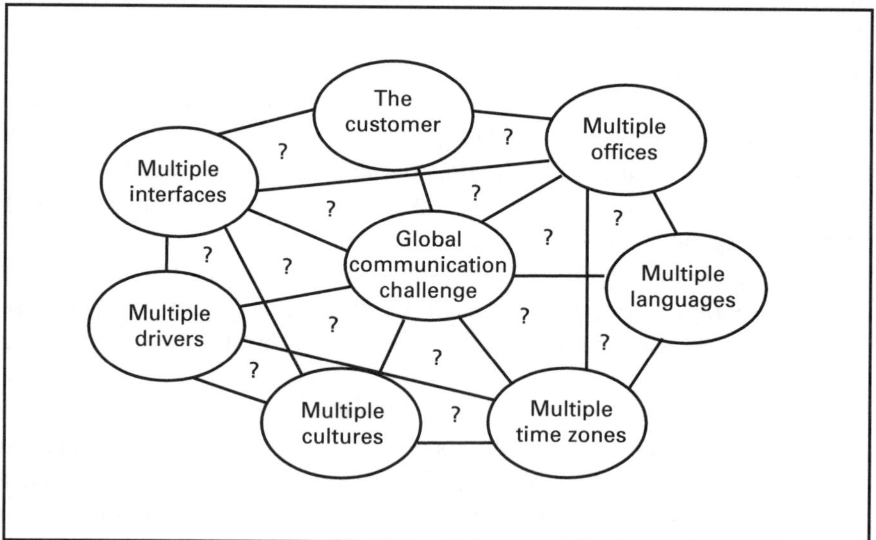

Figure 22.1   Communication challenges

responsibility (CSR) and the impacts of failures in corporate governance highlighted in cases like those of Enron and WorldCom.

The changing face of financial value has shifted from a traditional asset base to one that includes a greater emphasis on knowledge and organizational approach. Thus today not only does the executive leadership need to do the right things, they also have to spend considerable effort to be seen to be doing the right things. Again, the challenge is to manage the balance between what is necessary to maintain the external persona of the organization, against the need to have internal awareness of the strategy and the necessity to maintain a level of confidentially to protect innovation.

Added to this whole issue of visibility is the question of the sustainability agenda which, as we have already seen, creates many challenges and opportunities for the business community. In the evaluation of shareholders, the performance of the organization in relation to sustainable issues and overseas exploitation has created the need for a stronger focus on visibility and openness. PR management and brand protection are aspects that have expanded greatly since the introduction of enhanced communications technology. The smallest of issues on the other side of the world can now become a global media issue in hours, or sometimes even minutes.

Where visibility can be a help to some aspects of corporate life, it also has to be managed both internally and externally to ensure that the right levels of information are disseminated appropriately. Balancing these considerations is crucial to the whole process of strategic development and deployment.

I mentioned earlier the challenge that comes from trying to develop a strategy while looking at the future. Also that one of the obstacles is that everyone interprets what they see differently. In this environment, when seeking to release the energies within an organization and progress a strategy that is both understood and supported, scenario planning provides a structured approach that can provide the cohesion to the strategic implementation process.

As we have seen, the challenge is to develop a strategy in an uncertain world and this concept of scenario planning provides a common approach that can be deployed across the organization. Using agreed terminology can be very successful in helping organizations to focus on multiple projections:

Near-term future:	Up to one year
Short-term future:	One to five years from now
Mid-term future:	Five to twenty years from now
Long-range future:	Twenty to fifty years from now
Far future:	Fifty years from now.

Scenario planning is an approach that sits comfortably within the wider concepts of visibility and the stress that lack of recognition can induce: how we cope and plan for risk and uncertainty, or which trends and indicators are of significant enough influence to track going forward. Strategic planning is by its very nature one that spans an extended time-frame and this is an important part of separating overall and specific strategies and tactics into programmes that are able to be implemented.

Many would say that looking fifty years ahead is not realistic in a business context, but I would suggest that while it may exceed the working life of those who are employees today, it certainly would not exceed the lifetime of the local community. So when one starts to consider the long-term implications of sustainability (including environmental and local development growth) these time-frames are not unrealistic. The impact then is not so much about what we need to do in the next five years, but how that will project beyond the short-term horizons and into long-term investment.

It is people's attitudes to the future that shape the way in which they approach their current task, so any strategic change needs to be balanced to assess its potential over a series of time-based fire-breaks. This will also provide the framework for alternative planning solutions. It is through developing multiple time-phased projections that confidence grows in the short-term objectives. In understanding the various attitudes one can also see where it can be important to establish a corporate projection that everyone understands.

The fatalist will always be a challenge since they see no way to affect the future, while the traditionalist will be firmly planted in the belief that tomorrow will be the same as today. The pessimist, as we all know, sees everything from a negative perspective. The concept of discontinuity where nothing in the future will look like it does today is often an area of conflict for the optimist, who believes that progress and technology will ultimately solve every problem. There are those who perhaps are classified as unknowable who believe it is futile to try to predict the future, and they are often in conflict with futurists, who think that the future is rich with possibilities.

This range of perspectives can be found in every organization, and when developing a future strategy it is important to balance all views and consolidate a common strategy. These scenario projections are generally focused around a number of dimensions:

- Physical environment;
- Social and cultural;
- Legal, moral and ethical;

- Political;
- Economic;
- Military, defence and security;
- Science and technology; and
- The commercial marketplace.

These issues are common across many aspects of the business world, but often are only considered in isolation. In many cases it is the interaction that creates the multiplicity of potential outcomes, and when looking to project a background to strategic thinking it is important to consider these holistically.

It is all about rehearsing the future and looking to see the potential impacts of various approaches over a range of time-windows. There are many places where one can find projections from the CIA to Friends of the Earth with each focusing on what they would prefer the reader to acknowledge. The truth is that, like life itself, these organizations reflect only part of the trading backdrop and so should be considered together in order to engage the future in a robust strategy that is fully understood by the whole organization.

An effective scenario will project a vision of a possible future across all the previously mentioned dimensions and will, it is hoped, lead to more innovative thinking. It should also provide a platform for focusing on 'cause and effect' when developing and moving strategies forward. Using the scenario process will then enable the organization to engage jointly in building a profile that provides a common understanding of the basis for the strategic imperatives. In addition, it will help to focus on the need for change. Clearly, in adopting this approach as a foundation for future strategic thinking it is important to test the theory. In many ways, the approach can be very useful in itself, but perhaps it is even more valuable as a catalyst for helping to bring a common focus and visibility into the organization.

What I hope is obvious at this point is that in every sense the importance of establishing visibility as part of the process of liberating the force within organizations is crucial. The focus should be developed through 360 degrees, taking into account historical trends, current understanding, and the implications for future developments.

The most detailed of plans for the future that do not consider how others, whether competitors, customers or the regions and territories they frequent, may develop will be weakened. The development of strategic planning is even more dependent on considering these implications if it is to be effective. The key to all this visibility is to establish a common perspective that allows the organization to maintain a balance that allows it to harness all its energy towards solutions rather than debating the individual visions that detract from the overall strategic plan.

Where we have been will colour where we are today, and where we think we shall be in the future. The better the visibility and openness to share concerns and ideas for the future, the greater the prospect of avoiding strategic stress and building a solid platform towards success.

CHAPTER 23

Collaboration

The concept of partnering and collaboration is well established as an alternative operating approach to traditional conflict-based trading relationships. What perhaps has not been given wider consideration is collaboration and partnership both vertically and horizontally, for internal relationships across organizations. To exploit the energy of an organization fully it is essential to remove all barriers to co-operation.

The challenge is in developing and implementing an effective strategy that integrates these ideas into a practical approach to meet future business objectives. There is a commonly held view that collaborative relationships provide a comfortable, and some may say cosy, environment. The reality is that this type of trading relationship can offer new opportunities to add real value to the trading landscape. It does, however, require a strategic focus and the commensurate effort to develop an effective business model.

It should also be considered that the creation of a robust strategy often requires the integration of activities across organizations as well as across organizational boundaries. Such collaboration is perhaps something that starts with internal partners, though many will say that it is easier to collaborate externally than within the business family. International collaboration may be the least obvious but is frequently a key opportunity. Vertical and horizontal (see Figure 23.1) offer a variety of alternatives. The more effort that is put into the strategy the greater the prospect of success.

The objective of this chapter is to look at a structured framework against which to focus the strategic development process. It can often be simple steps that work from initially identifying the target areas where collaboration can open new opportunities, towards creating a joint implementation plan. At the same time, the failure of many strategic initiatives is that they focus on internal perceptions and fail to recognize the external influences that may aid or constrain the programme.

Outsourcing has become a key part of the business community in the quest to maintain competitiveness and develop alternative business models. This approach may take many different forms, from outsourcing of internal

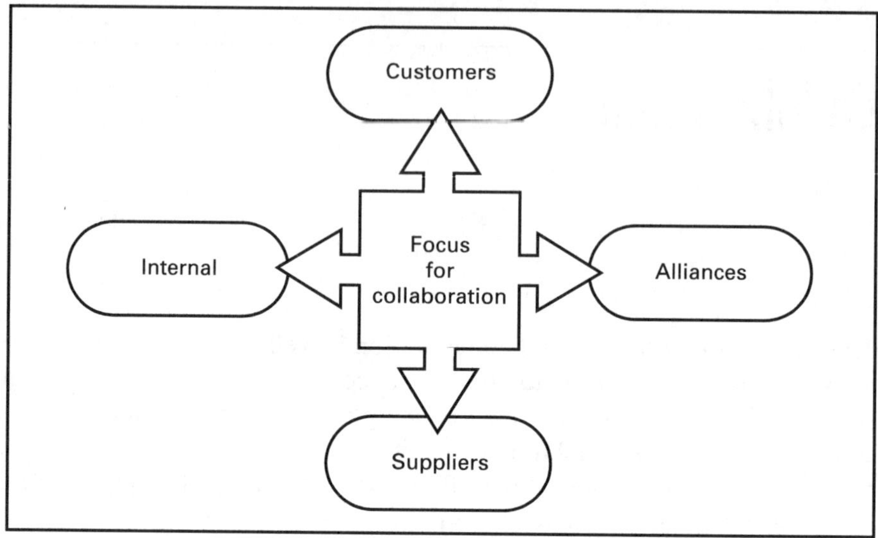

Figure 23.1   Recognizing collaboration links

support activities that are not core to the business profile, through to the external integration of business processes aimed at creating new business propositions through the concept of an extended enterprise.

This growth in outsourcing as a means of focusing resources and extending capabilities was seen initially as an effective tool in reducing costs; however, it quickly identified gaps in the existing business processes that may have been 'papered over' through internal collaboration. The failures in these approaches can also often be attributed to unrealistic expectations that govern the assessment of the satisfactory transfer of roles between organizations.

This is further risk-aggravated through the implications of others being in the front line of customer-facing delivery programmes. The impacts of poor performance and the potential vulnerability that might result from failing to meet acceptable corporate responsibility profiles call for the development of collaborative relationships. These allow organizations to develop a more open structure in the trading relationship to maintain the visibility and flexibility necessary to meet the challenges of today and exploit the potential of extended relationships more effectively into the future. Collaborative trading offers a new dimension to forward-looking business strategy.

Collaborative ventures involve time and effort, and must be able to demonstrate a value contribution that fits with the overall business profile and targeted objectives. In the same way, the risks of partnering need to be evaluated and a balanced view taken that reflects these same objectives.

Effective relationships can bring potential benefits, but conversely these will generate a number of limitations to the traditional way of working. Risk is an integral part of the business agenda, and risk management must run in parallel with any collaborative development programme.

Every business venture needs to build from its established objectives, but what frequently happens is the temptation to set objectives that are too far-reaching and have varying chances of success. Many of these desires and wish lists may be achieved through outsourcing and collaborative programmes; however, the cost of investment needs to be recognized.

For any organization to be successful, it must first understand its own requirements before trying to develop or integrate with those of an external organization. In most cases, the failure of external relationships is rooted in a failure to understand or define internal route maps. Focus and satisfaction (see Figure 23.2) highlight the principle opportunities for customer collaboration. This lack of clarity leads to confusion and misdirection, which in turn will result in the failure of the external organization to appreciate the implications of its own actions.

Creating an effective collaborative strategy must be founded not merely on desires but rather on a firm appreciation of the capabilities and sound assessment of the arena that will be encountered. It will be this assessment that has probably already identified the need to outsource and build alliances with others to overcome the obstacles ahead, or to create a proposition that the marketplace requires.

The quest to exploit the opportunities of the global market and the volatility of this market that can change business deals engenders a need to focus on managing risk. The growing new competition means that there is a dynamic culture against which to develop a flexible strategy. Technology has complicated the business environment, providing faster communications and raising the expectations of customers who now anticipate the benefits of global pricing while still focusing on traditional quality and performance. The implications for organizations are far-reaching and require a focus on risk management to ensure successful ventures.

Increased customer satisfaction	**Customer-focused solutions**
Expanded capabilities	Extended resources
Reduced costs	Economies of scale
Market research	Increased flexibility
Sustainable influence	Eco efficiency

Figure 23.2 Focus on satisfaction

The attraction of low-cost sourcing and manufacturing is certainly a potential opportunity for organizations. The challenge, then, is to adopt more flexible strategies that enable the maximization of the potential but retain effective management of the process and performance. The key to creating value is to understand fully the capabilities of collaborative partners and the resources they contribute. The more diverse these organizations are across cultural boundaries, the higher the likelihood of differing approaches to performance and management. The result is a higher possibility that organizations will create exposure by integrating activities.

In building alternative business models it is important to establish the roles and practices of the partners to ensure that a focused approach is taken not only towards the commercial benefits but also ensuring that processes are in place to address some of the wider market issues. For many in the business environment, risk management is a natural part of their corporate and management operations. What are not perhaps given as much consideration in this regard are the implications of collaborative relationships or the challenges of a less formal command and control model.

The strategy of developing strategic alliances in terms of building an effective approach takes on additional complications in order to realize the benefits of an extended enterprise. Strategic alliances may be formed by two or more organizations with the objective of developing new markets or providing a wider product/service portfolio aimed at jointly developing a growth profile. The challenge in considering this approach is to ensure a joint vision of integration that does not create its own frictions within the wider strategic operation.

Collaborative approaches provide the catalyst to help organizations integrate their operations and overcome many of the internal and cross-border frictions that may result from the transition from a traditional relationship to one of joint integration. The strategic alliance offers, particularly to medium-sized and small business ventures, the opportunity to extend their capability or market reach, or to develop alternative products.

The cornerstones of any effective business strategy are the relationships, at both a corporate and individual level, that connect the cross-functional activities within those operations. What is often overlooked is that, during the course of a business venture, these relationships will change through the impact of both internal and external influences, therefore what may have been adequate at one stage becomes stressed or less effective over time.

In a long-term relationship this evolution of the relationship needs to be tested and managed periodically. As collaborative ventures progress they build trust through the effective performance of the parties involved. There will, however, probably be changes in circumstances where refocusing the relationship can further improve performance. The investment in enhancing these relationship interfaces is a crucial factor in their overall success.

In today's business vocabulary we hear a great deal about the potential of the virtual organization, but how do we define that virtual organization? Collaborative programmes reflect the concept of linking complementary organizations, and this virtual idea can be described as 'A semi-permanent network or cluster of interdependent product and service providers who deliver supply propositions to customers by creating end-to-end value based solutions and configurations utilizing their individual assets without any single party owning the complete process.'

Figure 23.3 indicates the opportunities for virtual integration and the progression from traditional work units through to ultimate global alliance. The creation of virtual entities offers a new focus for business, although it incorporates many concepts that have been part of trading environments for hundreds of years. The new facilitator is the Internet, used to provide a flexible medium to create greater possibilities, rather than destroying traditional business. Technology, however, is only a part of the equation, which is only likely to succeed if it is based on robust and stable relationships.

The development of sustainable programmes requires the integration of multiple business relationships focused on building long-term operations that recognize the global implications and the furthering of local agendas

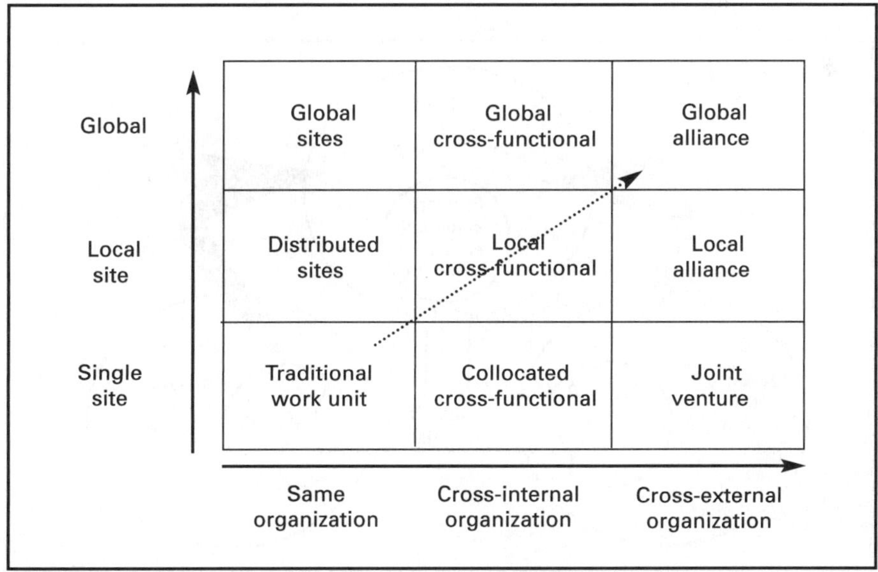

Figure 23.3 Opportunities for virtual integration

that support growing economies and add value to the business profiles of organizations.

The building of robust business alliances that can sustain continuous development of the value chain opens the opportunity of delivering improving quality and product development that prevents issues such as loss through absenteeism and health constraints. At the same time, partnerships that are built on cross-border training open the way to creating alternative business models that can be utilized as an export base rather than simply a single-flow trading process.

Eco-efficiency has the potential benefit of capturing cost savings and passing these to the bottom line, while simultaneously contributing to long-term sustainable agendas. The background to collaborative business and the deployment of partnering models as a means to improve competitiveness through collaboration can equally promote the sharing of knowledge and best practice in relation to sustainable growth.

Where integration of business ventures seeks to improve competitiveness through collaboration in design, manufacture, transport and distribution, these contribute to the overall framework of corporate social responsibility (CSR) both in terms of business strategy development and the market perception of organizations through the well-managed mutual exploitation of capabilities and skills. Sustainability has an impact on every aspect of business operations and in many cases only through a collaborative approach can these be addressed effectively.

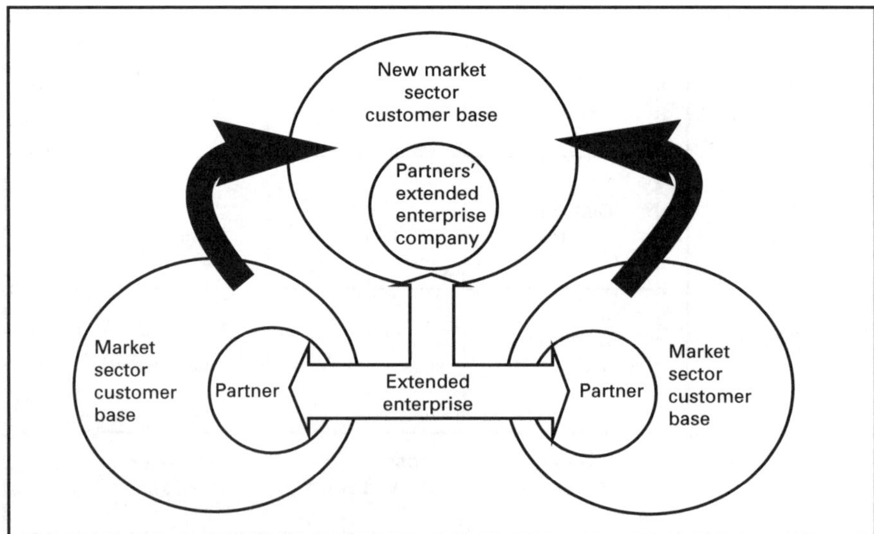

Figure 23.4   Developing an extended enterprise

The vistas of supermarket banks or gas companies selling insurance are examples of growth strategies based on exploitation of the extended enterprise approach (see Figure 23.4). The concept can be deployed in many aspects of business development, in terms of creating alternative outlets, linking skills into alternative solutions or combining skills to address new markets and sales propositions. In many cases, the extended enterprise approach is being adopted simply to build delivery processes that are based on complementary capabilities rather than on traditional investment and ownership, providing more dynamic and flexible market positioning. Collaborative approaches are being used more frequently than in the past to help manage the process of interdependence.

Creating a collaborative-based strategy must be approached in a holistic manner. The traditional integration within organizations may be well established, but the wider implications of the effects of failing to recognize the potential interactions on performance that can flow through from external relationships may be significant. Regulatory pressures, economic change and cultural difference or customer demands may drive this. Each will place pressure on the organization and its ultimate success.

The investment profile of any business needs to exploit the longest possible optimum return that will provide the highest return on investment. Short-term exploitation of any resource will not only limit the robustness of the business proposition, but it will also expose the organization to a multiplicity of new challenges. Successful collaboration is driven by the attitudes and expectations of the players, and if real value is to be created the first step must be to assess how well the organizations are positioned in relation to the challenges and envisioned objectives.

This aspect of creating a collaborative strategy is often the most difficult, since it needs organizations to 'get out of the box' and evaluate their own capabilities and approaches realistically. In many cases, organizations gloss over their own potential failings and pay the price later.

Innovative thinking is often constrained by the awareness of existing limitations, particularly within organizations. So often new ideas are not pursued because of a known lack of resources or a perceived lack of management support. The potential within the wider concept of virtual integration is that, for the right idea, there are no resource or skill limitations, since by linking with the appropriate organization these additional attributes can be adopted or incorporated provided there is a mutually beneficial commercial deal to be made.

The idea of innovation is often confused with invention, but in most cases innovation generally comes from linking existing ideas together or addressing specific operational issues. The process of developing innovative thinking often starts with two or more organizations simply reviewing what they traditionally demand of each other and examining why there is a need. This exploration moves into the area where there have been regular problems, which can be related to quality, delivery or performance. The sharing of information across the contracting boundaries can often identify practical solutions.

Effective collaboration must be driven from the top. Within many organizations the roles of leaders are generally defined in terms of what is expected of them rather than the skills and capabilities they may need to achieve results. There is also often confusion between management and leadership.

Collaboration within strategic programmes provides an alternative perspective on the traditional trading relationship. Beyond the commercial benefits that are usually the prime focus for pursuing partnering in terms of finding or improving a competitive edge, partnering offers a sound and mutual platform on which to support and develop new ideas, manage risk and help to underpin sustainability targets.

The characteristics of any successful business are the common factors in building effective relationships, and are able to move this integration even further towards success. Effective collaboration can be a crucial part of any strategic development, and this must be underpinned by developing trust through mutual performance. It is through this trust that more effective optimization and development can take place. This in turn will both identify opportunities for cost and time efficiencies, and at the same time create contributions to a wider social and sustainable profile.

The central factor in any venture that is based on collaboration is that not only will the organizations be integrated but at every level the employees of those organizations will also be working closely together. In defining the strategic imperatives and deploying them where close collaboration is a fundamental part of that strategy careful consideration must be given to ensure the building of interfaces across corporate boundaries.

CHAPTER 24

Agents and representatives

When looking to mobilize an organization effectively the general focus is always internal, whereas, as we have already highlighted, there are considerable external influences and resources to be considered. In a global marketplace one key ingredient that must be addressed in the marketing and operational mix is the role played by agents and representatives. Those who have operated only in a national context have perhaps not recognized the extended network that is a potentially valuable addition to the effectiveness of the overall strategy. Those experienced in working in a more global arena will appreciate that the performance of agents and representatives is frequently the critical factor in a company's success.

The activities of these external representatives of the organization can have a significant impact on the overall strategy, but often are not considered or consulted in the development of that strategy. Even worse, we find that in many organizations the existence of these external links is frequently not generally known or their role is not understood. This results in conflicts, both internally and externally, and confusion with clients not appreciating who talks for whom, which in turn leads to the strategy and initiatives failing to meet their full potential, or frequently failing completely.

The confusion starts by understanding the difference between the two roles, where an agent sells on a company's behalf, whereas a representative represents the organization. In reality, the edges are blurred and an effective relationship rests more on establishing a level of integration where agents are consulted and involved as if they were part of the organization.

In many organizations, the existence and practice of working with external representatives is often resented. Again, this may in part come from a lack of understanding of their roles, but also that many fail to appreciate the value that can be added in relation to what is often considered to be a high cost. The issues of whether these roles are a necessary evil or a valuable market link depends on how they perform and add value, which is often reflective of how the organization interfaces with them. What many fail to recognize is that in many parts of the world the necessity of having a local representative, or in some cases a direct selling agent is a mandatory regulation. In many parts of the world doing business is not possible without the establishment of a local partner and frequently it has to be a joint venture that has a minimum of 51 per cent local ownership.

In many cases these local links are treated as being only a legal requirement and as such many of the practical benefits can be lost. In others, the primary organization may fail to recognize the importance of the role that local organizations play and thus ignores their advice and contributions. In many areas, of course, the relationship has been developed to the point where these local organizations are integrated into the overall operation and are a key contributor to development strategy within their region.

There is no single solution for every organization, but I would suggest that if a company has resources that are not being exploited, it is missing some potential. In a strategic sense understanding where and how to develop and use external agents and representatives is crucial. Understanding how to ensure that these roles are accepted and utilized across the organizations is a key part of strategy implementation. Establishing clear rules of engagement and operating processes that ensure the maximum benefits are delivered.

For those who understand the complexity of trading overseas, the value of a local guide will be very much appreciated. As agents, they may be the only conduit to deliver a company's products and services into the market, and as representatives they provide the local networking links that are essential for successful business. In either case, they are also a critically valuable source of information and guidance in terms of understanding the local business culture and how to operate in it effectively.

Of course, the key challenge for any venture is to be able to pick the right partner, and this can be a most complex evaluation. It is perhaps in many cases a failure to focus on the selection process that creates a poor relationship, and in turn brings about the failure of the processes that follow. There are no absolutes in this regard, but what is certain is that the process of selection is linked specifically to the overall strategic aims. There will be many aspects to be considered, and in the case of the agents their market position and technical capability to support the product locally, assuming they are not simply trading on.

The representative is clearly a focus of their connections, networks and standing in the marketplace. What is often not recognized is that networks can be geographical, technical or social, and may often divide representatives, with value being strong in one sector but not in others. It is also important to know who else they are working with, as complementary or competitive relationships with the same representative can be a major factor in the selection. Often there are also customer considerations or influences to be taken into account; what may work well in one sector can be a barrier in another.

In addition to the obvious benefits of being guided through the local culture, there is also the potential to build extremely valuable information channels to understand and guide the strategic development. It is seldom a case of reading the local press but more often an issue of understanding local pressures and power balances. Providing a link to the local market and business network is perhaps the biggest contribution that can be made, but alongside this is the ability to use representatives to test approaches or identify weaknesses. This is a significant practical contribution that should be appreciated.

In the evaluation of potential partners consideration has to be given to a number of issues such as where a company is positioned in relation to their other clients, how much support they will need, and what level of education and technology transfer may be required to support them in the market. It should also be recognized that the more valuable the company is to them, the more focused they will be on the company's interests. This is one factor that often deflects focus in operations. Business is based on revenue, and when organizations trim commissions or remove profit streams from their representatives they should not be surprised when performance falls.

One of the most common strategic pressures that affect local representatives is where there are multiple agents, often resulting from mergers and acquisitions, bringing together previously competitive product ranges. The result of these mergers is to find a number of representatives in one region being in total conflict. This is often aggravated by internal conflicts supporting the historical relationships. It is strange that organizations move into mergers without understanding or establishing a strategy for future representation, which may be a significant factor in front-line marketing and is frequently left to flounder, resulting in loss of focus and sometimes even loss of markets.

We all understand the power of networks and this is the real value of the local representative. Even in cases where organizations have their own local offices the business network cannot be ignored. These networks may be driven by cultural differences, or religious or educational links such as the university, family and friends. The power of these should never be underestimated. Unfortunately, we frequently find those in organizations who feel the whole network is just a corrupt labyrinth that adds little value, and that eventually the product alone will win through. This tunnel vision may not be the accepted position overall within the organization, but often these views are found in sectors of the operation that should be closely supporting the local front line, frequently engineering departments, for example, which have perhaps less commercial awareness. When one really understands that the good local guy can find the customers' 'hot buttons' and can set you up to win, the lesson is well learned.

It is also worth considering another aspect that comes to the surface occasionally, and that is the local representative that has a split focus between what is good for the company and for him/her commercially, and what is good to support his/her more patriotic side. Finding oneself in a situation where the pressure is to reduce prices or enhance deals for local benefit can sometimes override the fees and commissions involved. This perhaps opens the way to raise the most delicate of issues in relation to working through or with overseas organizations to represent your company. The level of fees and commission is often reflective of the nature of the contribution the local team may make, and more often than not in certain regions of the world the level of influence that can be attracted to the proposition.

In polite circles, it is called facilitation payments, but in more open discussion we all know that bribes are a fact of life in many commercial business cultures. I should be clear here and say that I am not in any way supporting the practice, but simply recognizing what many prefer to pretend does not exist. It has to be appreciated that, for many parts of the world, the current practice is to assume that these payments go on, and thus wages are low, while in others these approaches may provide a route to a better future for families. If or when the balance of trading is stabilized, we may see the end of this practice, but in the meantime organizations and individuals have to decide what is acceptable for them.

There are many organizations trying hard to eliminate practices that many would see as both criminal and, more importantly detrimental to the long-term commercial development of many Third-World countries. The local representative or agent has often been seen as the ethical fire-break for many organizations that choose not to be directly involved but understand what is needed. These practices are often the reason that many people within organizations have considerable problems dealing with representatives, and as such this creates a friction that undermines all aspects of the operation and can frequently result in loss of business or a failure to maximize opportunities.

This raises a further key issue in respect of overseas representatives, which is the balance of risk and effective risk management. This may range from the issues of ethical trading and facilitation payments through to the impacts for IPR and knowledge transfer. To develop an effective strategy and bring the benefits of the external agents and representatives into the equation, there must be a focus on the risks involved. I believe that the more focus that is put on developing risk management approaches and risk mitigation, the more comfort is created, and thus also energy, which is centred on effective implementation. The more we understand about the risks we face, the more effort that can be directed towards success rather than failure.

From a commercial perspective, the long-term risk involved in transfer technology and IPR is perhaps of the greatest concern. Local agents overseas clearly need to understand the products and service they are offering, and in many cases they may require high levels of training to enable them to perform effectively. The challenge in the global trading environment of today is to exploit knowledge and technical advantage before the competition matches, copies or exceeds existing performance. When this knowledge also has been transferred by those who perhaps do not share the view of the representative regarding value, or questions the relationship on ethical terms, then the process is clearly flawed.

The major risk in a relationship that represents one's company is that the representatives are not focused fully on the company's objectives and strategic plans. It is very easy for conflicts of interest to arise, where perhaps multiple clients are looking for favours or support, and some will succeed. I have already mentioned the aspect of one network not being able serve multiple needs, and perhaps there might be a requirement for multiple agents but these need to fully understand their roles and focus.

There are clearly risks in some areas of the world that political change may neutralize local influence networks. It is also common that many locally actually understand who is doing what with whom and these situations can be exploited for political advantage, with the result that innocent organizations can lose out through no fault of their own. Reputation comes into this equation where a company might fail to conclude business simply because its representative is 'well known' locally both commercially and politically. The local 'fixer' might be the right link to get you a specific benefit, but perhaps this person will not offer the best image for the long term.

In more recent years the spectre of terrorism has added a further worrying dimension to the relationship between organizations and local companies. The relationship has to be properly understood and a level of confidence developed if the organizations are not to be at risk of contributing unwittingly to operations in which they would not choose to be involved.

It is not difficult to appreciate that, with all these conflicting and challenging issues linked to the role of the representative, many draw back from supporting the approach. It also follows that, if there is no clear focus for the organization, stresses will inevitably build, or important assumptions and links in the strategy are weakened. It would also be wrong to suggest that all overseas representatives are involved in ethically questionable practices. What is important is to recognize that the role provides a valuable extended capability which may in many cases be an essential part of delivering the strategic objectives.

Conflicts within the organization, between the organization and its representatives, between individual concepts or between representative companies where operations may be cross-border, will all result in a dilution of focus and energy. Given the potential importance of and effective need for local representation or partners in many parts of the world, it is an area that can have a significant impact on strategic intent. It is also certain that in the drive to mobilize the organization that the harnessing of resources is an important factor. In some cases, the deployment of multiple agents representing various organizations within an alliance can bring together considerably increased local influence.

Increasing the level of internal understanding and establishing well-defined rules of engagement creates a platform upon which the focus can be directed towards building an effective operation. Recognizing that conflicts could be generated, and that risk management must be integrated into the operations, provides the framework that will allow more open-mindedness and direction towards solutions. A clear corporate policy must encompass the issues that could divide the operation and dilute its energy.

The competitive nature of the global environment means that every available resource and advantage must be utilized to be successful. Few organizations can invest in the complete provision of wholly owned operations in all markets, so many regions will still require local participation. Thus developing a strategic approach and strengthening that strategy through effective implementation means that the role of the representative must be addressed among the spectrum of strategic stress issues.

GAINING ILLUMINATION

CHAPTER 25

Optimizing strategy

There can be few who do not recognize the complexity of developing an effective strategic approach. I hope that I have been able to reflect, in what has already been said, the potential impacts of failing to integrate the balance across the implementing organization. What should be clear to all in leadership roles is that the traditional concepts of deploying any strategy can be counter-productive. The idea of the CEO focusing the organization through a diktat such as 'Go to Beijing and call me when you have the contract' fails to take into account the dynamics of the market and the organization, which can frequently be seen to be in direct conflict.

To achieve sustainable success, organizations and strategy must to be in balance. It is this balancing of energy that enables the functional teams and project groups to focus on the outcome without the stresses and frictions that often constrain progress. The more established the organization, the more entrenched the traditional business processes and mind sets. Thus, when strategic plans focus on stepping outside the traditional boundaries or comfort zones, then stresses will quickly be seen.

The fundamentals of every strategy development programme are based on three key questions: what is the game or business scope; what are the goals and objectives; and how do you expect to deliver the results successfully? In a changing marketplace, the rules of engagement may be progressively stacking themselves against the traditional industrial regions. The pressures from new emerging economies and low-cost production and resource regions are placing new competitive strains on organizations. To maintain or grow market share or profits in this environment means taking a new look at traditional infrastructures, organizations and business approaches. The existing rules may no longer be valid, and if one cannot win within those rules, then changing the rules is the only alternative.

Creating new definitions of customer value often challenges organizations to redefine their business processes completely in order to move to another level of delivery or even into completely new business sectors. This step-change in strategic thinking needs to capture the energy of the whole organization in order to focus on success. Given the issues involved, it is obvious that failing to consider these factors within strategy developments will probably result in a weak strategic plan. Optimizing the strategic focus of the organization is a crucial part in being able to deliver both the promise and the vision.

Establishing a clear strategic road map for the organization is an important aspect of bringing the energy and focus of the organization to bear on its objectives and goals. The corporate business focus must also cascade down into the basic framework of delivery strategy, the 'four Cs' which relate to the effective **capture** of project opportunities; robust **contracts** that support the objective of the programme; the appropriate implementation plan to construct or deliver the **contact**; and the **close-out** of the programme.

These 'four Cs' represent the core steps in any business venture and highlight the need to consider, with strategic intent, the end-game as a crucial part of the development and implementation programme, and certainly the optimization of strategy. Understanding the final phase of any venture provides the envelope within which to develop the operation. The identification of an established process is often the major step forward, since it immediately becomes clear to all that there is a rationale behind the development.

What is equally important is to recognize that taking the process through to implementation requires the identification of feedback loops that can be used to test the strategy before full implementation (see Figure 25.1). It is, however, important to remember that over-testing results in death by analysis. Frequently, organizations are so busy testing the programmes and plans that they eventually fail to be implemented.

It is a difficult area between strategy and implementation, since in the first place it is crucial that initial strategic thinking should not be constrained by traditional evaluations of the resources used to deliver the vision. The balance between the visionary projection and the practical realities of the day is a critical part of optimizing the strategy. Poor strategy and implementation will obviously not deliver, but equally a poor strategy will probably not be recovered despite good implementation. And the right strategy can never deliver effectively if the implementation is weak. This may seem obvious, but matching the right strategy and implementation programme is the foundation of success.

It is not enough to have the right strategy alone; effective leaders will be those who can convert the right strategy into the required results through effective implementation. It is important to remember that strategy and planning should go together, and without effective action they are both a

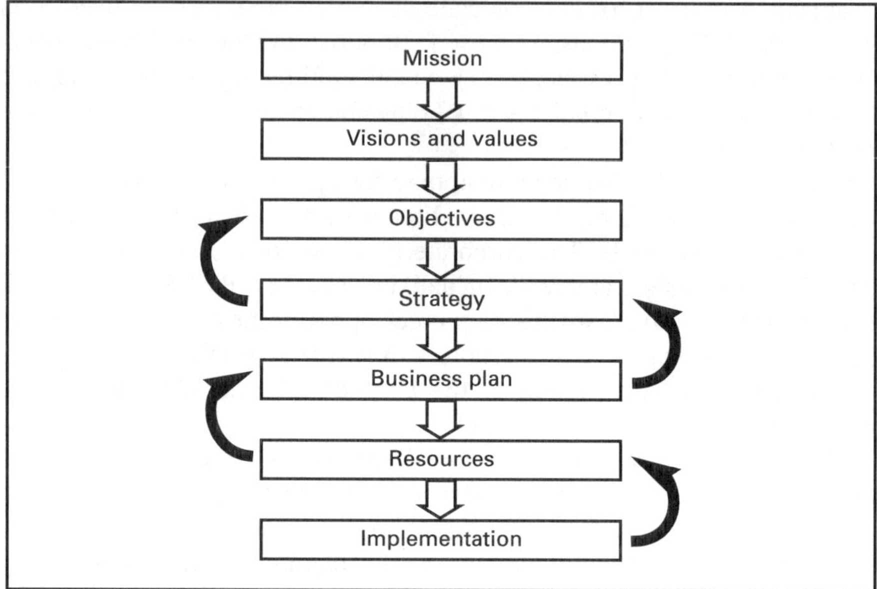

Figure 25.1   Feedback loops for testing strategy

waste of effort. The reverse can also be true: that action without strategy and planning is simply chaos. In the latter case, this can often be a result of failing to mobilize the focus of one's own organization rather than the result of others having a better strategic approach.

The four phases of the force-balancing process flow through the various aspects of strategic stress and provide a guiding focus for many of the elements that should be considered in the strategy validation process. Optimization is not simply about testing the premise and tightening the objectives; it is also about evaluating where the weaknesses are both internally and in the trading environment. It is also about building a holistic approach that considers, optimizes and ensures joined-up thinking. The more dispersed the organization, the greater the need to ensure that every fraction within it is working towards an integrated objective.

Strategic programmes can overwhelm organizations, and the more complex the product, the greater the dependency of the integrating subsystems. The more pressure on fast-track delivery, the greater the probability of and opportunity to trigger unplanned rework and waste, which dilutes energy and focus. The more unconventional the strategy approach, the greater the likelihood of needing to cut across conventional organizational structures and drive through the established functional silos.

The changing business landscape further complicates both internal stresses and external links as time and complexity increase pressures exponentially. Customer demands and the need for early financial recovery from business programmes create the need to move with greater speed but also increased accuracy. The complexity of the business environments and the expectations of customers places increased demand on product performance, which in turn means building strategic approaches that bring the optimization of delivery processes to the fore.

The strategic envelope then compounds around five key internal factors, and it is these that must be assessed and optimized in order to drive the strategy forward. Organizations provide the framework within which the strategy will have to be delivered. If this framework is restrictive or out of balance, the strategy is at risk from the start. The operating processes become the next major factor in that where these do not recognize the need for integration, the overall performance will clearly be affected. This becomes even more critical when the process is expected to operate over geographical boundaries, or organizational barriers in the case of external alliances.

Resources and skills form the next critical factors, since failing to ensure the appropriate capabilities are available or recognized within the developing strategy will lead to early conflict. Clearly, these two are closely linked, since often the disparity between quantity of resources and the quality of these resources provides a fundamental gap in the effective implementation. This has become increasingly obvious to those who have been involved in offshoring and outsourcing programmes, where a failure to appreciate the need for knowledge transfer and training may totally dilute the original perceived benefits in the short term.

Perhaps the most critical of factors, however, will be the impact of culture. In a global environment we can at least appreciate the culture diversity that exists, even if we fail to understand its implications. What is less obvious is the organizational culture that permeates every business, and when it fails to blend then the possibility for joined-up thinking becomes very strained. This is frequently the case where organizations have been through mergers, but should not be ignored when looking at multinationals that have allowed high degrees of autonomy by region or product line.

The culture will have a direct influence on performance, and thus must be a consideration in moving from strategy to implementation. The localized business generally has few difficulties with internal culture that has evolved over time and absorbed the local characteristics, but the more dispersed the organization, the more intrusive and significant the implications of cultural diversity. It is easy for organizations to say that they have a common culture, but many would not stand up to even a cursory investigation.

Clearly, the command and control structure may be established as a core structure and referred to as the culture, but even here local style will change its application. The core values of an organization may be clearly defined, but frequently these are driven by localized approaches that may even prevent effective collaboration. Competences will be a crucial factor in delivering a strategy, but these skills may well be subject to interpretation across a wide cultural spread that perhaps does not want to acknowledge weaknesses.

Perhaps the most difficult aspect of the cultural question is the ability of organizations to focus on cultivating a common approach and focus for its energy. Thus, when looking to validate any strategic intent, it is important to recognize the potential impact of culture and the need to promote a common culture that will support the implementation. Appreciating cultural impacts and potential conflicts may well force a consideration of the adoption of alternative implementation plans, whereas traditional relationships may be counter-productive.

The strategic development and contract development are in essence two sides of the same coin, and while one may initially drive the other the optimization process makes them largely interdependent. We mentioned earlier the 'four Cs' which define the operational phases of a business venture. They will provide some pinch points to consider in the strategy validation, but at the same time they need to be considered in terms of assessing the barriers to performance. These reflect in part similar aspects of strategic development, but should be used to test the strategic intent from the position of whether there are obvious obstacles to success.

The business environment is often a factor that has to be addressed but is frequently not one that organizations can control by themselves. It therefore represents a risk to the strategic intent and second-guessing the future is not a talent found in many corporate leaders. Therefore the business planning process often tries to develop approaches that provide some degree of flexibility. This demand for agility may, however, mean diluting the commitment and thus in some respects restrain the drive forward.

Once again we see the organization featuring as a clear potential risk in terms of meeting the performance expectations that the strategy has presented. As a perspective of performance, the way in which an organization is structured and controlled has a major effect on the ability of those within it to perform. In many cases the more novel and dynamic of strategic programmes have either been contained with (or segregated) skunk works operations that are freed from the constraints of the day-to-day business or developed as stand-alone projects that perform as virtual organizations with the existing structures. Understanding how the organization melds together can be a critical part of the strategic plan, while allowing the strategy to develop outside the box may be the difference between success and failure.

However organizations choose to structure their initiatives and move strategies forward, it is a certainty that current business processes will come under pressure. In many cases these will form firebreaks that prevent the devolvement of strategy across the operating groups. Thus in considering how to validate the strategic approach and to optimize the implementation the processes that span the operations need to be evaluated and either adapted or circumvented to avoid slowing progress.

Given these more definable aspects that can influence performance, there is a fourth element that in the end will be the governing factor, and that is people. Wherever organizations go and to a large extent whatever they try to achieve, the key ingredient will come from the people involved; and they represent the most complex element of any business operation. Machines and software can be developed, tested and frequently adapted to meet demands and changes. People, on the other hand, are the most complex of tools and resources that organizations have to work with.

People, in most cases, present the biggest potential barrier to performance. Despite training, education, rewards and incentives, their individual lack of confidence or commitment can be enough to thwart even the best of strategies. Understanding how people fit into a strategy and how they, as groups or individuals, may view the plan, may help to trim the programmes, and implement actions to avert negative impacts. This is certainly a complex area but one that frequently is ignored in the wake of financial projections and modelling. Yet the core assets of any business are its staff and its customers, neither of whom can be fully analysed by business modelling.

To put this into perspective goes back to Abraham Maslow's theory of the *hierarchy of needs* (published in 1970), which is still very valid today and provides a framework within which to consider the impacts and perspectives of individuals. Maslow focused on establishing the priorities that influence the thinking of individuals in relation to their environment. This also helps us to understand the way in which change may be viewed as a threat, which in turn no doubt affects performance.

At the foundation level is the **physiological** need for air, water and food. This in turn supports **security**, which is reflected in safety and freedom from threat. A **social** aspect follows and reflects a feeling of love and belonging, and above this is **esteem** created by recognition and achievement. With these aspects satisfied, Maslow suggests that only then will individuals move towards concerns such as a need to grow and seek **self-actualization** in terms of realizing one's potential. Given this structure, it is easy to see where the development of significant strategic changes could start to undermine or threaten even at the physiological and security levels.

Creating confidence and commitment as part of the strategic platform and avoiding dependence on parts of the organization that may well be affected personally by the strategy can help to stabilize implementation. Understanding the need to make provision for training and development will also help to centre the strategy and provide the people platform for delivery. Combining these people issues with the earlier comments around culture provide a complex matrix of issues that must be considered in the overall scheme.

The development of strategy starts by looking at the marketplace and developing optimization against the same background. In many cases the process of validation may well highlight the need for some adjustments, and these must be considered within the overall environment. As has been mentioned many times above, the strategy development process is not a linear one: it must be approached in a holistic manner and as such all the attributes that built up at the first pass must be assessed in any optimization.

The platform for assessing strategic stress was developed to capture the major elements of programme development. It also provides an aide-memoir in the optimization process. Considering what are frequently seen as issues that dilute the strategic intent and dampen the enthusiasm for success enables the validation to challenge the initial thinking. Given that the original focus was correct, it will provide the basis for looking at mitigation approaches rather than changing strategic direction completely.

The strategic analysis and profiling (see Figure 25.2) also provides a benchmark against which to measure impacts as the implementation proceeds. It is the complexity of the strategic environment that often creates obstacles to success, and by evaluating these within the validation and optimization that enable the focus to be maintained while ensuring, where practical, that a balance is maintained across the organization.

The essence of any sound strategy has to be based around its inherent risk management programme. Analysis of the programme, and hence its validation, needs to reflect the risk profile that was originally identified and then expand the review to consider where addition risk may be resulting from the moves towards implementation. The holistic perspective is an important element and one that is frequently ignored in favour of the prime objectives. One hopes that it is recognized that the end game may often be lost because of the secondary issues along the way.

It is the sign of a good leader that, having made a decision, he/she is

Strategic stress profiling

Goals and objectives
Leadership
Planning
Capability
Risk management
Financial management
Business environment
Customers
Competitors
Partners
Negotiations
Management
Change management
Communications
Marketing
Culture

Figure 25.2 Elements for strategic stress profiling

ready when necessary to adapt and vary their approach as new aspects emerge that can influence the outcome. Strategy is an iterative process that seldom stands still for more than a few moments in time, and will certainly require adjustment during implementation. The more agile an organization, the more flexibility needs to be contained within its business strategy.

Moving from the strategic high ground that ignores the practicalities to get outside the box towards the planning and implementation stages requires a level of pragmatism that is often lacking. It was perhaps possible in ancient times to lead on the basis of 'so let it be written, so let it be done', but today the business world has many more complications that must be acknowledged, even if eventually they are sidelined. Identifying the triggers for success will be different for every organization but in making progress towards implementation it is crucial to establish milestones and measures that are able to prove that the route is still valid.

Maintaining a balance and focus of energy across those who must deliver the strategy is a significant challenge and one that will not happen by default. The larger and more diverse the organization, the more crucial it is to establish a strategy that is robust but also reflects the strengths and weaknesses of the operators. Success may be measured in many ways and it is important in the validation of any strategy to identify clear stages where those involved may take extra confidence from interim achievements. This is particularly important where the strategy is perhaps pushing the envelope in terms of current experience.

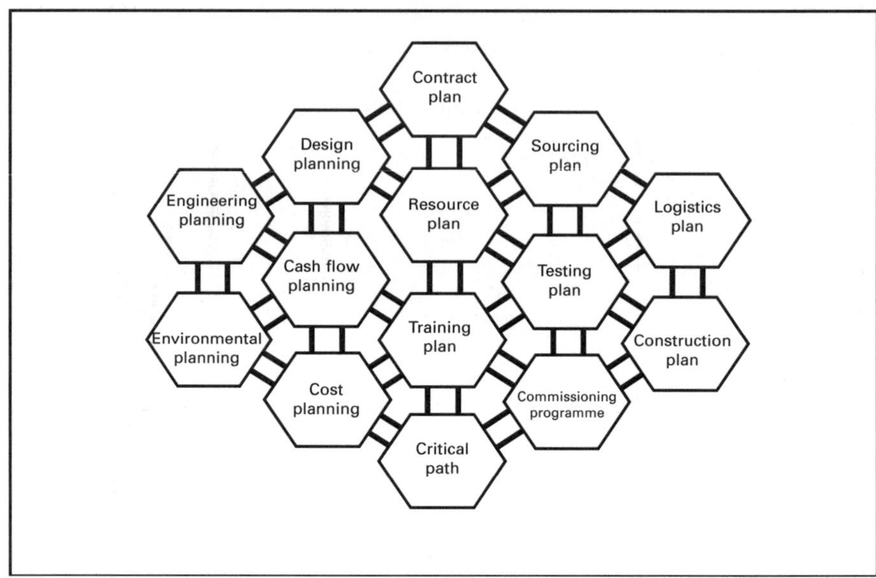

Figure 25.3 Integrated planning

The implementation planning will bring to the surface many issues and conflicts that may in themselves be minor but in total could provide a serious hindrance to overall success. Focusing the organization on pre-implementation planning enables every part of the process to be evaluated and balanced. Ensuring an effective feed process provides the opportunity to bring to the surface second- and third-level issues that could reflect back on the bigger picture.

Frequently one sees organizations that set a strategic plan at the highest levels then leave to attrition within the operation to smooth out the bumps. This makes a great deal of sense only when the full implementation programme has been trimmed. There is no substitute for planning, and while one often sees the success of entrepreneurs who went from strategic innovation to high profile returns, this ignores the many others who did not make it, and there are more of the latter than the former.

Often the entrepreneur's success is founded on relatively small organizations or isolated projects that operate outside the core structures of larger operations. The more fundamental the strategic change to the current business, the greater the dependence on the ability to carry every part of the organization forward towards a common objective. The development must be created considering the widest of holistic environments within a strategic planning framework (see Figure 25.4). The validation and optimization

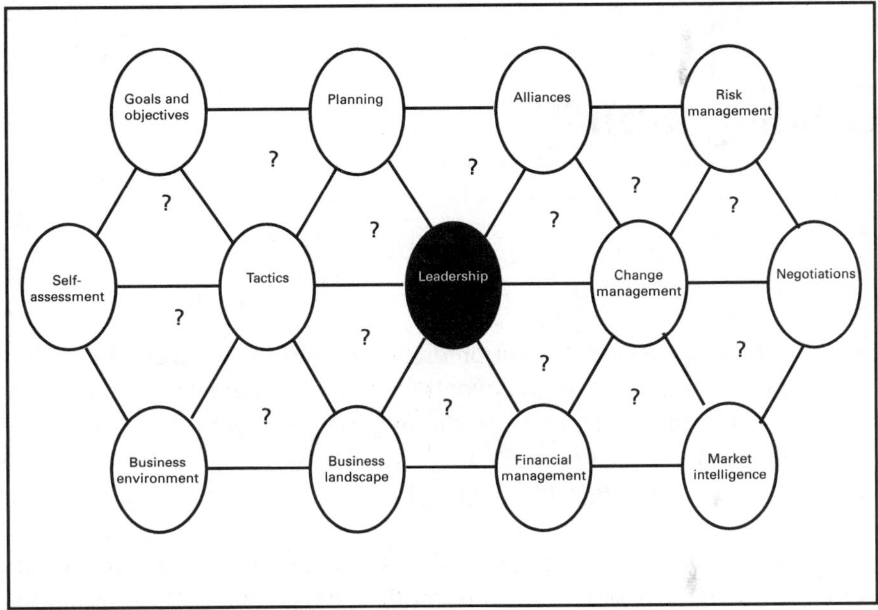

Figure 25.4 Strategic planning framework

must follow a similar, if not even wider, perspective, to capture as far as possible every potential limitation that might deflect success.

Strategy may be developed behind closed doors among a group of lateral thinkers, and often this is the only way to challenge the status quo, but eventually it must move outside into the wider organization. At this point the strategists must be prepared to be challenged and adjust elements to get collective energy behind the programme. Optimizing strategy requires a high degree of discipline to consider and address those aspects that must be balanced to ensure success.

CHAPTER 26

Creating destiny

Creating the future is better than predicting it, and the essence of developing a winning strategy is to go beyond the current parameters and focus on what might be. In my experience, the majority of organizations build the next strategic step based on what they already know. In this case, it is not difficult to appreciate that frequently this provides no significant shift in thinking.

The most effective strategic approaches are those that take a novel route to market or make a step-change in product development. The traditional view of military strategy was to do the unusual while convincing those observing that the standard routes are bing followed. In the business environment, where the competition are often leapfrogging each other, the importance of moving outside the traditional box is crucial to staying ahead of the masses.

In the context of strategic stress it is interesting that in a large number of cases, organizations' forward projections are constrained by what has happened in the past. The reverse applies to the people at an individual level in that they are generally only constrained by the limits of their imaginations. In this latter situation within a business environment, they too will generally be confined within the custom and practice of the organizations they represent. It therefore often happens that even where there is new thinking being put forward, it is suppressed by traditional boundaries, established practice and perhaps some degree of fear of stepping outside the comfort zone.

As was highlighted earlier, the practice of initiating corporate programmes designed to shift organizations to another level frequently fail because inertia prevails, causing even more stress and resulting in a dilution of enthusiasm. The discouraging aspect of this situation is that while organizations recognize that they need to move on and expand to new levels, they are anchored by only being able to assess these opportunities within their existing boundaries. Moving outside the comfort zone is hard enough, but when this involves challenging existing traditional tools and processes then it holds the prospect of serious conflicts at the individual, group and functional levels. It is fundamentally this contradiction that underlies the progressive decline of even the most successful of operations.

Since the 1970s many major global organizations have gone from being market leaders to being also-rans. In part this can be seen to be a result of stagnation and organizational baggage, but also their inability to break the mould and move on. Others looked to expand into new territories, industry sectors and markets, but failed to recognize that their strategic plans were based on their traditional skill sets. Thus when assessing the right way forward they were constrained by their experiences, and more importantly their traditional capabilities.

On the other side of the equation, the dot.com boom showed that one could not simply ignore the traditional values and create new business ventures that fly completely in the face of established thinking. Again, one sees the importance of perspective and balance in order to succeed. Stepping into new territory must be clearly evaluated and a combination of knowledge and imagination blended to capture the advantage without risking the complete collapse of traditional structures.

The entrepreneur will say 'Why not?' when traditional organizations tend to say 'Why?' and the strategist is stretching the boundaries by saying 'If only'. It is the concept of exploiting the 'if only' perspective that creates the next level of thinking. Sometimes this comes from internal imaginers but more often than not from listening to customers and collecting their thoughts on what would make life more interesting or comfortable.

Those who have made successful transitions generally developed new programmes outside the traditional comfort blanket, importing new blood and unleashing the thinking in a skunk works approach or isolated development environment until such time as the idea or initiative proved to be stable. For smaller organizations, the challenge is much harder because they do not have the luxury of spare resources and large investment budgets. Nevertheless, there is a curve upon which current capabilities and knowledge evolves. The further along the curve and the longer the current programme continues, the less of an opportunity to introduce refinements or innovation. Eventually, at some point, the current product or proposition must give way to alternative thinking and decline.

In the hi-tech industries, the lifespan of a product can be measured in months and the next generation is well into development before the launch of the current innovation. Even here, however, the limits of development must eventually give way to alternative technology thinking. Occasionally these conflicting technologies go head to head in the market. Many readers will remember the Betamax/VHS battle: the latter won the market despite many opinions that it was technically inferior. Capabilities and performance have increased progressively but now DVD is carrying the torch, and that is now not the newest technology.

These same pressures constrain all business ventures and trading fashions. As the marketplace changes, so the leading organizations tend to follow similar development routes. In recent times the drive to capitalize on cost-reduction opportunities of outsourcing and offshoring has seen a degree of hype among the many real strategic moves made by high profile organizations. These trends, though, are ones that the strategic thinking few lead and the rest just follow, often much later and with less impact or benefit. It should always be a focus for organizations to appreciate that by the time a particular approach has been generally accepted, the forward thinkers are already moving to the next level.

To some extent, investors can devalue organizations that are not following the trends, with the expectation being that if organizations are not adopting the current trends then they are falling behind, when it is perhaps more likely that following the trend for its own sake will in the end be determined by the investor and the company. This too was clearly visible in the late 1990s with the e-business hype that saw major corporations throwing money at schemes simply to satisfy the image of being in the leading pack. The aftermath saw significant write-offs and quietly dumped investment programmes. The sad part of this scenario was that many who had not even considered the possible opportunities stood back and congratulated themselves for not rushing in. The probable truth is that they never considered the long-term strategic value and will eventually fade in any case through failing to recognize the impacts of the status quo.

Many initiatives are constrained by resources, but in more recent times the growth in utilizing alliances and collaborative partnering business models has opened up alternative propositions. In essence, it is possible to achieve any objective without having to acquire or win the necessary resources provided one can find the right partners and develop a viable business plan. In the extreme, putting a man on the moon is only a question of bringing together the right partners and creating an attractive business case.

The alliance concept, which emerged strongly in the early 1990s to help reduce costs by eliminating overlaps and waste, has now evolved to enable the creation of extended enterprises driven by mutual benefit and sharing capabilities. In the dynamic global marketplace it is likely that the alliance business model will eventually become the more common one and as such presents an alternative contributor to the strategic modelling process. The investment profile provides much greater flexibility, linking organizations into adaptable delivery clusters that can mutate for new markets by changing only some of the constituents.

The cluster concept was originally promoted by Michael Porter as a means of creating industrial development pressure and growth is evolving into clusters of complementary organizations virtually integrated to provide time-base solutions or completely new market propositions. Technology has now provided the medium to link organizations globally and the multiple interdependent delivery and supply (MIDAS) cluster of complementary businesses creating a virtual operation, may be seen more and more in the future. It provides an approach that is founded in traditional partisan working models, and even more in the basics of strategic thinking going back to the era of Sun Tzu.

The concept is simple in that it looks to build a configuration of organizations to satisfy a particular customer need or to promote a new proposition. By being interdependent, the group is focused on mutual benefit and responsibility but avoids major individual investment. This approach provides the ultimate capability to exploit the 'what if or if only' analysis, since the solution is about finding the right partners rather than large investment programmes.

The danger with all strategic developments, however, is that while they may look for partners outside the current organization to foster innova-

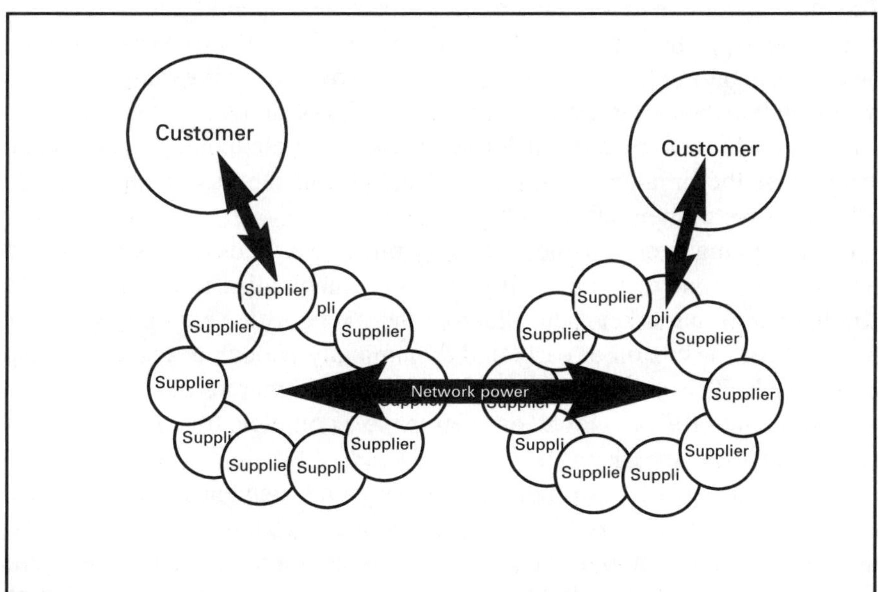

Figure 26.1   Harnessing network power

tion, even these groupings will over time be constrained by their joint experiences and knowledge. Thus over time the configurations and propositions will themselves eventually fall foul of innovation that comes from an alternative foundation. Thus organizations must always maintain some external view and test differing strategies to create the next level of value and market influence. All of which should sound a warning bell for those organizations that fail to adapt, or their leadership that fails to orchestrate the seed change in thinking to allow for the deployment of novel strategies.

In recent years there has been a decline in manufacturing in the industrial West, and given the opening up of low-cost economies it is not difficult to see why. Many companies competing simply on price are fated to meet disaster. The answer to these declining revenues was to seek strategies that moved the organizations away from a dependence on manufacture and towards a focus on the service and supply market. This strategy was consistent with the moves by major customers to reduce their own operating costs by outsourcing first non-core and later traditional core activities.

For some that adopted and promoted this strategic move, the strategy made complete sense. Unfortunately, though, they started from a point where their organizations were predominantly manufacturing-based and they failed to consider this core-manufacturing ethos of their operations. The result in many cases was a failure on both counts: they failed to convince customers of the new stretched service capability, and lost even more ground in their manufacturing activities. Recent experience in both the power-generating and mining industries provided clear examples of this mismatch between strategy, hype and the reality of delivery. Thus while the strategy might have been right for the market, the competences, skills and attitudes of the organizations failed to adapt and the leadership failed to drive the development effectively.

Underpinning every business strategy must be a focus on customers and their strategies and drivers. Taking the more imaginative route to making a paradigm shift in market focus means either being astute enough to capture the trends of the customer early and dynamically enough to respond ahead of the pack. The alternative is to look for customer trends and project beyond them to the next level, or even make a complete transition to a new proposition or approach.

Understanding the customer is a fundamental element of any strategy, and developing a strategy that captures the high ground depends on thinking beyond the traditional boundaries. As an example, one can look at the traditional supply hierarchy in the mining industry, which started with developers and went down through engineering companies to equipment providers and construction organizations. In the case of gold, which is often seen as a mineral or commodity but in fact is money, the driver is speed of exploitation to repay investments and get into the market. The traditional development process was exceedingly slow but could be totally transformed by redefining the extraction and processing plant. The fundamentals of customer profiling come back to price, quality or delivery: failing to understand these drive the customer leaves organizations floundering in the traditional market models.

In many industries there is also a reducing knowledge base, though regions such as China are producing hundreds of thousands of engineering graduates each year, thus in many industrial sectors the future strategic developments will become dependent on a greater level of collaboration between customers and markets. It would be pointless to undertake any development without considering the customers' perspective, so perhaps the logical thing to do would be to invite the principle customers to contribute to the strategic development process.

At the same time, if companies are going to consider pushing the boundaries of their business and venturing into alternative markets, business models or positions then they need to prepare their organizations for the transition. Creating the future is not only about modelling new ways to approach the market; it also has to be underpinned by equipping the organization to handle that change. Failing to recognize internal needs leads to pressures and imbalance that may well defeat even the soundest of strategies.

We come back to the pillars that support every business venture: its skill base, resources, processes and organization, but most important of all when creating a trading environment that will stretch the organization is to have the right leadership in place. It is perhaps this leadership issue that provides the biggest challenge: to develop alternative thinking and to have the confidence to take it forward. In the same way as we develop strategy based on the past, so too do we train our business managers via traditional programmes and established promotional ladders. Thus leaders brought to the fore have been to some extent conditioned by traditional thinking and then they are asked to be unconventional.

Organizations that want an alternative future and are focused on creating their destiny rather than following the market need to look closely at the their recruiting and training programmes. It is interesting that major investors look for charismatic leaders to produce dividends but expect them to employ the best traditionally-trained technologists and administrators.

Developing alternative positions means taking a different perspective on the concept of creating value. In the past, the traditional hierarchy of trad-

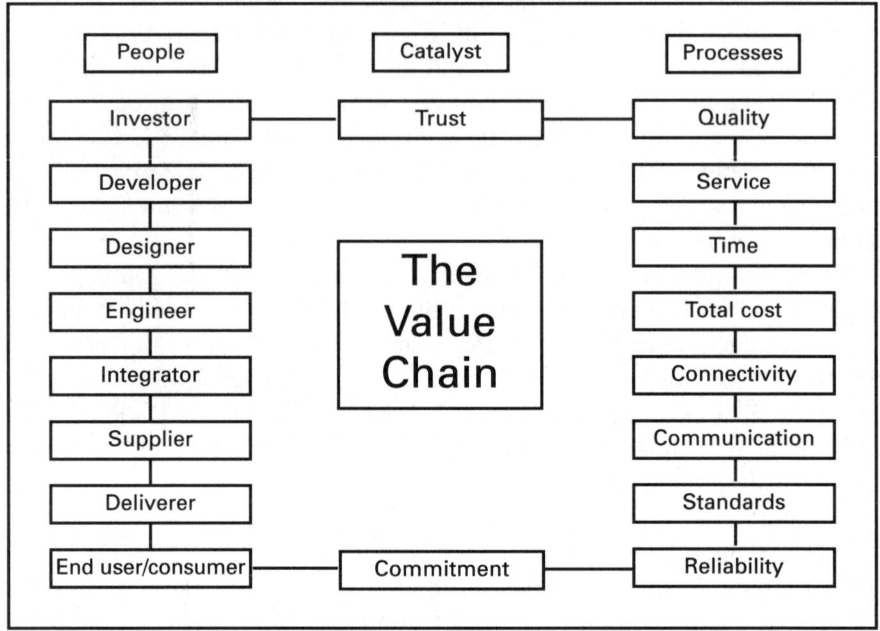

Figure 26.2   The value chain

ing relationships was based on the vertical transfer of responsibility down through the hierarchy. Moving to a new level of value means looking at the different stages of the business interface and the processes that make up that chain. While described as a value chain as opposed to the more traditional supply chain, the interconnected relationship is in fact more of a matrix that links all the parts through all the processes (see Figure 26.2). The catalysts for developing this connectivity and exploiting the networking value creation are commitment and trust, which are the foundations of business and trading concepts going back through the history of trade. Today the ability of technology to enhance these interfaces has provided a further catalyst that should be part of strategic thinking.

Releasing the fetters that constrain an organization is no easy task, but it is one that needs to be done in order to move to the next level. Again back to Charles Handy's view that 'what got you where you are won't keep you where you are': in this vein if one is going to push the boundaries, then the ethos of the organization clearly has to be prepared for failure and not enforce a traditional blame culture. To expect people to think the unthinkable and then hold them totally responsible does not engender innovative challenge but clearly carries a lot of risk where stretching the envelope may have an impact on corporate governance. The balance and energy of a company will not improve under conflicting pressures, and getting the mix right is what distinguishes market leaders from the rest.

Inspiring change to create destiny requires the focus to be on taking the current levels of thinking beyond their limits. What can be seen in the marketplace, though, is that major corporations frequently maintain their traditional positioning and watch like hawks the small organizations that do push the limits, then the larger companies swoop in once a proposition appears to be worthwhile. This strategy may be starting to flounder, however, given the ability of smaller organizations to attract finance and to be able to operate more effectively in the global market. The more flexible and agile smaller organizations may well be the catalyst for developing clusters that can defend themselves against this traditional exploitation. The result eventually could lead to the progressive demise of the major corporations that fail to consider the need to be more lateral and progressive in their strategic thinking.

This traditionalism is seen frequently where forward thinkers are unable to progress or even to be heard against the weight of established approaches. It is said that a prophet is seldom heard in his or her own country, and so often this applies to major corporations. One only has to look at the number of start-ups created by people who 'jumped ship' because they could not be heard. Ideas are the hardest thing to create, and many operations have tried to capture these through incentive schemes and initiatives, but what is less well published is how many ideas are ever developed, because they challenge the established boundaries.

Innovative strategy has to look beyond current horizons but still be anchored in reality. Consider the dot.com failures, they offer a current reflection of ignoring the balance. Yesterday is only a reference point for today, and today is only a stepping stone for tomorrow: sound leadership understands the difference and supports those who stumble. Maintaining the balance provides the platform for the future exploitation of the strategy and preventing the stresses on the organization from holding it back.

For many, the challenging environment itself pulls on the organization even while it is trying to make the next shift – similar to changing the wheel on a car while driving at 70 mph on a motorway. If everyone leans the same way, there is a chance one might make it happen, but if not, then failure is assured. It is all about balance, and the more adventurous an organization becomes, the more crucial the need to maintain the balance and energy that drives it.

Business survival and growth are very much dependent upon being ahead of the flock. This may be in product development, market reach, innovative alternatives or simply managing customer expectations. Those who follow will eventually fail, or at least never exploit their full potential; and those who lead must be ready for the next shift or may even be creating that shift.

To exploit this potential there is a need for imaginative leadership that can inspire and support alternative thinking. The next generation of managers must be given more tools to meet the challenges of the marketplace effectively, as these are rapidly outstripping traditional thinking. To get the best from any asset one needs to ensure preventive maintenance and development so too must organizations look to exploit these assets through maintaining balance.

Evolution or revolution? Organizations have to decide, but what they should not do is to try to combine the two as this only leads to confusion, which in turn will dilute the focus and reduce the chances of success. Creating destiny is not simply about having bright ideas; it also has to encompass how those innovative thoughts can be developed and delivered to the marketplace. Attention must be directed to breaking down the internal barriers that hold organizations back, and then mobilizing the people to move forward with confidence to ensure that they focus their energy on success. Gaining illumination is the core factor in helping the organization to understand where the leadership is going, and more importantly understanding people's roles in that process.

Today the business arena is perhaps more challenging and volatile then ever before. The range of opportunities and the strength of competition are creating a landscape that is pushing the boundaries of traditional thinking. It is no longer about being first, cheapest, available or trusted, it is about being what customers want, or perceive they want, today and guessing the trends for tomorrow. The importance in the complex market of creating an effective strategy and being able to balance this across the organization that must deliver it will certainly be a challenge to many.

Harnessing the force within an organization is, first, a question of decoding and understanding where it is holding back development or is constrained by the traditional processes within it. Energizing that force is about helping the organization to grow and develop in what is today a more complex environment than ever before, while holding on to the traditional values that must still be considered. The future will either be dictated by those who are ahead of the game or they will create a vortex that sucks the less prepared in behind them, where the turbulence will be most severe.

Maintaining the force

There can be no doubt that an effective strategic development planning process will differentiate the forward-thinking organization from the rest. The challenge, as we have seen, is to balance that process across the organization and bring together the focus of all that will be needed to deliver the results. Having considered the initial thinking and developed the implementation, it is not sufficient just to sit back and enjoy the ride, which if it is not fostered and fed will be short-lived.

The marketplace is dynamic, and so organizations must also be since nothing stands still for long. Just as an organization needs to remain agile in the market, so the resources within that organization have to be equally adaptable. Charging the organization with a clear strategic focus to exploit a forward-looking programme is an essential part of leadership, but ensuring the force is maintained is perhaps an even more challenging process. **Feeding the force** within an organization is a crucial part of exploiting good strategy.

Strategic stress is a constant threat to operations, and while efforts may have been deployed to address the initial hurdles as the strategy unfolds, it will certainly require some degree of modification and adjustment in direction. In creating a business planning process that recognizes the potential obstacles to success, one should also be thinking how that process could be used to test how the initial approach is progressing. More importantly, management programmes should be modified to create a feedback loop that highlights where frictions or lack of focus may be developing.

As was highlighted by Charles Darwin, being adaptable to change is the key that frequently is more important than pure strength alone. If that adaptation is to be used to capitalize on the position in the market, then a uniform understanding and delivery of course adjustments is critical. Failure to recognize this phenomenon will almost certainly lead to internal friction and loss of direction, with the result of losing impetus and reducing the potential for success. Change is a constant process, and the traditional command and control structure that pushes forward with strategic plans that are set in stone may well fail to extract the best focus. Without tempering, or at least periodic testing, the flow may result in inducing stresses that pull down the organization's energy levels. It will certainly bring a degree of imbalance into the equation which itself may create a loss of direction.

There is a concept that says if you stand still you must inevitably start to go backwards and this is particularly true for organizations that hold firm to their traditional business approaches while the marketplace moves on. In today's global marketplace this threat has been increased exponentially and must be a factor that organizations, and in particular their leadership, take into account. Failure to address changing trends, and more importantly to keep a watching brief on the future, may result in organizations finding themselves left behind. Many industries already have a very short focus on product life. Strategic direction must remain flexible enough to recognize and exploit the next potential shift, whether this is technology- or market-focused. When the competition wrong-foots the market, catching up is hard and quickly depletes the energy of those striving to maintain their position. Thus the balance must be kept trimmed in order not to be beaten to the next finishing line.

FEEDING THE FORCE

CHAPTER 27

Testing the temperature

It is unlikely that, despite the care and attention paid to developing a strategy, that every aspect will be perfect. In fact, the essence of any good strategy is to ensure that there is a degree of flexibility, and adaptability in implementation must be a feature of any winning formula. However, given that a strategy is robust and firm in its structure, it is even more unlikely that the environment around it will remain constant.

There is often a potential conflict between establishing a sound strategy and the need to reflect a large degree of adaptability. The conflict arises mainly where organizations fail to understand the nature of strategy, and cascade from vision to implementation without analysing properly the strategic intent and approach. It is perhaps this failure to take a structured approach that creates much of the stress within these organizations.

At the same time, organizations themselves evolve, as do the people within them, so it is probable that the constituents that existed when the strategy was created will have been reconfigured or changed within a short space of time. Key personnel may move, and one change can alter the dynamics of a group or function, particularly if that change is in the management structure. Beyond these internal changes there are the implications of mergers and acquisitions that even being part of or the focus of the strategic intent can significantly stretch the cohesiveness of the organization.

Change should be considered as a process, and not an event, and as such there is a need to monitor how alterations are affecting the progress towards strategic objectives. There is often a culture within organizations that emanates from the top, based on providing clear and unequivocal direction. The direction, having been set, provides no tolerance for deviation or challenge. There is the idea that maintaining focus avoids dilution of effort or consistency of direction on the established objectives and outcomes. One very successful CEO, Jack Welch of General Electric (GE), was reputed to work on the principle of 'my way or no way', and this approach certainly created an ethos that drove GE to become the global influence that it is.

The reality, of course, is that this is the exception rather than the rule, and in the majority of organizations the need to carry the confidence of the organization with the senior management is a crucial part of successful strategic implementation. The more obvious the need to reassess direction or approach, the more likely it will be that failure to do so will eventually bring the programme down.

In all of this there is one clear message, and that is that as the implementation moves forward there must be provision and structure to ensure that programmes are evaluated regularly in order to identify where a potential adjustment of approach may be necessary. This monitoring is also necessary to judge the progress and potential success of the venture.

Every organization is different, and so will be the impact of internal and external changes on its performance. The more radical the strategic approach, the more crucial it is to understand how that programme is delivering on its promise or where there could be opportunities to adjust and refine the approach. Testing the temperature also provides those involved with the reassurance that measures are in place to drive towards success.

This situation of measuring changes in influences is clearly not restricted to internal reactions; it also has to recognize that the marketplace itself does not stand still, and as a result the focus of the strategic approach can often be thwarted by external change. The market can be as unpredictable as the weather and while it may be possible to map out a forward plan there has always to be a clear understanding that the parameters that cannot be controlled will have a direct impact on an individual's or company's own drive.

Customers and competitors are a mix that often causes problems for organizations, and failing to appreciate the chemistry that can be created to either improve or constrain your programme has frequently led to high-profile organizations having to climb down on profit predictions.

A strategic approach is often developed on a given set of data frequently acquired from effective market intelligence and focused market testing. This level of knowledge and the assumptions taken from it have to be balanced against the wider considerations of how the customer will in fact react and respond, and what steps the competition may take to limit a company's success. The mixture of these can create an explosive situation that may scuttle even the most well-defined strategy.

There is another level that must also be considered within the testing programme, which is perhaps even less predictable, and that is the political and regulatory implications across a global marketplace. Understanding the potential impacts of the six dimensions of globalization is one aspect of setting the strategy in place, but understanding how to monitor the impacts of these influences is more complex. While it may be possible to read the signs in terms of some developments, there are clearly others such as the 9/11 tragedy that can have an impact on the strategic developments of a business in the short, medium and long term.

Security is one aspect, but economic trends can be equally hard to anticipate, though these can be scenario-mapped to provide a band of potential outcomes. The outputs of the options can then provide a series of fire-breaks and action points to be implemented. When these security issues then evolve into full-out war, the implications of the conflicts can completely distort many long-term plans. Some may see these as business opportunities, while others may find current directions being completely barred for extended periods.

Technology, on the other hand, will generally not have an impact in the short term unless it comes from a significant competitor release. In the longer term, predicting and building strategic plans based on technology developments is far easier to map. Regulation, particularly with respect to social and environmental issues, can be brought rapidly into play to respond to public opinion that is often divorced from commercial implications. All these factors are impacts that can have an influence on the delivery of strategic plans or those who are charged with their delivery, and as such must be considered as part of the monitoring platform that supports the initiative.

Strategies are generally based on a series of assumptions and objectives established at a single point in time. They take time to evolve and part of the strategic assessment must be to identify the appropriate points at which to test the water once again and validate the consistency of the programme. Selecting the right testing approach, and more importantly the frequency of testing, is as important as the defining of the strategy itself.

In creating a strategic approach, the issue of balancing the evaluation of objectives and resources should take into account the implications of strategic stress, but again these are fixed at a single point. Having identified where these pressure points may be and taking appropriate action to relieve the strain and release the constraints can only be related to the initial assessment. There are many influences that follow which can be counter-productive if not isolated and addressed.

Risk management approaches provide a multiplicity of mechanisms that can be deployed to provide options and fire-breaks in the implementation process, from the Options theory to the Monte Carlo simulation. The aim is to encircle those major issues or aspects that may endanger the potential for success. Frequently, however, the risk approach is focused only on the external aspects of the business and not on the potential to derail the programme from inside. If one can identify the traits and trends and convert these to measurements that can be tracked then one has a monitoring programme that can be integrated into the development and implementation process. It is an established concept that, if one cannot measure it, the outcome of the situation is that you will not be able to manage a situation.

There should be a clear understanding that the implications of internal stress and the impacts of external influences should be considered as part of the overall risk assessment and management process. Every action has a reaction, and the skill in developing an effective strategy that can mobilize the energy of an organization and maintain the balance through delivery is to cater for these variables within the overall programme.

Sound planning approaches must be a derivative of a strategic programme, and effective planning will provide the framework on which to isolate those elements that are critical to success. More importantly, the planning process will provide the platform on which to evaluate the sequences of impacts and thus enable organizations to target areas of vulnerability. From this structure, its follows that creating a critical path analysis will further refine the focusing of effort and ring-fencing of key impact areas. This identification of fire-breaks and pinch points is crucial if the organization as whole is to recognize the structured approach that aims to prevent rogue actions in response to changes that may well divert attention from the overall objectives.

Organizations are created around people, and while they may all share loyalty to the leadership there is still a strong influence that comes from not seeing the leadership being decisive and thus destabilizing the balance of focus. People may be a company's greatest asset, but they also represent a major risk. The more organizations try to capitalize on the intellect of these groups the more they risk the potential of free-range actions being implemented to react to change. The balancing of these two key influences is a major consideration for business leaders, and with more dynamic business models evolving, the greater the risk is of allowing the evolution of strategy to become disjointed.

The historical rule of successful military leaders was based on commitment, confidence and absolute discipline and this gave rise to concepts such as acceptable losses, where troops would willingly take on potentially fatal attacks for the greater good. In the business world this form of leadership is unlikely to be successful today. In the future, when organizations have virtually lost the traditional command and control structures the challenge to authority must be addressed through effective management and contingency planning.

Strategy cannot be set in stone, even though the objectives may be, and the importantance of recognizing the need to target key crossroads or decision points is crucial. Blind faith is no longer a management approach that has much chance of success and it will frequently lead up blind alleys, since it is mental dexterity and lateral thinking that should be developed across organizations, which enable the successful company to see the danger signs at every level and act to protect the objectives.

Good leadership should be able to sense the trends and pressures throughout the organization; listening to the people and feeling the energy are important factors in optimizing the focus. Meeting the objectives should not be compromised, but understanding how to maintain the balance is crucial if the organization is to move forward in a unified way.

There are many who praise those leaders that move forward at great speed, but this frequently ignores their inability to take the organization with them. The faster one goes, the harder it is for others to keep up, and as a result the leadership is often operating on a different plane and loses contact with the organization at large. This situation can often be seen when new leaders are appointed. The average life-span of a CEO is perhaps only two years before they either deliver results or are replaced. This situation can be seen even more blatantly in such people as football managers, who rise and fall with great rapidity. The stronger teams see a more structured approach that is focused on the long game; some of the more successful teams in a wide range of sports have seen years of failure before emerging as world champions. One only has to look at the history of Ferrari and its Formula One team.

The creating of a long-term strategy and being given the time to allow it to mature and deliver is the sign of an intelligent investor. Building a strategic approach and creating the team that will deliver it is seldom an overnight programme, but sadly too often there is pressure from shareholders to look for immediate returns. The resultant rush to deliver leads to increased levels of internal stress which dilutes the resolve and either prevents or limits success. Managing the stress from external sources and maintaining the focus internally during low times is a key factor in effective management. Monitoring the programme and being able to point to markers along the way is a key factor in developing a sustainable business.

This focus on maintaining the balance should not be seen as weak or fuzzy. Nor should it be interpreted as a reason to weaken resolve. On the contrary, it should be viewed as a valid supplement to managing a business that tempers the pace where necessary in order to strengthen the organization and concentrate on greater returns.

Periodic testing is one aspect of assessing the programme, but perhaps more important is the integration of key performance measurements into the fabric of the business process. Organizations often create or respond to public opinion and implement a wide and diverse range of key performance indicators (KPIs) in order to satisfy the many stakeholders that may be viewing the operation and assessing its performance. In an attempt to prove how well the organization is doing or to satisfy political or public criticism, the measures frequently become divorced from the realities of the business.

Whenever one visits a company today one will find charts and graphs that claim to depict an ever-increasing performance output and improvement, but these can be a smokescreen if not linked to the operation itself. In the political arena, the use of performance indicators has become as important if not more important, than the actual delivery of services. The impact of the anxiety to show progress rather than to deliver it has perhaps in many areas completely devalued the information and certainly diluted the focus and encouragement they were originally intended to promote.

For those in the organization who are charged with preparing the KPIs, or who are hoping to be enthused by seeing real progress, monitoring and measurement has become more of a burden than a stimulus. If performance indicators are to be useful they should meet certain parameters or be scrapped.

First they must be linked to actual outputs so that they can be collected and displayed regularly, whether good or bad. Second, they should be

Market	Competition	Customers	Shareholders	Employees
• Volatile	• Hungry	• Under pressure	• Dividend focused	• Employment security
• Political	• Aggressive	• Limited loyalty	• Risk aware	• Reward
• Changeable	• Competitive	• Cost focused	• Distant	• Recognition
• Variable	• Innovative	• Risk aware	• Short term	• Consistency
• Economics driven	• Flexible	• Short term	• Volatile	• Career development
• Competitive	• New players	• New ideas	• Sustainable returns	• Comfort zone
	• Ruthless	• Finance driven	• Volatile	

Figure 27.1 Stakeholder drivers

selected to reflect the key ingredients of the business venture, namely customers, productivity and people. All stakeholder drivers (see Figure 27.1) should be connected via these performance measures and not created selectively to satisfy one element. It is often ignored that people within the organization are also investors and members of the community at large, so what they see internally should also be reflected externally. Failure to be consistent is perhaps the worst management failing.

This openness is perhaps the hardest thing for CEOs and management boards to accept, and is perhaps why in recent years there has been more of a focus on corporate governance after outrages such as Enron and WorldCom. What is perhaps ignored in the quest to present the best possible picture to the marketplace is that, internally, the truth is well known and when organizations lose faith in themselves eventually nothing has any value.

There can be no substitute for the management 'walking the talk' and accepting the ups and downs of market challenges alongside those who are pressing to deliver more for less. This honesty also flows into the world of hype and fads that emerge and are seen by the market as measurements of forward thinking when in reality they are only appropriate for certain operations. Management's strategic plans should be strong enough to stand against the tide when it is judged not to be right for the business.

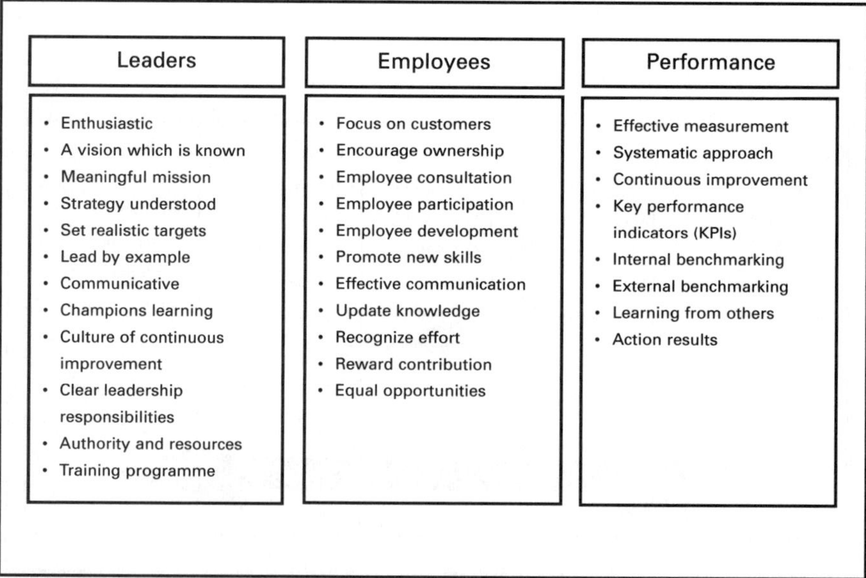

Figure 27.2   Best practice organizations

Best-practice organizations need to recognize the implications of change and market pressures, and develop approaches that link leadership and employees through effective measurement (consider Figure 27.2). In the wider context of management, strategic direction is crucial to push organizations to their limits of performance. In doing so there is a risk of distorting the balance of the operation and creating limitations on performance.

Taking the temperature is clearly an important part of validating the strategic approach and being able to turn the approach to meet local variables. Most of the impacts on any venture will be obvious and to some extent potentially predictable, and thus planning for change builds strength into the programme from the start. At the same time a measured approach to change gives confidence to those expected to deliver the plan. Ignoring the obvious will undermine the organization in the short term and is likely to dilute the energy that is being focused on results.

But, taking the temperature is only part of a continuous process of assessing progress and developing an approach through a structured programme that links the basic steps of development from objective to tactics, with clear definition, effective translation and implementation that is validated against these objectives. It then has to be flexible enough to accommodate the changes and variations that circumstances can present.

The measure of a good leader is one who is prepared to admit that change is necessary but is ready with an appropriate adaptation before an organization has developed its own independent thinking. Changing direction is not that common, but being ready to adjust the route should be high on the leadership radar. The larger the organization, the harder the task, similar to altering the course of a giant oil tanker which may take miles to slow down or stop. The crucial factor in any organization is that the commitment is there to accept that change has to happen, and there is a willingness to follow measured alternative routes with confidence.

CHAPTER 28

Adapting the direction

The speed of change in markets and the increasing number of variables this throws up have created a marketplace that on the surface appears to be a stormy maelstrom. While deeper currents may be more traditional it is this volatility that has an impact on the primary strategic focus and certainly has the ability to upset completely the balance of any organization. Daryl R. Conner captured the essence of this in his book *Leading Edge of Chaos*: 'the more volatile the market, the quicker an organisation's success formula becomes obsolete'.

Change, as we have seen, can be both a constructive and a damaging force that has the ability to divert energy from the main focus of strategic intent. Change is hard for many organizations to come to grips with as it moves people outside their comfort zones and can create high levels of fear. Constant change can be destabilizing and debilitating. Often change can be contradictory, which can further disturb the fundamental balance and focus of the organization.

There is an inevitable conflict in the volatile marketplace today that while we develop business training and processes to deliver consistent and stable operations these are grounded in traditional practices that perhaps hark back to the start of the Industrial Revolution and beyond. In many ways we have lost the fundamental essence of trading skills, which have been replaced by contracts, systems and mantra, all of which constrict our ability to think outside the box and accept the variations that can be carried on the tides of change.

To lead with a strategic focus means setting goals and driving them forward while maintaining a hold on value for shareholders, customers and employees. It is also important to remain open to redefining the game as it unfurls. The effective leader will also be able to upgrade or reinvent continuously methods of play and adapt the rules of engagement.

It has often been suggested that in negotiations the first rule is that there are no rules, the idea being that the more constraints that are artificially imposed the more rigid the approach and the less flexibility there is to exploit opportunities. Negotiations are a microcosm of trading relationships in general, and the more we continue to build business approaches based on defensive blockhouses, the less opportunity we have to exploit more flexible campaigns. In the book *Achieving Competitive Edge*, by Harry K. Jackson, the author promotes 'the success and rate of progress in achieving a world-class competitive business are directly proportional to the participation of its managers and executives' Leaders have to be ahead of the game in order to set the frameworks within which the organization can develop and respond to change.

What clearly is crucial is the need for adaptability at every level of the operation and a strategic and business framework that does not constrain the ability of the organization to respond to the market. Reaction to change, however, must be measured and controlled, recognizing that over-reaction to a trend or event can often lead to imbalance and confusion which ultimately magnifies the impact of a change rather than capitalizing or exploiting the opportunity by being attuned, responsive and ahead of the competition.

In the sailing community the most successful sailors are those who have the ability to sense the wind and respond while the rest react and clearly lose advantage. Many reports and writing on military conflicts over hundreds of years have reflected the ability of great generals to pull success from the jaws of defeat. Many leaders have commented on the point at which intuition or genius grabbed their victories when perhaps others saw the battle as being lost. They have an ability to maintain focus even when the odds seem heavily stacked against their winning. Others may suggest that these situations were just a result of luck, whatever that is. Most would suggest that people make their own luck by understanding when to play and when not.

Luck or judgement, either way the crux of this situational reversal or exploitation is that, having made a decision, the troops – or in the business sense, the organization – is willing, capable and focused enough to be able to respond when asked. As we have seen, traditional command and control structures are less effective in today's knowledge-based business world, therefore ensuring that the culture of the organization is able to reflect the trends and challenges of a changing marketplace is of fundamental importance in the global trading environment.

The strength of any organization is its ability to adapt, but at the same time the traditional thinking that persists makes this key ability one that is frequently hard to energize. In large organizations, maintaining the balance between driving forward and the confusion that comes from changes of direction are hard to manage. The followers in any community take time to fix their focus on the strategic imperatives that have been set, and then if they are asked to leave this established course this creates stress and imbalance. Frequently these changes have to be implemented at speed and thus not being able to convey the rationale leaves a void which, if not addressed, will cause a vacuum that will act to constrain progress.

Increasing the pressure without giving people any reason for it is one of the main frustrations for many across organizations. The more frequent the changes of course, the less realistic the strategy appears and then, as we have seen already, the focus wavers and the effort lessens, thus creating its own failure. Organizations today have to be educated to a much higher degree than in past traditional structures, to understand the volatility of the marketplace and the need for alternative thinking in order to ride the waves of change.

In every situation where change is a factor one does not have to leave it totally to chance; there is still an evaluation and monitoring process that should be used to assess impacts and options. These stages involve understanding the inputs, process, outputs and the key elements of the feedback from customers, which fine tunes every aspect of business operations, or at least it should. As effectively put by B. Joseph Pine, 'Customers do not want more choice. They want exactly what they want, when, where and how they want it.' Even at times of change, the impact on the customer must be paramount in the deployment of variations and changes of approach. There must also be a clear linkage to the big picture and the overall strategic programme.

The buzzword for many today is **innovation**, and this is clearly an important factor in staying ahead of the competition. This term frequently gets confused with invention, which is the creation of something new, whereas innovation is about enhancing what we already know or applying what we know in a different or more imaginative way. Innovation should not, however, become a cause in itself which often happens in organizations where moving to another level is seen as more important than the overall aims of the business. The engineering environment is one that is particularly prone to trying to improve constantly without knowing whether the improvement actually adds value.

In a world where we train engineers for excellence it is understandable that they are always looking to enhance whatever their particular environment may be. Innovation should always be focused on supplementing the strategic direction, not changing it. It is often the personal challenge that becomes an overriding influence and loses sight of the main objectives.

It should be recognized that, if strategy is well grounded and the implementations programme well defined it should not be derailed by change and in fact will be likely to absorb change and innovation to enhance the outcome. This will, of course, very much depend on the ability of the people who have to deliver it.

There are certainly external pressures that frequently force adaptations and many are often poorly founded. On the one hand there is the novel opportunity that presents itself as a strategy unfolds. It may be the case that the overall approach can be improved, or that advantage can be gained for future developments without compromising the current aims. What should be viewed with much greater care and consideration, though, are those changes that come from market hype. The investment market is a classic example of how what one organization does is seen as the benchmark for every business. The next impact is that every organization that does not follow the trend is viewed as being less robust and therefore devalued. Since the 1990s we have seen clear examples in the dot.com boom, and more recently the rush towards offshoring.

In both these trends and other hyped concepts there are many real benefits if they are truly integrated into the business strategy and in fact add value to the business in question. What should also be clear is that, for many, the approach is not right, either for the business or the customer base, and as such chasing artificial targets simply deflects attention from the core business approach.

Understanding the differences between opportunity, hype and panic is crucial in being able to address the need and method of adapting to variables. The more confidence the organization has in its leadership, the more opportunist it can be, but failing to understand the difference between these drivers can be a major factor in creating a lack of balance across the organization.

In the main, as I have said before, change is a process not an event, although it must be recognized that occasionally freak conditions do arise. In the main change is a process that proceeds at varying speeds dependent on when, where and how it emerges as an influence to the business approach. This concept of constant change has perhaps only emerged since the 1960s, often linked directly to the technology drivers. These have certainly had a major impact, but perhaps their biggest influence has been to accelerate changes that would have happened in any case over time.

New markets and new competitors are perhaps more easily accessible, but this would have come in time. Understanding that the new world order is one where change is inevitable should be encouraging organizations to look more closely at their internal structures and strengths in order to ensure that they have the infrastructure and ethos to become more adaptable and flexible. The stronger the organization, the more agile it will be and the less vulnerable to changes that could have an impact on strategic programmes.

Certainly, the leading organizations monitor trends in the market but more often than not they lead the charge rather than following it. Those that follow will obviously not enjoy the maximum benefits, with perhaps the exception of those that are looking to exploit technology platforms preceding them in the market. 'Hitchhiker' technology exploitation is perhaps the one area where it can be better to be second and focus on delivery opportunities rather than on trying to be the technology leader.

Strategy should provide a framework for deployment and not a definitive and rigid route map that allows no flexibility. It is certain that in any strategy not every aspect can be known or fixed, and thus accommodating adaptation must be a core part of strategic thinking. Promoting this across the organization should be providing the foundation to accept change without diluting the focus and energy needed to deliver the key objectives. Creating options, however, gives rise to another risk in the overall leadership, because picking the right option at any point makes leaders vulnerable and as these choices cascade down through the organization the skills and confidence levels cause a significant risk to implementation. Doing what you are told is much easier than deciding which option to take. It is this dilemma that causes a great deal of stagnation within organizations where careers may be protected by not getting outside the box.

As outlined earlier, while adaptability may be a key ingredient for success it must also be integrated within a wider risk management infrastructure. Decision tree analysis provides many with a simple process of blending adaptation and options with the ability to assess along the route rather than committing every aspect up front. The skill of strategic thinking is to build in options and alternatives while maintaining a focus on the long game. The concepts then have to be communicated in order to ensure that the organization understands the direction and alternatives.

Shifting the focus can be essential but is very dangerous, and effectiveness relies on the ability of the organization to absorb change while maintaining a cohesive approach. Often the answer is to isolate adaptations and allow only part of the operation to be affected in the short term, until a full-blown solution has been established.

Clearly, in a strategic context the more adaptable the approach the more likelihood there is of exploiting opportunities during implementation. The downside is that the greater the degree of freedom and flexibility, the more likely the dilution of focus towards the core objectives. The issue is one of balance and of maintaining that balance across the operation and often across the entire organization. Options may provide more confidence of success initially, but as the programme progresses these multiple options will cause conflict and confusion, which in turn will harm the probability of maximizing success.

Setting the 'go–no go' parameters for adopting strategic options at the outset does provide organizations with a greater degree of confidence when moving forward. Unfortunately, in many organizations these options are often introduced to create compromise and establish management consensus, which later reopens the debate even though guidelines have been established. As highlighted earlier, strategic stress and loss of balance can frequently come from internal agendas and egos.

One aspect of adaptation that often gets ignored, given the desire to move forward, is the tactical retreat, where it is possible to draw back and consider the implications before stepping forward. This is frequently viewed as being indecisive, but the truth is that when a decision is not needed immediately why make it if one has the time to consider it further. On the other hand, sometimes the decision is obvious and it is only a desire for more analysis that holds managers back. Perhaps organizations should institute the 'brolly test', in that if it is raining you either stay in or go out and get wet, the only real question being how wet you get, and does that matter.

Changing approach or direction also needs to encompass partners and allies that are crucial to the programme. If these external organizations are part of an integrated approach, then clearly any variation may have an impact on their operations. Frequently, when alliances begin to crack, it is not because they were not built on a solid foundation but that when changes come along they are not jointly addressed. The result is that the operations start to diverge and eventually the pressure and stress starts to pull them apart.

In the future there will probably be more developments built around alliances and flexible networks. This arena will stretch the current breed of organizational and management programmes. It will be crucial in these relationships to see partners as an integral part of the strategic approach, and thus the balance and energy must be projected and harnessed across organizational boundaries.

When the need for change arises, and perhaps this is the only certainty in business, then evaluating the impacts and reactions is a crucial part of effective leadership and management. These impacts cover a wide range of internal and external perspectives, including shareholders, customers and competitors. Shareholders, as we have seen, can be a major stimulus for change, but often without fully understanding the implications of the drivers they pursue. In a similar vein, the impacts of the investor community may have a significant impact on the strategic direction, and changes often need to be presented in a manner that allows for an understanding of the implications. This is likely to be even more of an issue in the future, where sustainability factors may override the investors' return on investment.

Competitors need always to be a factor when considering how to adapt an approach or implement a change in direction. On the first level it is important to ensure that they are not pre-warned and able to influence the market perception ahead of time. On the more fundamental level though, any adaptations or strategic imperatives must be robust enough to hold the lead while the next generation of developments goes through the strategic process.

The customer is ultimately the real judge of successful strategy, and of the ability of organizations to bring that balance and focus to delivering customer satisfaction. Customers seldom influence short-term direction but can certainly be influenced by strategic adaptations that cut across their current thinking. It is in balancing these external factors and the impacts of internal imbalance that must be addressed in order to ensure that the energy and focus of the organization is maintained towards success.

CHAPTER 29

Building for the next shift

Nothing lasts for ever, and whatever initiatives organizations adopt these will only have a certain life-span during which to capitalize on market position and prepare the platform for the next leap forward. In this digital age, the product cycle has condensed from the traditional three- to five-year programmes to those that appear and decline within perhaps only a year. This pressure is in itself perhaps more than many organizations have developed the ability to handle, but this is only the tip of the iceberg and there are many more factors that squeeze strategic thinking and constrain more traditional organizations' capability to respond to the demands of today's customer expectations.

There are many variables, from market movements and consumer demands to customers and competitors. More widely, there are the influences of regulatory pressures and political change. Since the 1970s we have seen the rise and fall of the tiger economies, along with the collapse of the communist bloc and the move towards a free economy. This has been further complicated by the growth in size of the European Community (EC), which itself has seen great change. In the background, China has been progressively building up its new economic model, which is predicted to be the most significant market builder of the coming decades. Already China has become a market-maker, through influence perhaps more than design, but this is only the first stage. As that influence consolidates, so market driving will take over from simple influence.

Clearly, the strategic programmes of organizations now have to consider the global influence, and perhaps more importantly have to consider how to stay ahead of the pack in this volatile environment. Certainly maintaining market position means thinking beyond current restraints and this in turn means considering strategies that will surely test the majority of traditionally structured organizations. Delivering these strategies will call for more focus on how to optimize the performance of organizations by removing the imbalances that dilute the focus and energy.

Scenario planning may help to push the focus beyond the established mindsets and performance matrices, but it will be the strategic imperatives that organizations adopt that will support the transition to what will surely be a more diverse and unstable business environment of the future. Financing planning may be the benchmark of the modern investor, but the recognition that perhaps it will be the softer issues that in fact define success is beginning to be appreciated. As Albert Einstein commented, 'sometimes what counts can't be counted and what can be counted doesn't count'.

Strategy for the next paradigm shift will be focused more on how to exploit knowledge and influence across networks of relationships that are as yet not even on the business community's radar. Globalization will continue to shrink the gaps in time and accessibility, but the melding of cultural diversity will be a much longer evolution. Thus, for the immediate future, trends, desires and passions will shape and influence organizations, both externally and internally. The capacity to manage the external impacts will largely be dependent on the skill of handling the internal pressures and imbalances that the cultural changes will bring about.

Innovation, invention and R&D programmes need to be deployed, and developed, ensuring the external stimulus that cannot come from traditional close-focused operations. Academics need to be listened to, but perhaps they should not be the only source of innovative thinking, since even in their ivory towers of research they base the next level of thinking on the historical platforms they have created. Therefore, the creation of innovative technology clusters and communities may themselves implode in time from a lack of stimulators.

We need 'blue sky' thinkers in the business community as well to look at the innovative ways of exploiting what we already know rather than waiting for a flash of technology to arrive. This in its own way will test the resolve of organizations and their ability to absorb and deploy approaches that run counter to the way they have evolved. It is likely that many traditionalists will simply drop out of the race. It will therefore be crucial to start evaluating how we train the business leaders of tomorrow to mange these complex and volatile environments.

Performance is a major part of the equation in terms of how we assess and develop our people, systems, processes and supply networks to evolve and adapt to meet the challenges of the next generation of business models. We only learn and improve if we evaluate what we have done right and what we could have done better, then consider the next configuration of processes, tools, networks and people. While we must evaluate to improve it is also important to recognize that the parameters of the future business environment will probably be very different and less predictable based on current assessment baselines.

The creation of integrated networks of relationships would seem to be one of the obvious developments, to be able to meet demands for flexibility. Alliances and partnerships will take the place of ownership and acquisition, bringing with the change a whole new set of complexities that must be managed and focused. Recognizing these impacts will be a key factor in managing successful delivery programmes of the future. The internal frictions and conflicts that can evolve from no longer having a joint organizational responsibility towards one that is mutually interdependent will test the best leaders. All this while trying to meet the challenges of the new market entrants and shapers, many of whom will have to be part of these new dynamic business models if they are to succeed in some sectors.

Virtual integration offers a multiplicity of solutions for some of the coming challenges and developments. We are already seeing brand management becoming a more influential factor than asset ownership and national identity. It is now difficult to establish the nationality of many products, and this is likely to increase in the future. The result of this will be that strategic imperatives will increasingly have to be carried and balanced across organizations and cultural boundaries without the comfort of traditional management structures. Success is more than ever being driven by the ability of organizations to maintain a focus on their strategy and carry other organizations with them.

For many sectors, the future will also mean a change in emphasis from manufacturing to more service-related approaches that move them up the hierarchy. The long-term initiative will be the horizontal and vertical integration that focuses on who does what best rather than who owns what, creating virtual organizations that exploit technology, resources, skills and knowledge by concentrating on continuous improvement and the optimization or exploitation of capabilities against markets. In these fluid, extended enterprises the impacts of failing to focus energy and maintain balance will be more readily visible, and the impacts more immediate.

Considering these challenges and developments, there is a certain need to evaluate how we create the new breed of leaders and managers who can exploit this less stable business landscape. The systems and processes to support them will also need to be addressed, but perhaps today we focus far too much on the technology rather than on the relationships that make these systems and processes work. We must assess current training and development programmes to tune them to the future demands of operating outside the traditional command and control structures.

The loss of ownership and the complexities of loosening social interaction, or what some might call the 'coffee machine comfort zone', offers the prospect of having to rewrite many management development programmes. We must remember that, while we drive towards greater exploitation of the digital age we are still dealing with real people and the unique combination of issues and stresses that each has. Real people in unreal environments will probably lead to increased stresses and loss of effective balance across the operations, with the inevitable loss of energy and performance.

The evolution in business thinking and opportunities that occurred in the second half of the twentieth century is likely to be overshadowed by the developments of the next two decades of the twenty-first century, both technically and politically. Developing strategies to contend with these evolutions and managing the effective deployment of these strategies is still being created, based on processes and structural thinking that pre-date the technology advances and political evaluations.

We often hear about the next paradigm shift but seldom see anything other than some minor evolution in what we already know and understand. But if one wants to leap ahead of current thinking, one has to break free of current thinking. The focus on core skills and the exploitation of knowledge dispensing regarding expensive assets that constrain financial developments is crucial to building the next level of thinking.

More importantly, these developments need to be worked through at the delivery level to ensure that people who understand and support the strategic imperatives can implement the next shift. Organizations will have to consider the increased use of contained developments that stay outside the traditional operation until they can be demonstrated and communicated. For wherever people will be involved in the delivery process we have to recognize the implications of their individual drivers and concerns that will have an impact on the strategy.

Exploiting knowledge is the cry we hear more than any other today, but seldom do we see realistic programmes that can do just that. Perhaps the first point that organizations need to appreciate is what knowledge they have and what is held within the minds of their key personnel. The trends towards outsourcing of manufacture and offshoring of services activities is perhaps a short-term strategic move to save money in the long term, but one hopes that these same organizations are retaining the skills to move the service or function again.

Managing a third party means understanding the role and one's fears that these short-term strategic moves may backfire in a very short time. Since the mid-1990s the economic increases of once low-cost markets has already seen significant moves, and this cycle will increase, so retaining the core skills and project management capability to deploy them should be considered as part of the 'family jewels'.

The World Wide Web has provided a unique source of knowledge and was originally conceived to make all information available to everyone. A very laudable aim, but perhaps not one that the business community would share. Certainly, the lawyers would not be very happy but there is perhaps some thinking that organizations should be doing. Many spend considerable effort on not exploiting their knowledge while endeavouring to protect it. In many cases what they work so hard to protect is already in the public domain or will certainly be so within a short pace of time.

Elements of some operations will pull back from major strategic moves to protect what they think of as their technology, which frequently is only a reflection of the investments made and not the true inventive content. Given the pace of change and the need to capitalize on market opportunities, perhaps organizations should invest more effort in speeding up the route to market rather then investing in protecting the intellectual property. The sooner a company reaps the benefits, the sooner it can reinvest for the next leap forward – standing still is not an option. Commercial advantage versus short-term protectionism is a serious question that should form part of future strategic thinking.

All aspects of current strategic thinking should be looking also to lay the foundations of the next evolution, recognizing that the changes introduced today will be the basis upon which a company moves forward tomorrow. In the midst of this complexity, the people who have to deliver the strategy must also understand their roles today and be trained and developed progressively for their roles of tomorrow.

As one looks forward there can be little doubt that if today we find it difficult to manage the impacts of strategic stress and maintain the balance within organizations, then the challenges of tomorrow will be even greater. It is often said that if it does not make sense then it will not make money. This can be reflected in the environment, where free thinkers are expected to deliver a strategy that does not make sense to them and thus it will probably never deliver its potential.

To capitalize on the force and energy of any operation there is a need to ensure that players understand their own roles and recognize the objectives and values they are being asked to deliver. In this situation it will be the leadership that makes the difference, and those leaders must be close enough to relate to other people, but also far enough ahead to motivate them.

We have moved since the Second World War from organizational thinking based on rigid structures and compliance to the more dynamic perspective of cross-functional performance. Future business models and approaches will probably devolve from alliance concepts to flexible complementary clustered networks with little or no hierarchical structure. Yet the basis of how we look at organizations in the main has not changed and certainly management tools have not kept pace.

The certain truth is that the more complexity there is in the market, the greater the dependence on a sound strategic approach. This, however, must also be linked to an understanding of who the strategy will be received by and how it will have an impact on those who have to deliver it, since without their commitment the strategy is merely an academic exercise. The key to success is developing the right strategy, and the key to implementation is to recognize within that situation how to optimize the strategy across the broad organization.

Strategic stress is the commonest cause of strategy failure, when the aims and objectives fail to mesh with the thinking and approach of those who have to deliver the product. This creates an imbalance that is crucial for any organism to survive, and businesses are organisms. This lack of balance in approach then deflects the focus of the organization and thus in turn reduces the energy that is directed towards the real challenges. Identifying the peaks and troughs of strategic stress allows organizations to address the major issues that can undermine their strategic intent. It also provides a basis to assess over time how the organization is evolving.

Exploiting the full potential of an organization must draw upon the systems and processes in place, but predominantly it requires an optimization of the energy that the organizations can generate through its people. Maintaining the balance across organizations, particularly those that are now nationally or globally dispersed, is a crucial part of managing the skills and capabilities that can be deployed, but equally it can pull against itself.

Looking to the future, the challenge will become even more testing: while the alternative business models may well break down the traditional infrastructures, the impact of failing to balance the energy and focus across multiple organizations will dilute the forces that should be concentrated on outcomes. Technology may well be seen as the new business medium, but behind the wired connections will be real organizations that need to be integrated with the process and strategy.

Failure can be divided into those who thought and never did, and those who did and never thought. To this end, the aim of *The Bending Moment* has been to stimulate debate and raise the focus on those many issues that can, if ignored, drain the energy from an organization and have a serious impact from within the potential success of even the most well-developed strategic approach.

Bibliography

The author would like to acknowledge the following works which have contributed to the thinking behind the development of this book.

Daryl R. Conner, *The Leading Edge of Chaos* (John Wiley & Sons, 1998).
Peter Drucker, *The Age of Discontinuity* (Transaction Publishers, 1992).
Gary Hamel, *Competing for the Future* (Harvard Business School, 1994).
Michael Hammer, *Re-engineering the Corporation* (Nicholas Brealey, 2001).
Michael Hammer, *Beyond Re-engineering* (HarperCollins, 1996).
Charles Handy, *The Age of Paradox* (McGraw Hill, 1995).
Harry K. Jackson, *Achieving Competitive Edge* (John Wiley & Sons, 1996).
Tom Peters, *Liberation Management* (Pan Macmillan, 1994).
B. Joseph Pine, *Mass Customization* (Harvard Business School, 1999).
Michael Porter, *The Competitive Advantage* (Simon & Schuster, 1998).
James Tompkins, *No Boundaries* (Tompkins Press, 2000).

Index